Revolution

READINGS IN POLITICS AND SOCIETY

GENERAL EDITOR: Bernard Crick
*Professor of Political Theory and Institutions,
University of Sheffield*

ALREADY PUBLISHED

W. L. Guttsman, *The English Ruling Class*
A. J. Beattie, *English Party Politics*
Frank W. Bealey, *The Social and Political Thought of the British Labour Party*
Edmund Ions, *Political and Social Thought in America 1870–1970*

Forthcoming volumes
William Thornhill, *The Growth and Reform of Local Government*
N. D. Deakin, *Race in British Politics*
Maurice Bruce, *The Rise of the Welfare State*
Louis Blom-Cooper and Gavin Drewry, *Law and Morality*

Previously published in this series by Routledge & Kegan Paul

David Nicolls, *Church and State in Britain Since 1820*

Revolution

THE THEORY AND PRACTICE OF A EUROPEAN IDEA

Edited and introduced by

KRISHAN KUMAR

Lecturer in Sociology,
University of Kent at Canterbury

WEIDENFELD AND NICOLSON
5 Winsley Street London W1

Editorial and introductory material © Krishan Kumar 1971

ISBN 0297 00289 9 Case Bound
ISBN 0297 00290 6 Paper Back

Printed in Great Britain by
Cox & Wyman Ltd, London, Fakenham and Reading

Contents

CONTENTS

General Editor's Preface

The purpose of this series is to introduce students of society to a number of important problems through the study of sources and contemporary documents. It should be part of every student's education to have some contact with the materials from which the judgements of authors of secondary works are reached, or the grounds of social action determined. Students may actually find this more interesting than relying exclusively on the pre-digested diet of textbooks. The readings will be drawn from as great a variety of documents as is possible within each book: Royal Commission reports, Parliamentary debates, letters to the Press, newspaper editorials, letters and diaries both published and unpublished, sermons and literary sources, et cetera, will all be drawn upon. For the aim is both to introduce the student to carefully selected extracts from the principal contemporary books and documents (the things he always hears about but never reads), and to show him a great range of subsidiary and representative source materials available (the memorials of actors in the actual events).

The prejudice of this series is that the social sciences need to be taught and developed in an historical context. Those of us who wish to be relevant and topical (and this is no bad wish) sometimes need reminding that the most usual explanation of why a thing is as it is, is that things happened in the past to make it so. These things might not have happened. They might have happened differently. And nothing in the present is, strictly speaking, *determined* from the past; but everything is limited by what went before. Every present problem, whether of understanding or of action, will always have a variety of relevant antecedent factors, all of which must be understood before it is sensible to commit ourselves to an explanatory theory or to some course of practical action. No present problem is completely novel and there is never any single cause for it, but always a variety of conditioning factors, arising through time, whose relative importance is a matter of critical judgement as well as of objective knowledge.

The aim of this series is, then, to give the student the opportunity to examine with care an avowedly selective body of source materials. The topics have been chosen both because they are of contemporary importance and because they cut across established pedagogic boundaries between the various disciplines and between courses of professional instruction. We hope that these books will supplement, not replace, other forms of introductory reading; so both the length and the character of the Introductions will vary according to whether the particular editor has already written on the subject or not. Some Introductions will summarise what is already to be found elsewhere at greater length, but some will be original contributions to knowledge or even, on occasions, reasoned advocacies. Above all, however, I hope that this series will help to develop a method of introductory teaching that can show how and from where we come to reach the judgements that are to be found in secondary accounts and textbooks.

University of Sheffield   *BERNARD CRICK*

Foreword

This book is a hybrid. It aims to stand somewhere between a collection of historical documents on revolution, and a collection of 'readings' on revolution by modern academics. Inevitably it partakes a bit of the nature of both. But I hope it will serve its main purpose of introducing students to some of the principal concepts and theories of revolution, as they have been held by the most important writers of the past. To this end I have not tried to be fair in my coverage of particular revolutions. If a lot of interesting things were said about 1848, for instance, and not so many about 1871, the former figures disproportionately, from a purely historical point of view.

One limitation deserves special mention. I have not tried, either in the Introduction or in the documents, to deal more than in passing with the twentieth-century revolutions of the 'Third World'. As I explain in the conclusion to my essay, I think these revolutions demand separate treatment from that given to the revolutions of the European world. There is, certainly, a temporal and intellectual connection between the concepts as held in the different areas; but the differences of historical experience demand a far more detailed analysis than is possible here.

The documents are, of course, partly illustrative of the argument of the Introduction. But they also give points of view opposed to it, and cover topics for which there was no space in the essay. The Introduction referred to in the prefatory notes to the documents is the introductory essay to the book, and in this Introduction the numbers in square brackets refer to the documents.

I have been helped in many different ways by Chimen Abramsky, Bernard Crick and George Webb, and I should like to thank them.

Canterbury, February 1970   *KRISHAN KUMAR*

Acknowledgements

The editor and publisher would like to thank the following for permission to quote from copyright sources: George Allen & Unwin Ltd for Robert C. Tucker, *The Marxian Revolutionary Idea*; Hannah Arendt, *The Origins of Totalitarianism*; Jack Lively, *The Works of Joseph de Maistre*; and J. Burckhardt, *Reflections on History*; Martin Secker & Warburg Ltd for Raymond Aron, *The Opium of the Intellectuals*; The University of Chicago Press for Paul Milyeukov, *Russia and its Critics*; Hamish Hamilton Ltd for Sir Lewis Namier, *Vanished Supremacies*; F. F. Seeley for 'The Heyday of the Superfluous Man in Russia'; K. C. Chorley for *Armies and the Art of Revolution*; Oxford University Press for Victor Serge, *Memoirs of a Revolutionary*, translated and edited by Peter Sedgewick; Chatto & Windus Ltd for Raymond Williams, *Modern Tragedy* and, with Mr David Garnett, for Alexander Herzen, *My Past and Thoughts*, translated by Constance Garnett; Macmillan & Company Ltd for E. H. Carr, *A History of Soviet Russia*; McGraw-Hill Book Company for G. Mosca, *The Ruling Class*, © 1939 by McGraw-Hill Inc.; International Publishers for Mao Tse-tung, *The Selected Works*, and Karl Marx and Friedrich Engels, *The German Ideology*; The Harvill Press Ltd for *The Recollections of Alexis de Tocqueville*; The Macmillan Company for Georges Sorel, *Reflections on Violence*, trans. J. Roth and T. E. Hulme, Copyright 1950 by the Free Press, a Corporation; C. A. Watts & Co. Ltd for *Karl Marx : Early Writings*, edited by T. B. Bottomore; Allen Lane the Penguin Press for Herbert Marcuse, *An Essay on Liberation*, © 1969 by Herbert Marcuse; *The Political Quarterly* for Hugh Seton-Watson, 'Twentieth Century Revolu-

ACKNOWLEDGEMENTS

tions'; Ernest Benn Ltd for Gustave Le Bon, *The Psychology of Revolution*; Holt, Rinehart & Winston Inc. for Leon Trotsky, *Our Revolution*, translated by Moissaye J. Olgin, all rights reserved, Pathfinder Press, Inc. for Leon Trotsky, *The Permanent Revolution*, Copyright © 1969 by Merit Publishers; Mlle M. Bonnet and Victor Gollancz Ltd for Leon Trotsky, *History of the Revolution*; The Macmillan Company of Canada and Macmillan & Company Ltd, Basingstoke, for R. C. Bridges, *Nations and Empires*; Doubleday & Company, Inc. for Karl Marx, 'Critical Notes on "The King of Prussia and Social Reform"', from *Writings of the Young Marx on Philosophy and Society*, edited and translated by L. D. Easton and H. K. H. Guddat; Routledge & Kegan Paul Ltd for Emile Durkheim, *Suicide: A Study in Sociology*, translated by Hans Gerth and C. Wright Mills; William Heinemann Ltd for Peter Kropotkin, *The Great French Revolution 1789–93*; Collier-Macmillan for Robert Michels, *Political Parties*; The Porcupine Press for Pierre-Joseph Proudhon, *A Hundred Years of Revolution*; New Park Publishers for Trotsky, *The Revolution Betrayed*.

Introduction

1 THE HISTORICAL CONTEXT

The modern idea of revolution, like the modern idea of democracy, was invented in the eighteenth century in Europe. There is no intrinsic connection between the two ideas; nevertheless their origin at the same time in the same place gives them a characteristic affinity. The eighteenth-century Enlightenment discovered Man, as opposed to mere men. It proclaimed him to be a creature whose essence was freedom and rationality. The immoral and wasteful organisation of society had suppressed that freedom and corrupted that rationality. Some thinkers, such as Voltaire, looked towards a pious and enlightened monarch for the restoration of man's original nature; others hoped to achieve this through a political system based on universal suffrage. It was the French who, seeking to bring some sort of constitutional order into their chaotic polity, stumbled upon the idea that revolution was the means by which man was to be made free. From the time of the French Revolution of 1789, it would have been difficult to disagree with Condorcet's conviction that 'the word *revolutionary* can be applied only to revolutions which have liberty as their object' [1.1]. A contemporary dictum makes the same point in a neat contrast: 'Rebellion is the subversion of the laws, Revolution that of tyrants.'[1]

The actual course of the French Revolution shattered any easy optimism that freedom was the inevitable consequence of revolution. The mercilessness of the Terror and the rise of a military dictatorship could not be denied. But the concept of revolution as conscious human action had become deeply lodged in the European mind. After the French Revolution, it was impossible to return to

[1] OED, quoting an anonymous writer of 1796.

a pre-revolutionary innocence, an innocence displayed in large measure even by the actors of that Revolution itself. Now we find professed revolutionaries, working for revolutions in the future and studying those of the past. Revolution was seen as the sovereign means of re-structuring society, and so man. It was the act by which man asserted his ability totally to change the institutions to which he was subject; an act of willed destruction and replacement of a whole system of society, in which man found and secured his freedom. Even those who opposed revolution were now defined by the accomplished fact of revolution: they were *counter-revolutionaries*, men, as Condorcet said, 'who wish to produce a revolution in reverse [*en sens contraire*], a *counter*-revolution'. Such men could no longer be passive defenders of an old order, even if they were not faced with an actual revolution. Conservatism too, henceforth, was a matter of active policy, of continuous search and destroy, of stealing, where necessary, the revolutionaries' clothes. Metternich did not understand this, and escaped from the revolution ignominiously hiding in a laundry-basket. Bismarck, by contrast, is the best example of the conservative statesman who used the forces of revolution to forestall the revolution.

The French Revolution of the eighteenth century inspired practically every important statement about revolution in the subsequent century and a half. In writing about its causes, Alexis de Tocqueville produced the most important single book on revolution, *The Ancien Régime and the Revolution*. The Revolution provoked the critical reflections of Burke, Chateaubriand, Joseph de Maistre, and Friedrich Gentz. It provided Hegel with the outstanding example of the disaster that must follow any attempt to establish a state on the basis of abstract rational principles, unaccompanied by the development of an appropriate subjective consciousness on the part of its subjects. For Marx, it remained always the model of revolution as such. It identified for him the elements by which he could analyse the English Revolution of the seventeenth century, and which also suggested the requirements for the proletarian revolution of the future. As Peter Kropotkin wrote at the end of his history of *The Great French Revolution*, it was 'the source and origin of all the present communist, anarchist, and socialist conceptions. . . . The one thing certain is, that whatsoever nation enters on the path of revolution in our own day, it will be heir to all our forefathers have done in France'.[2]

The theorists of revolution were, of course, also practitioners: actual or would-be. Here again the influence of the French Revolution was irresistible. In vain did Marx urge that 'the social revolution of the nineteenth century cannot draw its poetry from the past, but only from the future' [5.6]. Men were mesmerised, not only by their zealously acquired knowledge of the stages of the French Revolution, but also by the conviction that all revolutions had to run the whole gamut of that Revolution. As Hannah Arendt writes, 'their trouble has always been the same: those who went into the school of revolution learned and knew beforehand the course a revolution must take'.[3] In any revolution, they expected, there would be a 'Fourteenth of July' (the fall of the Bastille), a 'Ninth of Thermidor' (the fall of Robespierre), an 'Eighteenth of Brumaire' (the coup d'état of Napoleon). They knew, of course, that this sequence always spelled the end to the revolutionary aspiration to freedom, that it delivered the revolution into the hands of the strong man who promised the restoration of order. But such had been the course of the 'great' French revolution, and such, they supposed, was the inherent logic of revolution. Even Lenin, the most sophisticated and self-conscious of revolutionaries, felt obliged to place himself in the tradition. 'A Frenchman,' he said to a French Communist in 1920, 'has nothing to renounce in the Russian Revolution, which in its method and procedures recommences the French Revolution.'[4]

Knowing the plot of revolution, some actors sought to stop the play after they had made their big entrance, and were basking in the applause of the audience; others equally determinedly tried to hurry on the action to the end, where the good characters, after much misfortune, get their just deserts. Such foreknowledge was bound to distort the 'pure logic' of revolution. 'One reason why history so rarely repeats itself,' says E. H. Carr, 'is that the dramatis personae at the second performance have prior knowledge of the denouement' [3.13]. And Trotsky spoke of the German bourgeoisie

[2] Peter Kropotkin, *The Great French Revolution 1789–1793* (London, 1909), pp. 581–2.
[3] Hannah Arendt, *On Revolution* (London, 1963), p. 51.
[4] Quoted C. R. A. Behrens, 'The Spirit of the Terror', *New York Review of Books*, 27 February 1969.

of 1848 as being 'shabbily wise with the experience of the French bourgeoisie'. But what was perhaps more striking to contemporary observers was how little this knowledge seemed to affect the basic course and outcome of the nineteenth-century revolutions. The very participants seemed almost resigned in advance to making their bow at the appropriate time and then passing on. Marx was able to write a tract derisively entitled *The Eighteenth Brumaire of Louis Napoleon*. In this he observed that

from 1848 to 1851 the ghost of the old revolution walked about. . . . An entire people, which had imagined that by means of a revolution it had imparted to itself an accelerated power of motion, suddenly finds itself set back into a defunct epoch and, in order that no doubt as to the relapse may be possible, the old dates arise again, the old chronology, the old names, the old edicts . . . [5.6].

Alexis de Tocqueville too, as participant and observer, was forcibly struck by the imitation and theatricality in the French Revolution of 1848.

The men of the first Revolution were living in every mind, their deeds and words present to every memory. . . . It seemed to me throughout as though they were engaged in acting the French Revolution, rather than continuing it. [5.5].

The Revolutions of 1848 in Europe failed everywhere, and everywhere the outlines of 1789–99 could be discerned: sometimes boldly as, most appropriately, in France, sometimes faintly and distortedly, as in Germany, Italy, Austria and Hungary. One could easily conclude from this that revolution was the god that had failed. It seemed predestined to follow the path of a particular curve or cycle that began in freedom and ended in despotism. This idea had already been sketched by Hegel from the experience of the first French Revolution; and it haunted the minds of Western European liberals after the experiences of 1848. Being liberals, it was unthinkable that they could altogether relinquish the right of a people to revolt: were they not admirers of John Locke and the English Revolutions of the seventeenth century? The right of revolt, said the German liberal Bluntschli, belonged to 'any people who can save its soul in no other way. Once the hope of reform perishes in the heart of any brave people, the desperate

4

condition of revolution sets in.'[5] At the same time revolution seemed to open the way to anarchy. It seemed incapable of stopping at the achievement of the political settlement desired by the liberals, but pressed on to the destruction of property, order, and culture. Revolution therefore for ever retained for European liberals its Janus-head: one face showing it as the noblest striving for freedom, the other revealing it as the precipitator of nihilistic violence and terror which always ended in tyranny. After 1848, European liberalism was primarily on the defensive against revolution; but its ambivalent attitude towards it made liberalism the prey of the forces both of the Right and of the Left.

In Western Europe after 1848 the revolutionary tradition continued in the various forms of militant socialism: Marxist, anarchist, syndicalist, and others. Even in these, the ambiguous nature of that tradition did not allow an unswerving commitment to revolution. Socialists at the end of the century were deeply divided on how far socialism was 'evolutionary', and could be achieved gradually and peacefully through parliamentary politics; and how far it had to be revolutionary, only attainable through a violent confrontation of the existing social order. But outside Western Europe the meaning of revolution still seemed clear, its performance still essential. This was true above all in Tsarist Russia. The Russian gentry had corresponded with the European Enlightenment and welcomed the French Revolution. On the death of Alexander I they attempted to effect their own liberal revolution, and failed dismally. The seeds of this failure nourished the principle of revolutionism marvellously. After the Decembrist rising of 1825, every critic or opponent of the regime had to be a revolutionary, and was certainly treated as one by the authorities. Revolution came to carry the aspect – Theodor Schieder writes – not simply of a political, but of an ethical and religious principle.

No other nation – not even the French, the 'demiurge' of bourgeois revolution – had embraced the idea of revolution in the same manner as did the Russian intelligentsia about the turn of the century, when they prophetically interpreted the whole of Russian history as a coming revolution and created the revolutionary as a human type whose very

---

[5] Quoted Theodor Schieder, 'The Problem of Revolution in the Nineteenth Century', in his *The State and Society in Our Times* (London, 1962), p. 7.

5

outward appearance is at variance with his surroundings and who submits himself to the forms of a sort of monastic life [1.10].[6]

A number of Russian writers, of whom Alexander Herzen was the best, proclaimed the bankruptcy of the revolutionary potential of the West, especially after 1848. The West, it was admitted, was the inventor of the revolutionary idea, and that was to its everlasting glory. But it had no permanent proprietary right over it. The right lapsed with the capacity to exercise it. Russia, having that capacity, was now the natural bearer of the revolutionary idea.[7]

In our own century a host of other societies have laid claim to be the bearer of that idea. The course of events in Russia after the Revolution of 1917 suggested that she, too, had betrayed the revolution, which still remained to be made. The European idea of revolution, usually in a Marxist form, reached out to Asia, to Latin America, to the Middle East, and to Africa. In his defence speech at the Moncada trial in 1953, Fidel Castro showed that the very existence of Cuba was an inheritance of the European revolutionary tradition, and he ransacked that tradition in defence of his actions.[8] Mao's China, Tito's Yugoslavia, Castro's Cuba, Nasser's Egypt, Nkrumah's Ghana, or that collectivity, the 'Third World' of industrially undeveloped nations: all at various times have claimed or had claimed for them the role of the consummator of the revolution. If none of these claims carries complete conviction, it may be because the aims of revolution as enunciated by the French Revolution are inherently incapable of realisation in a society of men; or because these societies are trying to disguise the apparent fact that here, as with the European societies of the past, the 'logic' of revolution has driven on to its tyrannical conclusion. At any rate, if we ask, 'What is revolution?', we must still echo Archbishop Temple's celebrated answer to a similar question about man: 'Not yet.'

[6] Schieder, ibid., p. 28.
[7] See especially Alexander Herzen, *My Past and Thoughts*, 4 vols., trans. Constance Garnett (London, 1968 rev. ed.), vol. IV, pp. 1560–73.
[8] Fidel Castro, *History Will Absolve Me* (London, 1967), pp. 95 ff.

2 WHAT IS REVOLUTION?

We have not, in fact, so far directly put the question, 'What is revolution?' and must do so now. The point of the preceding section has been to show that the concept of revolution is essentially *historical* in nature. It takes its meaning and resonance from the fact of its origin in the French Revolution, as modified and elaborated by subsequent historical events. Undoubtedly that historical inheritance is complex. It has led some students of revolution to write in terms of a sort of ecstatic bewilderment, as of 'a mysterious, lustful virago, who gives herself to all, intoxicates all, promises all things, and calls herself Revolution'.[9] We need to take away some of the mystery from the concept; and no attempts to do so are likely to be successful that ignore the historical meaning and context of the term.

There are at least two things we can do about definitions in the social sciences. We can establish what are called 'operational definitions': concepts like 'law' or 'revolution' only have meaning in relation to the methods or operations that have been employed in establishing them.[10] Concepts therefore are linked to phenomena, met with in society or history, that are quantifiable, measurable, observable, or in some other way amenable to the operations of the investigator. The recipe for a cake defines the cake; intelligence is the intelligence quotient as measured by IQ tests. There is no problem about what 'really' or 'essentially' is the meaning of a concept, and the analysis of the concept is tied neatly to the available set of empirical techniques. Every time we use the word 'revolution' we should know precisely what phenomenon we are referring to, since we have defined it in terms of practical operations; conversely – although this is not always relevant – every time we meet the phenomenon in the real world of society or history we should know what it 'is'.

Basically the procedure is entirely arbitrary. It leaves the scope and significance of the social reality referred to by the concept

[9] Marcu, quoted in George Pettee, *The Process of Revolution* (London, 1938), pp. 2–3.
[10] See Harry Alpert, 'Operational Definitions in Sociology', *American Sociological Review*, vol. III (1938), pp. 855–61.

entirely up to the wilfulness of the writer, who, by the use of concepts with a traditional importance and complex historical content, entices us to a reading of what often turns out to be footling and trivial matters. The writings of Talcott Parsons on the concept of power seem to me a good example of this technique; but modern sociological writing, with its 'arid desert of definitions' is in any case replete with it, not least, as we shall see, in the case of writing on revolution.

The other way of treating definitions is methodologically more messy, but substantially more rewarding. It accepts the basically historical and *social* nature of our concepts. It therefore does not expect a definite 'fit' between a concept and any empirically given instance of its content. If we look at the different usages and applications of a particular word, we are likely to find a certain common meaning, or perhaps simply a common set of associations; but we shall not find some single, absolutely unequivocal meaning. Common usage reflects the whole historical experience embodied in a word and, as we have seen in the case of revolution, that experience is often ambiguous and contradictory. Wittgenstein has warned us against the search for some quintessential meaning implicit in a concept, and advises us rather to look for 'family resemblances' between different uses of a word.

But this, of course, need not leave us in a hopelessly vague situation. This would be the case only if we accepted something like 'operationalism' as the only form of conceptual analysis. Herbert Blumer has suggested that such a procedure is quite inappropriate to the social world, and that we must rather look to 'sensitising' concepts as providing the gateways to social reality. Such concepts – of which 'revolution' seems pre-eminently one – have no rigidly fixed empirical content, but guide us towards the analysis of concrete expressions which have certain similarities. In turn, the working through of such concrete and distinctive expressions elaborates and refines what is common to the concept. As Blumer puts it, 'what is common (i.e. what the concept refers to) is expressed in a distinctive manner in each empirical instance and can be got at by accepting and working through the distinctive expression'.[11]

[11] Herbert Blumer, 'What is Wrong with Social Theory?' *American Sociological Review*, vol. XIX (1954), pp. 3–10.

The procedure is far from simple. It is not simply a matter of inspecting an array of current usages and concrete instances, finding something common in them, and so defining the concept. It is a complicated process of moving from the concept to the investigation of the concrete events referred to by the concept, and back to the concept again. And that movement must not be confined to one point in time: it has to move through time, dialectically. The events of a particular time affect the meaning of the concept, which then has its own effect on subsequent events, by which it may be further modified, and so on. Definitions, in other words, are not created; they emerge.

Perhaps one need not labour the point: a brief recital of some of the many uses of the word 'revolution' should sufficiently shake any complacency that might exist as to the complexity of the problem. We have the French Revolution, the Freudian Revolution, the Scientific Revolution, the Industrial Revolution, the Managerial Revolution, the Greek Revolution (in artistic development), the Technological Revolution, the Student Revolution. Nor is the chaos contained by any firm commitment to a temporal span within which the alleged revolution has to happen. Two anthropologists, Hockett and Ascher, speak of 'the human revolution', that 'drastic set of changes that turned non-humans into humans'. These drastic changes, they agree, 'may have required a good many millions of years; yet they can validly be regarded as sudden in view of the tens of millions of years of mammalian history that preceded them'.[12] Gordon Childe wrote of 'the urban revolution', 'the thousand years or so immediately preceding 3000 BC', and which succeeded the more drawn out 'neolithic revolution'.[13] E. P. Thompson talks of 'the bourgeois revolution of the fifteenth to the eighteenth centuries' in England.[14] Today, our journalists write of revolutions occurring annually, sometimes monthly and weekly, in describing the succession of dictatorships in Latin America, the Middle East and Africa.

One can just about make out the family resemblance in these

[12] Charles F. Hockett and Robert Ascher, 'The Human Revolution', *Current Anthropology*, vol. v (1964), pp. 135–68.
[13] V. Gordon Childe, *Man Makes Himself* (1936), ch. 7.
[14] E. P. Thompson, 'The Peculiarities of the English', *The Socialist Register* (eds. J. Saville and R. Miliband) (1965), p. 319.

various uses. But one gets the impression that the family contains a lot of freaks, and probably bastards.

There would not, however, be any disagreement to the proposition that all these uses of the word 'revolution' turn on the notion of *change*. This change is, moreover, seen in two ways. It is in some sense *fundamental,* not always nor often very accurately specified; and it is in some sense *sudden,* an acceleration of previously existing rates of change, or of the rate variously conceived by different writers as 'normal'. In popular usage, and certainly in popular imagery, it is the aspect of the suddenness of the change that predominates; the notion that such change is fundamental is felt, but obscurely and incoherently. It is in this respect that revolution carries its associations of 'divers tumults, seditions, battels, burnings, and bloodsheddings'; its Promethean imagery of fire and thunder; its ominous sounds of tumbrils rolling and guillotines falling.[15] More scholarly investigations of the concept have preferred to concentrate on the problem of what constitutes the 'fundamental' change alleged to have been accomplished by the revolution.

Any concept of revolution then must incorporate somehow the notion of fundamental and accelerated change. It is clear that we are not likely to get much further than this so long as we confront the manifold uses of the term *en bloc.* We cannot expect to find a definition that substantively can be applied in all the different social spheres: political, economic, intellectual, artistic, religious. The Freudian Revolution, whatever it is, is bound to need expression in very different terms from the French Revolution. We should do better, therefore, to speak of revolutions in the political sphere, in the economic sphere, in the intellectual sphere, and so on.

To do so is not to commit ourselves to a view of the autonomy of the different spheres: either in the sociological sense of regarding the different developments as unrelated to each other, or in the

[15] These popular associations of course long antedate the modern idea of revolution, having their roots largely in pre-industrial millennial movements. See on this Melvin J. Lasky, 'The Prometheans: On the Imagery of Fire and Revolution', *Encounter* (October 1968); and 'The Metaphysics of Doomsday', *Encounter* (January 1969). George Orwell was probably right to suggest that for the English an important source of these associations was Dickens's description of mob riots in *Barnaby Rudge,* and of the Terror in *A Tale of Two Cities.*

etymological sense of regarding the different usages as being unrelated to each other. As far as the former is concerned, a good case could be made out showing that political revolution is closely associated with revolutions in many other spheres. For the latter, we shall see that the different usages of the word have always had a decisive effect on each other's meaning.

The reason for separating out the uses into the different spheres is that we can ask and answer the question, what constitutes fundamental change in the political sphere, the economic sphere, and so on, more easily than what constitutes, in a substantive sense, fundamental change as such. And when we do separate them in this way we can also see that there is a common pattern to all revolutionary change in a strictly *formal* sense. This pattern is formed by the fact that *revolution is a change of style*.

Since this idea is taken basically from the history of art, we had best turn there first for an illustration of the procedure by which it is arrived at. Following the work of Heinrich Wölfflin, a number of art historians have been led to speak of the 'revolution of the Baroque' in European art and architecture. Wölfflin himself expounded the nature of this revolution in his book *Renaissance and Baroque*. In this, he takes 'style' to be the basic organising concept of art history. He does not here give us a clear definition of style, but one sufficiently in keeping with the spirit of his usage is provided by Paul Schrecker. 'A style,' says Schrecker, 'is a model of structure, a norm more or less general, unwritten . . . and most frequently ineffable, which is specified, made effective and individuated by the work of the artist, which it helps to determine.'[16] Wölfflin delineated the stylistic norm of the Renaissance as one of calm and contemplation, of perfect proportions creating a sense of harmony and satisfaction. During the sixteenth century, this norm was steadily undermined, beginning in Rome under the auspices of the Renaissance masters themselves: above all Michelangelo. In their works there emerged a new stylistic norm which Wölfflin designated as 'painterly', characterised as aiming at an illusion of movement, and conveying a state of dissatisfaction and restlessness rather than fulfilment. The period between 1520 and 1580 was one of revolutionary change in artistic development; by 1580 the

[16] Paul Schrecker, 'Revolution as a Problem in the Philosophy of History', in *Revolution*, ed. Carl J. Friedrich (New York, 1966), p. 44.

fully-formed Baroque style had come into being, and the revolution was accomplished.

Schrecker's concept of style is specifically related to the arts, but it seems to be general enough to be economically used as a generic term for what he himself calls 'the generative principle' governing the norms of any mode of activity. Thus, in economics we can talk of 'styles of production' as an equivalent of Marx's 'modes of production'. Using 'style' in this general way, the history of science provides another good field for exemplifying the basic idea that revolution is a change of style. In his stimulating book *The Structure of Scientific Revolutions*, Thomas Kuhn argues that it is possible to identify revolutions in the development of science, as in other spheres of human activity; and that such revolutions are constituted by changes of 'paradigm'. It is not, I think, a serious distortion of Kuhn's concept to see it as very similar to our use of 'style'. Paradigms, says Kuhn, are 'universally recognised scientific achievements that for a time provide model problems and solutions to a community of practitioners'. He further explains: ' . . . I mean to suggest that some accepted examples of actual scientific practice – examples which include law, theory, application, and instrumentation together – provide models from which spring particular coherent traditions of scientific research'.[17] Scientists are always working under the rule of a dominant paradigm: articulating it, elaborating it, testing it, pursuing the many implications often only hinted at by it. Such are the periods of what Kuhn calls 'normal science', and they easily constitute the major part of the history of science. But sometimes 'normal science' runs into more than ordinary difficulties. A new element or planet is discovered that casts doubt on all the existing assumptions in the field; an unexpected observation is made in the course of normal experimentation; current theories are persistently falsified in crucial experiments. Then begins a period of revolutionary crisis. There are fundamental debates about the methodology of science, and conflicts of substantive theory, both of the new and the old, and of varieties within the new. Finally, and more or less gradually, a new paradigm establishes itself within the scientific community, inaugurating a new style

[17] Thomas S. Kuhn, *The Structure of Scientific Revolutions* (Chicago, 1964 ed.), pp. x, 10.

of 'normal science'. The old guard either gives way gracefully or, more commonly, its members remain opposed until death to the new paradigm, so that the accomplishment of the revolution is often disguised and seen only in retrospect.[18]

Kuhn makes a number of points about such revolutionary changes of paradigm that are particularly important for the political concept of revolution. He insists that the 'differences between successive paradigms are both necessary and irreconcilable'. A new paradigm cannot be old wine in new bottles; it cannot, like so many alleged revolutions, be the old priest in the guise of the new presbyter. Paradigm changes, says Kuhn, are 'changes of world view'. It is not simply that they tell us different things about the population of the universe and that population's behaviour; these are the substantive differences between different paradigms. But

paradigms differ in more than substance, for they are directed not only to nature but also back upon the science that produced them. They are the source of the methods, problem-field, and standards of solution accepted by any mature scientific community at any given time. As a result, the reception of a new paradigm often necessitates a redefinition of the corresponding science. Some old problems may be relegated to another science or declared entirely 'unscientific'. Others that were previously non-existent or trivial may, with a new paradigm, become the very archetypes of significant scientific achievements. And as the problems change, so, often, does the standard that distinguishes a real scientific solution from a mere metaphysical speculation, word game, or mathematical play. The normal scientific tradition that emerges from a scientific revolution is not only incompatible, but often actually incommensurable, with that which has gone before.[19]

And Kuhn shows how such fundamental changes of world view were demonstrably the effect of the paradigm changes brought about by Newton and Einstein in mechanics, or Lavoisier in chemistry.

[18] The process so closely resembles the standard account of political revolution that it is not surprising to find that Kuhn draws a close parallel between the two (ibid., pp. 91–2). Schrecker, too (see n. 16, above), discusses revolution as a parallel process in politics, religion, the arts, etc. But interestingly both he and Kuhn seem to have been inspired in the first place by the conventional *political* concept, and to have applied this to the other fields. Since I have in a sense done just the opposite, the implications I draw from the parallel for the concept of political revolution can be and are very different from theirs.

[19] Kuhn, *The Structure of Scientific Revolutions*, p. 102.

It does not matter much, from the point of view of the present argument, whether or not Wölfflin and Kuhn have got their history quite right. It does not even matter whether or not we agree that the concept of style can be used as a generic term for paradigm or mode (of production, of philosophy, etc.), or any other 'generative principle': it is simply a matter of convenience to use it in this sense here, and it is not stretching customary usage too far. The point is that, within each of the fields of human activity, students can and often do reach a large measure of agreement as to what constitutes fundamental change within that field. The criteria for speaking of change in whatever 'generative principle' governs the norms in the particular field are far better established than they ever can be for *all* 'generative principles' or styles, taken together. It is perfectly sensible for Hockett and Ascher to talk of 'the human revolution' within the context of mammalian development, just as Gordon Childe could easily justify speaking of the neolithic and urban revolutions within the context of the whole of human history. On the same principle, economic historians can designate as revolutionary the transition from an economy based on agriculture to one based on industry; historians of ideas can legitimately speak of 'the Darwinian revolution', showing how Darwin's theory of variation and natural selection completely undermined the existing explanatory principle in biology. In each case the criteria, as regards their nature, time and scope, differ greatly; but in each case there is good hope that they can be agreed upon. What remains, when the substantive differences are abstracted, is a formal concept of revolution as a change of style, of the 'generative principle' governing the norms of an activity.

3 THE CONCEPT OF A POLITICAL REVOLUTION

What then is a revolution in the sphere of politics? What constitutes a change of style within it, corresponding to a change in the fundamental stylistic principle determining artistic practice, or in the paradigm governing scientific practice?

The principle of the political is rule or power. Political revolution is the transformation of power.

But we can go further than this. We know what sort of transformation must occur to entitle us to speak of revolution. It has to be a shift in the basis of power from its monopoly by the state to its effective possession by associations of the state's citizens. Only then do we know that we are dealing with revolution, and not repetition or restoration in new clothes. Only then does the change in the style of politics approach that transformation of world view, that new *praxis*, which is the consequence of a change of paradigm in science.

The reasons for this are historical rather than logical. Conceivably, if history had gone another way, political revolution could have been a transformation of power in some other direction. But political revolution is a modern idea inseparably connected with the development of the modern state; and that development, as Max Weber showed, has been in the direction of the exclusive appropriation of force by the state against other centres of power. Hence Weber's definition of the state in terms of its means, its possession of physical force. 'A state is a human community that (successfully) claims the monopoly of the legitimate use of physical force within a given territory.'[20] Other writers, such as Hobbes, have called this monopolistic power, sovereignty – as Bodin defined it, that supreme power, unrestrained by law, over all citizens and subjects.

Political revolution aims to change the style of politics based on the state's monopoly of armed violence. It aims at the dissolution of sovereignty, which is to say, the dissolution of the state. It is in this action that it recognises political freedom. In this sense, a revolution is anarchic, and Proudhon is right when he says that 'it implies a contradiction that a government could ever be called revolutionary, for the very simple reason that it is the government' [1.6]. This can also be seen as the implication of Weber's remark that 'if no social institutions existed which knew the use of violence, then the concept of "state" would be eliminated, and a condition would emerge that could be designated as "anarchy", in the specific sense of this word'.[21] The revolution lasts so long as the monopoly of force is broken, and the organisation of social groups is anar-

[20] Max Weber, 'Politics as a Vocation', in *From Max Weber: Essays in Sociology*. trans. and ed. H. H. Gerth and C. Wright Mills. (London, 1948), p. 78
[21] Weber, ibid., p. 78.

chistic. It ends, or is defeated, when one or a number of groups emerges and effectively reconstitutes the sovereign power of the state.[22] This is the counter-revolution, the revolution 'in a reverse direction'.

The revolutionary tradition provides ample support for this view, expressed in our own time by Camus when he declared that 'freedom . . . is the motivating principle of all revolutions'.[23] We have seen Condorcet making an assertion in similar terms, and from that time it could not be denied that, whatever the actual outcome of attempted revolution, its object was freedom. If we allow for differences of language, indeed, we find a similar conception prevailing at the time of the English Revolution of the seventeenth century. As was appropriate to the time, the terms used were those of restoration and 'reformation of government', but the aim was that of securing freedom, even though this was seen as something to be recovered, not made anew. Thus the English Parliamentarians in their declarations of 1642 insisted that they were acting in defence of the existing free and ancient constitution, against the usurpation of the Crown. The Levellers contended that man had set up government to give him 'safetie and freedome', that by usurpation his rights had been taken away, and that now the Civil War offered the opportunity of re-establishing civil society by a new agreement of the people, establishing a purified government with popular guarantees against usurpation. The Diggers went furthest of all, with their call to 'break to pieces the bands of property', and to restore society to its state of pristine equality, free of all oppression. All three were varieties of revolutionary Puritanism, for the Puritan, as R. C. Latham says, 'was born, as it were, into the opposition . . . . The whole of history was to him a challenge to restore to the spoilt works of creation their original perfection.'[24]

The practice of attempting to secure political freedom while at the same time denying that any novel precedent was being set,

[22] At least one other contemporary writer takes the same view: 'A revolution prevails when the state's monopoly is effectively challenged and persists until a monopoly of power is re-established.' See Peter Amann, 'Revolution: A Redefinition', *Political Science Quarterly*, vo. LXXVII (1962), p. 39.
[23] Albert Camus, *The Rebel* (London, 1962), p. 76.
[24] R. C. Latham, 'English Revolutionary Thought 1640–1660', *History*, vol. XXX (1945), p. 59.

persisted in the later political upheavals of the century in England. Curiously, it can be seen in the fact that Clarendon and the monarchists designated the Restoration of 1660 a 'revolution' – using this word in its older sense of the turning of a wheel or cycle, and signifying thereby that things had returned at last to their true and original condition of constitutional liberty, after the fanatical experiments of 'the Great Rebellion'. The Whigs turned the tables in 1688 by using the word 'revolution' in precisely the same sense; but this time they were expelling a King, and declaring that by flouting the laws he had broken the social contract. In this way Locke was able to argue that the King was the real rebel, for by his actions he had thrown society back to the original point in the constitutional cycle at which the contract could be re-made. Once the contract had been re-negotiated, the cycle was completed and the revolution had occurred.[25]

The English Revolution and, to a lesser extent, the American, succeeded so well in maintaining their conservative and legitimate pretensions, that they may genuinely have been unaware that they were pregnant with new conceptions and new forces.[26] But the men of the English Revolution were certainly clear that the enemy was sovereignty, although typically the Parliamentary lawyers invented a largely mythical legal history in fighting it. 'Prerogative I know is part of the law', declared Sir Edward Coke, 'but "sovereignty" is no Parliamentary word.' The Levellers had even more cause to know what was the main issue at stake. John Lilburne had suffered from the sovereign claims first of the King's Star Chamber, then of the House of Lords, then of the House of Commons. He was therefore in a good position – while imprisoned in Newgate in 1645 – to realise that what was required were no more sovereigns of any kind save only the sovereignty of the people as a whole, expressed through fundamental laws which no government, however 'popular' its claim, could touch, and through short-term Parliaments which would allow for popular control of its activities. The experience with Cromwell and the New Model

[25] See Vernon F. Snow, 'The Concept of Revolution in Seventeenth Century England', *The Historical Journal*, vol. v, no. 2 (1962), pp. 167–90.

[26] The 'American Revolution' was not called such until 1789; while the 'English Revolution' of 1640–60 had to wait until 1826 for the French historian Guizot so to call it, and then again by analogy with the French Revolution of 1789.

Army confirmed all these convictions. 'We were ruled before by King, Lords and Commons, now by a General, Court Martial and Commons; and we pray you what is the difference?'[27]

But it took the French Revolution to make explicit, and defiantly so, what had been implicit in these earlier revolutions. Hannah Arendt has written of the enormous 'pathos of novelty' experienced by the revolutionaries of the time: their feeling that they were attempting something grand and unprecedented in the history of mankind: the making, by a conscious act of will, of a new order of freedom.[28] Observers at the time were similarly struck by an irresistible feeling that they were witnessing a new beginning. 'Bliss was it in that dawn to be alive!' exclaimed Wordsworth. 'How much the greatest event in the history of the world and how much the best', Charles James Fox greeted the fall of the Bastille. Goethe declared that the victory of the revolutionaries at Valmy marked a new era in man's history. Hegel waxed ecstatic over the fact that the French Revolution had discovered that history was governed by Reason:

> Never since the sun had stood in the firmament and the planets revolved around him had it been perceived that man's existence centres in his head, i.e. in Thought, inspired by which he builds up the world of reality. . . . This was accordingly a glorious mental dawn. All thinking beings shared in the jubilation of this epoch.[29]

The French Revolution also clearly revealed what the form of this new order of freedom was to be, and so pointed to the other central element of the revolutionary idea. While the Third Estate and its supporters formed themselves into the Constituent Assembly and sought to direct the Revolution from the centre in Paris, the Revolution had already found new political forms. These were the 'sections' of Paris, the communes that were the organs of the municipalities, the popular clubs and societies that sprang up alongside all of these. As early as the fall of the Bastille, the 'municipal revolution' was under way, displacing the old incumbents of the councils, and claiming for the communes something

[27] See G. P. Gooch, *Political Thought in England from Bacon to Halifax* (London, 1950 reprint), pp. 62 3.
[28] Arendt, *On Revolution*, p. 27.
[29] Hegel, *The Philosophy of History*, trans. J. Sibree (New York, 1956 ed.), p. 447.

like complete autonomy within the municipality and the surrounding districts. From August of 1789 on, writes Georges Lefebvre, 'towns started to conclude mutual assistance pacts, spontaneously transforming France into a federation of communes'.[30] For much of the time the communes acted independently of events in Paris; but even they were not allowed to be sole rulers in their particular areas. No formally constituted body could be entirely trusted not to act self-interestedly, and so continuous pressure was applied to the communes by a host of spontaneously formed clubs and societies, which had no officially designed purpose whatsoever [2.2]. Together with the Parisian 'sections', these clubs and societies – the *sociétés populaires* – represented the most basic form of popular political activity in the Revolution, and as such were the distinctive political expression of a Revolution whose end, as Robespierre said, was 'the conquest and conservation of freedom'.[31]

Robespierre himself recognised that the clubs and societies were synonymous with the Revolution. He saw their aims as being 'to instruct, to enlighten their fellow citizens on the true principles of the constitution, and to spread a light without which the constitution will not be able to survive'. The survival of the constitution depended upon 'the public spirit' which existed only in 'assemblies where the citizens could occupy themselves in common with these (public) matters. . . .' In September 1791 he spoke before the National Assembly against the proposal to curb the political power of the clubs and societies. If, he said, the end of the Revolution was freedom, then the popular societies were the only places in the country where this freedom could actually show itself and be exercised by the citizens; they were the true 'pillars of the constitution', they constituted the very 'foundation of freedom', and among the crimes against the Revolution, 'the greatest was the persecution of the societies'.[32]

Robespierre spoke in very different terms once he himself had gained power, and fought for the suppression of all the 'so-called

[30] Georges Lefebvre, *The French Revolution: From its Origins to 1793*, trans. Elizabeth Moss Evanson (London, 1965), p. 126.

[31] Alfred Cobban estimates that by 1793 there were between 5000 and 8000 political clubs alone. See his *A History of Modern France*, 2 vols. (Harmondsworth, 1961), vol. 1, p. 173.

[32] All quotations in this paragraph are from Arendt, *On Revolution*, pp. 242–3.

B

popular societies' except for his own Jacobin Club. But this very change of position with accession to office revealed all the more clearly that the struggle was really one between the centralised sovereign power of the state and the diffused power of the popular organs that had been summoned up by the Revolution. The actual form of these organs was not itself novel. It went back at least to the communes of the medieval towns, and had close parallels in the democratic organisation of many of the Protestant sects in seventeenth-century England, as well as in the townships of the North American colonies. But it was in the French Revolution that the popular organisations could be first seen as an achievement of *revolution,* indeed as the spontaneous and almost natural manifestation of the revolutionary enterprise to make the ruled into rulers.

If revolution aimed at 'the conquest and conservation of freedom', it could not do so simply by transferring power from a single delegate – the King – to an Assembly of delegates. There was no reason to think that an Assembly would be less dictatorial: indeed it was likely to be more so, since it would claim to express the will of the whole people. Its very presence implied a custodianship that made further participation by the people unnecessary, and probably harmful. Thus freedom could only be conserved if the people, who always made the revolution possible, continued to act politically, in their own persons, in bodies which were in immediate contact with the environment affecting them, and where political education was a product of political participation in debates and decisions made by the very people whose concerns they directly touched. To preserve this arrangement would be to continue the revolution in being, to make it what all revolutions aspire to be, a permanent activity.

The popular organisations – clubs, communes, councils, *soviets, Räte* – have been thrown up by every real revolution since the French. And in nearly every case they have appeared spontaneously: unanticipated, unsponsored, and usually undesired by the revolutionary parties and their leaders, who struggled to subvert or submit them to their centralising direction. In the February Revolution of 1848 in France they took the form of the political clubs and the organised crafts, the *corporations ouvrières.* In 1871 they reappeared as the Paris Commune, which, as Marx noted,

'was to be the political form of even the smallest country hamlet'. The Russian experience of 1905 produced a new word
for the form: the *Soviet*, which came to be applied to all
the popular councils of later Revolutions. Thus it was used
not only of the workers', peasants', and soldiers' councils of the
Russian Revolution in 1917, but also of the soldiers' and
workers' councils in Germany and Austria in 1919, and of
the Revolutionary and Workers' Councils of Hungary in 1956
[2.1].

The Paris Commune and the Russian Soviets are especially
significant because they supplied a missing part to the most influential theory of revolution, that of Marxism. Up to 1871 Marx had
given only the barest account of the form to be taken by the
'dictatorship of the proletariat', as the political expression of the
coming proletarian revolution. This was deliberate: Marx disliked
drawing up blueprints for the future. Unexpectedly, although quite
consistently with his theory, the activities of the Paris workmen
in 1871 showed him what the 'dictatorship of the proletariat'
would be like. He hailed the Commune as 'the glorious harbinger
of a new society', since it did not 'simply lay hold of the ready-made
state machinery, and wield it for its own purposes', but was a
'completely new historical creation . . . which breaks the modern
State power'. He emphasised especially 'the suppression of the
standing army, and the substitution for it of the armed people';
'the police was at once stripped of its political attributes, and turned
into the responsible and at all times revocable agent of the Commune'. Nor did the Paris Commune aspire to dominate France,
unlike all previous revolutionary regimes, but offered to 'serve as
a model to all the great industrial centres of France' as well as to
the rural provinces [2.3].

For all Marx's later qualifications as to the significance of the
Commune, his most serious followers accepted that his experience
of this spontaneous revolutionary organisation of the working
class, marked a decisive step in his thinking.[33] As late as 1891
Engels summarised the aims of the Commune as follows:

It was precisely the oppressing power of the former centralised

[33] For the general influence of the Commune on revolutionary theory, see
Theodor Schieder, 'The Problems of Revolution in the Nineteenth Century',
p. 21.

government, army, political police, bureaucracy, which Napoleon had created in 1789 and which since then had been taken over by every new government as a welcome instrument and used against its opponents – it was precisely this power which was to fall everywhere, just as it had already fallen in Paris.

And he concluded:

Of late, the Social Democratic philistine has once more been filled with wholesome terror at the words: Dictatorship of the Proletariat. Well and good, gentlemen, do you want to know what this dictatorship looks like? Look at the Paris Commune. That was the Dictatorship of the Proletariat.[34]

It was above all Lenin who seized upon Marx's writings on the Commune as the scriptural basis for his analysis of Russia's own experience of 'communes': the Soviets that appeared with equal spontaneity in the Revolutions of 1905 and 1917. Not that he had any better understanding of them at the time of their first appearance than most revolutionary theorists have had when confronted with new revolutionary forms. E. H. Carr writes that 'the earliest of these new-fangled institutions seem to have been the result of spontaneous action by groups of workers on strike . . . During the next few weeks [of October 1905] more or less organised Soviets sprang up in nearly all the main industrial centres.'[35] Lenin was as surprised as all other revolutionaries, and was inclined to belittle them as 'not a workers' parliament and not an organ of proletarian self-government'.[36] They had no place in his tactics at the time: they were non-party, and, especially, out of the control of the Bolsheviks. It was Trotsky – not surprisingly, as the last president of the St Petersburg Soviet – who most fully appreciated the significance of the new organisations. 'The Soviet,' he wrote immediately after the suppression of the 1905 Revolution, 'is the first democratic power in modern Russian history. The Soviet is the organised power of the masses themselves over their component parts.' Up to this time there had been revolutionary

[34] Friedrich Engels, 'Introduction' (1891) to Marx's *The Civil War in France*, in K. Marx and F. Engels, *Selected Works in Two Volumes* (Moscow, 1962), vol. 1, pp. 483, 485.
[35] E. H. Carr, *A History of Soviet Russia*, vol. 1 (London, 1960), pp. 46–7.
[36] Lenin, quoted ibid., p. 47.

organisations *among* the masses, seeking to influence them; but 'the Soviet is an organisation *of* the proletariat; its aim is to fight for revolutionary power'. And it was a sign of genuine insight, considering the novelty of the phenomenon in Russian revolutionary experience, for Trotsky to predict that 'the first new wave of the revolution will lead to the creation of Soviets all over the country' [2.5].

This was precisely what happened in February 1917; and this time Lenin, though he had still not paid much attention to the Soviets in his thinking, adopted them wholeheartedly as the sole repositories of revolutionary power [2.6]. In his 'April theses', to the consternation of his own party, he stated the goal of the revolution: 'Not a parliamentary republic . . . but a republic of Soviets of Workers', Poor Peasants' and Peasants' Deputies throughout the country, growing from below upwards.' The more theoretical pronouncements of these months elaborated the point. Drawing on Marx's writings on the Commune, he quoted Marx on the need to 'smash . . . the bureaucratic-military machine' as 'the preliminary condition for every real people's revolution'. The proletariat could not simply take over the old state machinery, however radical its policies. It had to construct a new sort of state altogether, and 'this new type of state machinery was created by the Paris Commune, and the Russian Soviets of Workers', Soldiers' and Peasants' Deputies are a power *of the same type*'. In listing the revolutionary features of the Soviets, he echoed Marx closely. The Soviets replaced the standing army of the past with the people armed; it eliminated bureaucracy by being an organ of direct democracy; it made reforms quicker and more effective through its close contact with all the crafts and professions; and it was a unique instrument for the political education of the masses, so long excluded from political life. As late as the end of 1918, when the Bolshevik party was already draining away the power of the Soviets, Lenin was still declaring that 'the Soviets are the Russian form of the dictatorship of the proletariat' – a direct echo, this time, of Engels' remark on the Commune.[37]

'The Soviets,' Franz Borkenau has written,

---

[37] The most important of Lenin's theoretical discussions can be found in his *The State and Revolution* (1917), included in the *Selected Works in Three Volumes*, vol. II, pp. 305 ff.

as the direct representatives of the masses, dependent on their local and professional structure and their ever-changing moods, were the natural organ of revolt. Their continued domination would have meant the perpetuation of the situation of revolt, the free federation of professions and districts with a policy continuously changing.[38]

As a statement of the aim of revolution this can hardly be bettered, just as it makes quite clear when revolution ends. Revolution ends with the suppression of the popular councils and their promise of 'a policy continuously changing'. Sooner or later this has occurred in all revolutions to date. Nor is it usually the forces of the *ancien régime*, the 'counter-revolution' in the conventional sense, that bring about this end. It is precisely the revolutionary parties themselves who, in their successful elimination of other contenders for power, heal the breach in the state's sovereignty which has been effected by the revolution, and so become the heirs of their pre-revolutionary predecessors. In England this was accomplished by Cromwell and the New Model Army; in France by the Jacobins and, more definitively, by Napoleon. The end of the Russian Revolution was especially poignant. At the outside it was over by 1921, when the Kronstadt 'rebellion' was put down by Trotsky's Red Army – a symbolic as well as an actual end, since mutiny in the Kronstadt fleet had sparked off revolution both in 1905 and 1917. The revolt was naturally styled by the Bolsheviks a 'White' plot and a 'counter-revolution', thus precisely reversing the true position. Lenin at least knew better: in Kronstadt, he said, 'they do not want the White Guards, and they do not want our power either'.[39] 'Soviets without Communists' was how the Kronstadt sailors themselves put it, so indicating clearly that the real victims were the revolutionary organisations of the Soviets, suppressed now by Lenin's party just as Robespierre suppressed the revolutionary clubs that he had once championed.

The persistent failure of revolutions to fulfil themselves, to make secure the conditions of freedom when once they have achieved the dissolution of sovereign power, enables us to see why political

[38] F. Borkenau, 'State and Revolution in the Paris Commune, the Russian Revolution, and the Spanish Civil War', *Sociological Review*, vol. XXIX (1937), p. 58.
[39] Quoted L. Schapiro, *The Communist Party of the Soviet Union* (London, 1963), p. 205.

revolution has been so rare and fleeting a thing, and gives substance to Camus' remark that 'there has not yet been a (political) revolution in the course of history'.[40] This is not quite right. There have been revolutions, but they have never managed to continue in being, by recognising clearly the conditions that gave birth to them, and so attempting to establish these on firm foundations. As a result they have had something of the character of happy accidents, reminiscent of Trotsky's description of them as the 'mad inspirations of history'. They come into being for reasons the participants do not understand, flourish briefly, in the process producing some of man's most creative achievements, and die away, leaving behind a structure of power that differs from that of the *ancien régime* largely in its superior effectiveness.

This sequence perhaps points to a new perspective for considering an ancient paradox about Western social development. It has often been remarked that we can speak plausibly about economic and technological progress, and about progress in scientific ideas and the arts; it is far less easy to speak convincingly about political progress. Now we do not have to mean by progress, a movement *towards* some ultimate goal, conceived as Absolute Truth, or some perfect standard of artistic representation. We can mean rather – as Kuhn points out in the case of science – a history of change or evolution *from* earlier states, such that the particular activity experiences repeated changes of 'style', and its practitioners are agreed in recognising a series of fundamental changes, however they assess them in terms of 'better' or 'worse'. Progress in this sense amounts to having a revolutionary history; and it is in this sense that there has been progress in the arts and sciences, and almost none in politics. This is reflected in the fact that political problems seem to have changed hardly at all since the political speculations of the Greeks. The reason is that the nature of the polity itself has changed so little. There have been many revolutions, many changes of style, in man's technological and intellectual activities; there have been no clearly successful ones in his political activity. Unlike the succession of styles in the case of the former, introducing new paradigms and new world-views, developments in the latter have reverted again and again to the pre-existing style, expressed in the principle of monopolistic power and

[40] Camus, *The Rebel*, p. 77.

sovereignty. There have been local variations in this style: the rule of the few over the many, which was the general custom until about the eighteenth century; and the rule of the many over the few, which has been the custom ever since and which is commonly more vicious. But the general principle has continued to exert an apparently irresistible attraction. Revolutions have been but brief interruptions of its rule. Like Pareto's remark about aristocracies, history is their graveyard too.

4 A CRITICISM OF CURRENT CONCEPTS OF POLITICAL REVOLUTION

John Stuart Mill once had occasion to observe that '"the Revolution", as a name for any sort of principles or opinions, is not English'. English would speak of particular events, like 'the French Revolution', or 'the English Revolution'. The general usage, which derived from France, was to be deplored. 'It proceeds from an infirmity of the French mind, which has been one main cause of the miscarriages of the French nation in its pursuit of liberty and progress; that of being led away by phrases, and treating abstractions as if they were realities which have a will and exert active power.'[41]

The average speech of almost any revolutionary over the last century would testify to the need to heed this formidable warning. Against this, there is the hope that an examination of a common but cloudy concept might make it yield some profitable meaning. The justification of the concept as I have sketched it is two-fold: there is a tradition of thinking of it in this way that derives from the birth of the modern idea in the eighteenth century, and that has been upheld by the most influential theorists of revolution subsequently; and the concept thus understood enables us to approach, with better understanding and more hope of benefit, some of the most instructive phenomena in history. My criticism of current concepts parallels this, in a certain sense. Their weakness seems to me to be due largely to the fact that their meanings depend upon certain traditions, but that they are either ignorant of or indifferent

[41] J. S. Mill, letter of October 1872, in *Letters*, vol. II, pp. 347–8.

to these traditions, one of which vastly pre-dates the eighteenth-century creation of the revolutionary idea; and that this fact is responsible for devaluing and largely emptying the concept of revolution.

There are broadly two types of definition of revolution in the current literature. One is a legal or constitutionalist type; the other a Marxist or sociological type.

(a) *Legal and Constitutional Concepts*

To take a few examples of the first type: most are an echo in one form or another of the Oxford English Dictionary definition: a revolution is 'a complete overthrow of the established government in any country or state by those who were previously subject to it; a forcible substitution of a new ruler or form of government'. Thus L. P. Edwards saw revolution as 'a change . . . whereby one system of legality is terminated and another originated'. For George Pettee 'a great revolution is a reconstitution of the state'. Crane Brinton defines it as 'the drastic, sudden substitution of one group in charge of the running of a territorial political unity for another group'. Arthur Hatto falls back on the OED definition: 'Let "revolution" continue to do good work by pointing the way to crucial events involving a shift of power in the state swifter than "evolution".' J. C. Davies takes revolutions to be 'violent civil disturbances that cause the displacement of one ruling group by another that has a broader popular basis for support'.[42]

The trouble with these definitions is not that they do not point to real, identifiable phenomena; but that it is making very poor

[42] See, in order of quotations: L. P. Edwards, *The Natural History of Revolution* (Chicago, 1927), p. 2; G. Pettee, *The Process of Revolution*, p. 3; Crane Brinton, *The Anatomy of Revolution* (rev. ed., New York, 1952), p. 4; Arthur Hatto, 'Revolution: An Inquiry into the Usefulness of an Historical Term', *Mind*, vol. LVIII (1949), p. 517; J. C. Davies, 'Toward a Theory of Revolution', *American Sociological Review*, vol. XXVII (1962), p. 6n. And see also Tanter and Midlarsky: 'A revolution may be said to exist when a group of insurgents illegally and/or forcefully challenges the governmental élite for the occupancy of roles in the structure of political authority.' 'A Theory of Revolution', *Journal of Conflict Resolution*, vol. XI (1967), p. 267; Peter Calvert: Revolution is 'the change by physical force by citizens of those in power over them'. 'Revolution: The Politics of Violence', *Political Studies*, vol. XV (1967), pp. 2–3.

27

use of a much more worth-while concept when revolution is reduced to a mere transfer of power from one group to another. These definitions are, moreover, highly abstract and a-historical, with a concept where this is least defensible and least likely to be valuable. This is not simply seen in the fact that they ignore the central associations of the revolutionary idea since the eighteenth century. It is more significantly shown up by the fact that they are fragmentary relics of an ancient philosophy of history whose meaning and purpose they entirely ignore.

The use of the word 'revolution' to mean fundamental transfers of power or changes of regime derives from the cyclical view of history prevalent in classical antiquity. In this view the events of history were seen to follow sequences as regular as those in nature, and especially to fall into those cycles of growth and decay so abundantly illustrated in natural processes. Since particular changes were simply the successive stages in the whole movement of the cycle, it was strictly correct to call them 'revolutions', since they were 'turnings' or even 're-turnings' of the cycle. Plato sketched one such sequence of 'revolutions' in Book VIII of the *Republic,* when describing the successive forms of degeneration from the ideal state. There is a deterioration first to timocracy, then to oligarchy, and so on through democracy to tyranny. Plato did not here quite complete the cycle of political development. This was left to Polybius, who generalised Plato's sequence into a fully cyclical theory of political change. States begin with kingship, and inevitably return to it after passing through a number of forms: ' . . . such is the cycle of political revolutions, the course appointed by nature in which constitutions change, disappear and finally return to the point from which they started'. From Plato and Polybius, Cicero took over the idea of cycles of constitutions, and wrote of contemporary political changes as natural turns of a circle or wheel (*orbis*).

Such a cyclical conception of change was common enough in the Graeco-Roman world for J. B. Bury to describe it as 'the orthodox theory'.[43] It is not surprising then to find it pervading the Renaissance usage of the word 'revolution'. Machiavelli followed strict classical precedents in describing a cycle of constitutional changes from monarchy, through necessary stages, to popular government,

[43] J. B. Bury, *The Idea of Progress* (London, 1923), p. 12.

which in turn led to licence and anarchy and back to monarchy. 'Such is the circle which all republics are destined to run through' (*Discourses*, I.2.). It was this sense of political changes which could not be influenced by human power that the word *rivoluzione* connoted in the political upheavals of the medieval Italian states. Bodin, too, accepted the theory of constitutional cycles, and it is within this context that we must understand his influential definition of revolution as a displacement or transfer of sovereignty.[44]

The very special limitations of the concept of revolution within this tradition are even more apparent when we consider that the very word – *revolution* – which was applied to the changes of the political cycle, had its origin in the science of astronomy; and that throughout the Middle Ages, and right down to the end of the seventeenth century, it continued to be used predominantly in its astronomical sense. Here, as in Copernicus' *De Revolutionibus Orbium Coelestium*, it reflected precisely its etymological root, designating the regular, lawfully revolving motions of the stars, beyond the influence of man and hence irresistible. As Hannah Arendt has written, 'if used for affairs of men on earth, it could only signify that the few known forms of government revolve among the mortals in eternal recurrence and with the same irresistible force which makes the stars follow their pre-ordained paths in the skies'.[45] Its application to political events almost invariably carried the astronomical connotation, and we have seen how this affected contemporary interpretations of the English Revolutions of the seventeenth century. It was only in the eighteenth century, in the course of the French Revolution, that the word acquired its modern meaning. It was only then that 'revolution' ceased to be a phenomenon of the natural or divine order, made by non-human, elemental forces, and became part of a man-made, conscious purpose to create a new order based on reason and freedom.[46]

[44] G. Sabine, *A History of Political Theory* (London, 1951), p. 350. For Bodin's influence on modern concepts of revolution, cf. C. A. Ellwood: 'As Bodin long ago pointed out, the mark of revolution is a change in the location of sovereignty.' Quoted Dale Yoder, 'Current Definitions of Revolution', *American Journal of Sociology*, vol. XXXII (1926–7), p. 437.

[45] Arendt, *On Revolution*, p. 35.

[46] For the history of the word 'revolution' I have used especially the articles by Hatto and Snow, cited above; also Hannah Arendt, op. cit., ch. 1; Karl Griewank 'Emergence of the Concept of Revolution', in *Revolutions in Modern European History*, ed. Heinz Lubasz (New York, 1966), pp. 55–61 (a translated section of

To earlier writers, then, the concept of revolution had a limited but clearly defined meaning within a general theory of history and politics. Modern writers have inherited their usage while jettisoning the framework that gave it meaning. The word 'revolution' has come into the political vocabulary as a gloss upon a certain type of political change discussed by Plato, Polybius, Cicero, Machiavelli, Bodin, and a number of seventeenth-century writers; but few who now use the word accept the cyclical theory of change that went with that use. It is this that makes the definitions quoted earlier abstract and rather barren. Shorn of their general context and purpose, there remains no informing principle to point them to any interesting and illuminating phenomenon. Revolutions as 'changes in the location of sovereignty', as the originators of different constitutional forms, are of great interest if one is concerned with tracing the recurring patterns of political rule through which all human societies pass. This gives one a certain independence of position, removed from a belief in the intrinsic significance of these impermanent forms, and allows one to look for the real significance of human history in other spheres, in cosmology or religion. Such revolutions are far less interesting, however, if they simply mark the passage from the rule of some to the rule of others, unadorned by any philosophy except perhaps the weary one of *eadem, sed aliter*. It is a conception that seems to point to a timeless sequence in which nothing really changes or can change. The study of history must be profitless since all it will reveal is more of the same thing that we already experience in abundance.

The suspicion that these current concepts are not dealing with 'fundamental change' at all is heightened by a further consideration. It has often been said that ours is a 'century of revolutions', and that in this respect we seem to be re-living the experiences of the city-states of ancient Greece in the time of the Peloponnesian War. There is indeed a famous passage in Thucydides which could stand as a remarkably accurate account of the political experiences

---

his important work *Der Neuzeitliche Revolutionsbegriff* [1955]). The work of Eugen Rosenstock-Huessy, *Revolution als Politischer Begriff in der Neuzeit* (1931), remains untranslated but is the basis for most later accounts. For good summaries of it, see Eugene Kamenka, 'The Concept of A Political Revolution', in *Revolution*, ed. Carl Friedrich, pp. 122–35; and Sigmund Neumann, 'The International Civil War', *World Politics*, vol. 1 (1949), pp. 333–50.

of this century. Writing of developments within the Greek states
during the war, he says:

> . . . practically the whole of the Hellenic world was convulsed, with
> rival parties in every state. . . . Revolution broke out in city after city,
> and in places where the revolutions occurred late the knowledge of what
> had happened previously caused still new extravagances of revolutionary
> zeal, expressed by an elaboration in the methods of seizing power and by
> unheard of atrocities in revenge. . . . The tie of party was stronger than
> the tie of blood, because a partisan was more ready to dare without
> asking why. . . . Love of power, operating through greed and personal
> ambition, was the cause of all these evils. To this must be added the
> violent fanaticism that came into play once the struggle had broken out.
> Leaders of parties in the cities had programmes which appeared
> admirable – on the one side political equality for the masses, on the other
> safe and sound government of the aristocracy – but in professing to
> serve the public interest they were seeking to win the prizes for them-
> selves. Here they were deterred neither by the claims of justice nor by
> the interests of the state; their one standard was the pleasure of their
> own party at that particular moment. . . .[47]

This is an admirable summary of the course of so many so-called
'revolutions' since the eighteenth century; and just as a Cromwell
or a Napoleon came forward as the saviours of society torn apart
in this way, so Philip and Alexander of Macedon brought order to
the city-states, at the price of their independence. But the important thing to point out is that Thucydides is not speaking of revolution in our modern sense. He is speaking of *stasis*, and to the Greeks
this had a meaning the very opposite of the change, novelty and
freedom associated with the modern idea of revolution. The common translation of *stasis* as 'revolution', both in Thucydides and
in Book V of Aristotle's *Politics*, is gravely misleading, and is an
important source for the current devaluation of the concept.
Stasis derived from *histemi*, which the Liddell and Scott lexicon
variously translates as 'stand', 'bring to a standstill', 'stay', 'check'.
In its non-political use *stasis* could still mean 'standing still',
'stationariness'; and in its political use it fully echoed its derivation.
Here it denoted a violent upheaval in the state, the less capable
of effecting real change in proportion to the degree of this very
violence; and by an easy transference it also came to be used of

[47] Thucydides, *The Peloponnesian War*, bk. III, ch. 5 (trans. Warner).

the factions that were the protagonists of this senseless play, full of sound and fury, and signifying nothing. To a Greek writer, the mental picture conjured up by repeated experiences of *stasis* would have been of a society shaken by the automatic spasms of a sort of social tetanus, locked in the struggles of two parties, alternately rising and falling in power, and by the very fanaticism of their conflict destroying any chance of real change. It was such societies that Thucydides so brilliantly described, and his account should make it clear that where there was *stasis* there could be no revolution. If our century is indeed retracing the paths of the states of ancient Greece, exhausting itself in wars until it submits to the deathly peace of a world-empire, then we may choose to call it the 'century of *stasis*'; but of revolution it will have known very little.

(b) *Marxist and Sociological Concepts*

Definitions of revolution of the legal and constitutionalist type I have criticised as unhistorical abstractions, devoid of the meaning given to earlier uses by a specific historical context or particular framework of their own. Current definitions of the Marxist and sociological type suffer from a similar failing. They owe their origins largely to Marx, but have become divorced from Marx's theory and philosophy of history. Consequently they lack the specific content and meaning given to the concept in his usage, and indeed imply a view of change similar to, and as superficial as, definitions of the first type.

The characteristic feature of sociological definitions of revolution is to emphasise its social content. Revolution is seen as the transformation of the economic and social structure of society, the actual political act of the overthrow of state power being no more than the consolidation of, or perhaps the necessary midwifery to, these more fundamental social changes.[48] Political events, however violent, which did not involve such changes, Marx dismissed as 'partial, merely *political* revolution which leaves the pillars of the

[48] For a succinct account of this concept, see Karl Marx, 'Preface to "A Contribution to the Critique of Political Economy" ', in *Selected Works*, vol. I, pp. 362–3.

building standing' [1.4]. Thus Engels wrote: 'Every real revolution is a social one, in that it brings a new class to power and allows it to remodel society in its own image.'[49] More recently we have Sigmund Neumann defining revolution as 'a sweeping, fundamental change in political organisation, social structure, economic property control, and the predominant myth of a social order'. Alfred Meusel says that 'a re-casting of the social order is . . . a far more important characteristic of revolutions than a change of the political constitution or the use of violence in the attainment of this end'. Eugene Kamenka writes: 'Revolution is a sharp, sudden change in the social location of political power . . . the transfer of social power from one governing class to a new class.'[50]

Briefly, Marx conceived the fundamental change brought about by revolution as follows. A society was essentially structured by its mode and level of economic production. Within this mode was contained a certain set of property relations, expressing the basic social relationship between the classes in the population. So long as there were no significant changes in this 'infrastructure' there would be no basic changes in the life of society as a whole, in the 'superstructure' of political, intellectual and artistic activities, which mirrored, at the level of social consciousness, the particular mode of production. But economic processes were dynamic. Technological developments, new methods in credit and commercial exchange, all tended to be cumulative and eventually to press against the existing property relations. Since the new developments favoured some classes at the expense of others, the conflict was bound to express itself as a conflict of classes. Such a conflict, moreover, ultimately had to become revolutionary in the sphere of politics. For part of the old social order was the control of the state by the economically dominant class, for whom the state was an instrument of repression in the perpetuation of their privileges,

[49] Engels, 'On Social Relations in Russia', in Marx and Engels, *Selected Works*, vol 2, p. 53.

[50] See, in order, Sigmund Neumann, 'The International Civil War', p. 333n.; Alfred Meusel, 'Revolution and Counter-Revolution', in the *Encyclopaedia of the Social Sciences*; Eugene Kamenka, 'The Concept of a Political Revolution', p. 124. And cf. R. K. Merton: 'When rebellion becomes endemic in a substantial part of society, it provides a potential for revolution, which re-shapes both the normative and the social structure', *Social Theory and Social Structure* (rev. ed., Glencoe, 1957), p. 191. See also Chalmers Johnson, *Revolution and the Social System* (Stanford, 1964).

and generally of a social pattern favourable to them. For the new, economically advancing class fully to exploit the new mode of production, it would have to wrest political power away from the old ruling class. Thus, so long as society was divided up into classes, social development was necessarily revolutionary in manner: 'It is only in an order of things where there are no longer classes and class antagonism that *social evolution* will cease to involve *political revolution*.'[51] With the seizure of political power and the consolidation of the political position of the new class, the revolution could be said to have been substantially completed. It remained for its implications to work themselves out fully – as they inevitably would – in the superstructural realms of philosophy, art, political theory, and legal codification.

A number of things need to be noted about this view of revolution. The sort of structural changes it entails can be mapped out only on a very broad plane of history. It follows that for Marx revolutions have been singularly few, and have been successful only where change in the underlying economic structure favoured the classes making or supporting them. England in the seventeenth and France in the eighteenth century experienced true revolutionary change: in both cases the outmoded, feudal type of production, together with its exponent, the nobility, broke down under the revolutionary impetus of a rising bourgeoisie basing itself on the forms of capitalist production. The European revolutions of 1848 were, however, abortive precisely because the bourgeoisie was too weak as against the landowners; or because it was fearful of a proletariat that was as yet too weak as a class to establish a proletarian state, thus delivering up both parties to the reaction [5.7].

The Marxist concept of revolution therefore sets itself against a purely romantic conception of revolution as willed, spontaneous action. It was the poets who had nurtured the idea of revolution as an almost personal, individual, act of defiance against the whole social and even cosmic order. This Marx saw as a typical echo of bourgeois individualism. 'Men make their own history,' he wrote, 'but they do not make it just as they please; they do not make it under circumstances chosen by themselves, but under circumstances directly encountered, given and transmitted from the past'

[51] Marx, *The Poverty of Philosophy* (1847) (New York, 1963), p. 176.

34

[5.6]. For much of the time, the social fabric remains refractory to revolutionary enterprises: such attempts are futile while there is still capacity for development within the existing economic order. Thus Marx emphasises the objective dimension of revolution, the need for social conditions to be 'ripe' for revolution:

No social order ever perishes before all the productive forces for which there is room in it have developed; and new, higher relations of production never appear before the material conditions of their existence have matured in the womb of the old society itself. Therefore mankind always sets itself only such tasks as it can solve; since, looking at the matter more closely, it will always be found that the task itself arises only when the material conditions for its solution already exist or are at least in the process of formation.[52]

The Marxists saw themselves as the representatives of the third and final phase of the concept of revolution. To use Rosenstock-Huessy's terms, the first phase was the *naturalistic*: the use of revolution in its astronomical sense which, when applied to politics, implied an objective, elemental, non-human force: the cycle of history, the wheel of fortune. The naturalistic meaning was still there, perhaps for the last time, in the celebrated dialogue between Louis XVI and the Duc de la Rochefoucauld-Liancourt when the latter informed the King of the fall of the Bastille. '*C'est une révolte,*' exclaimed the King. The Duc corrected him: '*Non, sire, c'est une révolution*' – by which he meant that this was a force of nature, and hence irresistible. In the course of the French Revolution the naturalistic concept was displaced by the *romantic* concept: revolution was now the assertion of human subjectivity, made by man as the master of his own history. Marx could claim to have inaugurated the third phase, the phase of the *realist* concept, and to see this as the dialectical synthesis of the two preceding phases. Naturalism was preserved in the insistence that revolutions are not simply the products of human will, but depend upon objective conditions which make a society 'ripe' for revolution. Romanticism was preserved in the view that nevertheless revolution was a human, not a superhuman, phenomenon, and that objective conditions were not sufficient to bring about revolution. There had in addition to be a class, fully conscious of its revolutionary role,

[52] Marx, 'Preface to "A Contribution to the Critique of Political Economy" ', p. 363.

articulating this in revolutionary ideology, and embodying it in a revolutionary political organisation. There were, in other words, both objective and subjective components to revolution. In recognising this, revolution was to be removed from the realm of astrology and of poetry, and to become part of science.

But 'scientific' only in the rather special Marxist sense: which is to say, that revolution still took its main significance from its pivotal place in the Marxist philosophy of history. There is a sense indeed in which revolution is for Marx a category of the whole of human history. History has a revolutionary stamp, for 'the whole of history is nothing but a continual transformation of human nature'.[53] Robert Tucker expresses this by saying that history for Marx is the 'process of man's revolutionary evolution . . . the growth process of humanity from the primitive beginnings to complete maturity and self-realisation in future communism'.[54] But if history itself is the Revolution, then the particular revolutions within history have to be seen as stages or 'moments' in the making of that Revolution. They could not be studied in isolation as self-sufficient phenomena; their pretensions to be final and consummating acts of liberation had to be inspected critically. If this were done it would be found that the claim to be bringing about a general order of freedom was bound to be spurious. For the social conditions necessary for such an order have not yet existed. All that revolutions could do was to introduce new forms of the division of labour, different variations on the old theme of class rule, of oppressors and oppressed. As Marx put it, 'in all revolutions up till now the mode of activity always remained unscathed and it was only a question of a different distribution of this activity, a new distribution of labour to other persons . . .' [1.5]. The classes which made the revolutions naturally proclaimed that they were acting for the liberation of all; but this was simply one of the inescapable conditions of a successful revolution waged by a class striving to impose its rule. For

no class in civil society can play this part unless it can arouse, in itself and in the masses, a moment of enthusiasm in which it associates and mingles with society at large, identifies itself with it, and is felt and

[53] Marx, *The Poverty of Philosophy*, p. 160.
[54] Robert C. Tucker, 'The Marxian Revolutionary Idea', in *Revolution*, ed. Carl Freidrich, pp. 219, 222.

recognised as the general representative of this society. . . . It is only in the name of general interests that a particular class can claim general supremacy [1.4].

But the true meaning of each revolution soon reveals itself as the victory of particular interests over the rest of society. This gradual revelation is the setting for the next stage of class conflict, the next revolution marking another stage in the general liberation of humanity. Marx once wrote that 'revolutions are the locomotives of history';[55] and in this graphic phrase he expressed perfectly the idea that revolutions are the driving-forces of man's successive attempts to tear himself from the realm of necessity into the realm of freedom, to leap from 'pre-history' into 'history'.

The proletarian and communistic revolution of the future was to be the final act in the process of human liberation. It would be the first revolution in history that could both speak of 'general interests' and genuinely act in those interests. For 'the communistic revolution is directed against the preceding *mode* of activity, does away with *labour,* and abolishes the rule of all classes with the classes themselves, because it is carried through by the class which no longer counts as a class in society . . . and is in itself the expression of the dissolution of all classes . . . within present society' [1.5]. All revolutions had proclaimed freedom as their end, but it was the social circumstances of the proletariat alone that would enable it to establish a form of society 'in which the free development of each is the condition for the free development of all'.[56] The mechanics of the proletarian revolution Marx saw as formally similar to those of earlier ones; but the proletariat's special structural and temporal position in the development of man's productive forces marked its revolution decisively off from all preceding ones.

In his writings on the proletarian revolution, and on such possible foreshadowings of it as the Paris Commune, Marx placed himself in, and furthered, the Enlightenment tradition that associated the idea of revolution intrinsically with the idea of freedom. But it was precisely on this matter that his particular delineation

[55] Marx, 'The Class Struggles in France 1848–50', in *Selected Works,* vol. 1, p. 217.
[56] Marx and Engels, 'The Communist Manifesto', *Selected Works,* vol. 1, p. 54.

of the concept of revolution carried an equivocal legacy for his sociological successors. Two points especially stand out. Since, for Marx, the association of revolution and freedom could only be a reality in the case of the proletarian revolution of the future, all revolutions of the past were 'historicised' by a philosophy that radically depreciated their aims and practices. Freedom came only at the end of a number of historical stages, each marked by a 'revolution' which was incapable of realising its 'ideological' programme of general emancipation because social conditions were not yet 'ripe'. The historical revolutions were thereby devalued, both as fields of study for general propositions about revolution, and as authentic, realisable, and perhaps imitable attempts to create an order of political freedom. The aspirations and achievements of men in the past had to be seen as incomplete: real enough for their own times, of course, but necessarily limited by those times and, since they were 'taken up' and 'superseded' by later developments, of no real value as guidance for the present. Revolution had to be considered more or less exclusively as an ambition of the future, as a special 'project' of a special class. The conditions favouring or retarding the revolutionary organisation of the proletariat came to be seen as the central study of the sociology of revolution. Uninformed by an interest in and knowledge of past revolutions, such an approach not surprisingly has yielded little of lasting value.

This aspect of Marx was, of course, largely a problem for Marxist sociologists. Other sociologists, seizing on another aspect, evaded this problem by renouncing what was distinctively Marxian in the schema of revolution. It was not a very large step, especially for the academic students of revolution, to come to regard the concept of a liberating proletarian revolution as utopian and apocalyptic, while at the same time retaining Marx's formal notion of revolution as the transformation of the social and economic 'infrastructure' of a society. A variation on this was to regard revolution as 'structural' or 'systemic' change: society was conceived as an integrated system with a 'core institutional order', which the revolution replaced with an entirely new order, a new social system. Both varieties of this concept give rise to acute difficulties of analysis; but this problem belongs to another discussion. What is important here is to see how closely the sociological definition of revolution parallels the constitutional definition. Just as the latter's 'changes in the location of sovereignty' was an abstraction from a full theory of history, so the former's notion of a transfer of power based on economic dominance was an abstraction from Marx's philosophy of history. Marx had integrated the ideas of revolution and freedom by means of his version of evolutionary anthropology. His successors pulled these ideas apart. Revolutions simply marked the attainment of political power by new economic classes: there was no longer any suggestion that they might be attempts to intervene in and change this apparently natural and unchanging order. As such, the sequences of the rise and fall of classes had something of the irresistibility, and even the absurdity, of the turn of Fortune's wheel, or the rhythms of the cycles of the classical world. At the very least they were a far cry from Marx's fundamental premise that man makes his own history.

At a more immediate level, the sociological and the constitutional concepts of revolution come together in a view of revolution as *restoration*: in this curiously but quite unconsciously echoing the practice of Royalists like Clarendon in calling the Restoration of Charles II in 1660 'a revolution'. Revolution is seen as basically re-constitutive: of a new 'system of legality', of a new ruling group, of a new equilibrium of the social system. Power is transferred from one group to another; social credit runs out, and new groups claim to have the confidence of the masses, and with it the right to rule. But the fact of power remains, and indeed is usually strengthened; the principle of rule is upheld. In the language of American sociology, 'revolution is fundamentally a process whereby accumulated imbalances between major elements of society . . . are eliminated, and a new state of relative integration achieved'.[57] The underlying image is often that of a sick man being restored to health through necessarily drastic remedial treatment; and it is not surprising to find writers like Talcott Parsons making the image explicit and seeing revolution as a fever of the body politic. Crane Brinton, too, borrows the language of pathology: 'We shall regard revolutions . . . as a kind of fever.'[58]

Sickness only has meaning in relation to health. If the health of

[57] Pierre L. van den Berghe, 'Dialectic and Functionalism: Towards a Synthesis', *American Journal of Sociology*, October 1963.
[58] Brinton, *The Anatomy of Revolution*, p. 16.

society is seen in terms of an organised and effective system of power, then revolution, which aims to dissolve that power, must be considered as disease. But doctors can agree on what constitutes the healthy individual far more easily than sociologists on what constitutes the healthy society. Current concepts of revolution usually lay claim to a respectable intellectual or at least ideological pedigree; but they are in fact based on assumptions about the nature of society by no means shared and often explicitly rejected by the thinkers that they appeal to. As compared with Robespierre on the clubs, and Marx on the Commune, contemporary theorists seem unable or unwilling to acknowledge that the varieties of change conceived of by their philosophies might be mere local variations, when set against the mutations of revolutions.

5 THE CAUSES OF REVOLUTION

Revolutions, I have suggested, are interruptions in the pattern of sovereign rule. In this section I want to examine the causes of these 'interruptions'. To do so it is necessary to clarify the relation between revolution as I have defined it and the 'great Revolutions' so called by the historians: the 'English Revolution of 1640', the 'French Revolution of 1789', the 'Russian Revolution of 1917', and others. In what follows, the use of the Capital 'R' will always denote a set of events that have been conventionally termed 'revolution', whether deserving the name or not.

It follows from the concept of revolution that I have adopted that what I identify as revolutions are not single events, however momentous or cataclysmic they may have seemed at the time or since. Rather we should speak of revolutionary *periods* or epochs. The effective dissolution of centralised power, and not simply the brief pause while one palatial group takes over from another, cannot take place in one or two years. It may take decades and, in the context of a certain sort of society, as much as a century. Typically in the *coup d'état* or the *putsch,* one ruling group replaces another more or less noisily and bloodily. It is unusual for the whole structure of the governmental bureaucracy to be seriously affected, and there is therefore little change in the pattern of rule. It has often been remarked of France, for instance, that it combines a high degree of governmental or regime instability, with a very high degree of administrative stability. Since the establishment of a strong centralised bureaucracy by the first Napoleon, France has gone through two monarchies, two empires, and four republics; but what is remarkable is the uniformity and consistency of the bureaucratic administration underlying all these regimes. The French bureaucracy, like all well-organised bureaucracies, is largely self-sustaining, and even initiates most of the legislation it administers. So long as it remains confident and intact, political rulers can be thrown out, parliamentary assemblies seized with cataleptic fits; but there will be no new French Revolution [6.3, 6.4].

These remarks have to be borne in mind when considering the relation between revolution and the classic 'Revolutions' of the historians. For while in most cases there is, empirically, some overlap in meaning between the two, they are far from coinciding completely, and may indeed come to represent totally opposed aims. The relationship may be expressed briefly as follows: in most cases the opening stages of the classic Revolutions are the *final* stages of the revolution proper, the revolutionary period. The classic Revolution is the continuation of the revolution already in being. If we look at the *anciens régimes* of the various Revolutions, the striking thing is the extent to which the ruling authorities have already lost effective political control over their subjects. Sovereignty is an empty legal formula, in the conditions of such societies. The decrees of authority can be evaded, often through the protection of a powerful patron himself engaged in a struggle with the central power, but equally often because the institutions of authority have been so gravely undermined at every level that they are blatantly inefficient. Groups at all levels of society are struggling to make ground, exploiting the political vacuum which is often not consciously noticed, and certainly not intended by any particular group. It was such a state of society that Alexis de Tocqueville depicted so vividly in his study of France before 1789; and Hugh Brogan summarises that condition aptly when he writes of 'men at odds, institutions crumbling, subversive ideas springing up

41

like weeds in a fertile garden run wild'.[59] What to one eye looks like decay, to another looks like revolution. Well before the spectacular events of 1789, or 1917, the revolution was in full flood in each society.

The classic Revolutions are born out of these continuing revolutions. The revolutionary situation is so fluid, so full of tensions, that open conflict can break out given any of an enormous number of possible precipitating factors. In France, this was provided by the bankrupt Exchequer's need to summon the Estates-General; in Russia, by the defeats of the First World War. Again, the different groups which define themselves in the course of this organised conflict have different aims. Some, as we have seen earlier in this essay, are seeking largely to formalise the existing state of revolutionary consciousness; whether in the form of clubs or communes or soviets. Others wish to establish an efficient institutional framework for matters of commerce, law, or administration. Still others hope to fashion out of the conflict a strengthened and resilient *status quo*. But, whatever the aims of the different groups, the Revolutions of the past have had one outstanding consequence. They have ended the revolutions which gave birth to them. Under the pressure of internal struggles and foreign intervention, some group emerges which reconstitutes the fragmentary authority of the revolutionary period and the early years of the Revolution. The Revolution turns into the counter-revolution, indeed makes this its explicit aim. It becomes the solution to the problem of divided sovereignty. It was in documenting this hitherto unobserved fact about the French Revolution that de Tocqueville thought he had made his main contribution; and the course of other revolutions subsequently has amply borne out this conclusion [6.1].

We must be careful, then, to say what phenomenon we are seeking the causes of. We are not looking for the causes of, say, 'the French Revolution of 1789', or even of 'the French Revolution of 1789 to 1815', for at different stages that Revolution had a quite different meaning and character. We are trying to account for that process of the disintegration of political authority which essentially constituted the revolution, and to which the occurrence of the Revolution so-called appears as a coda, concluding a much

---

[59] Hugh Brogan, 'Introduction' to the Fontana edition of de Tocqueville, *The Ancien Régime and the French Revolution* (London, 1966), p. 18.

longer period of revolutionary activity. We shall, in other words, be interested in the causes of such phenomena as the peculiar state of French and Russian society in the fifty years or so preceding their respective Revolutions.

Two generalisations about the causes of revolution stand out for their suggestiveness and range of applicability. One we owe to Plato, the other to de Tocqueville.

In his study of French society before the Revolution of 1789, Alexis de Tocqueville wrote, in what is probably the most influential single passage on revolution:

It is not always by going from bad to worse that a country falls into a revolution. It happens most frequently that a people, which had supported the most crushing laws without complaint, and apparently as if they were unfelt, throws them off with violence as soon as the burden begins to be diminished. The state of things destroyed by a revolution is almost always somewhat better than that which immediately preceded it; and experience has shown that the most dangerous moment for a bad government is usually that when it enters upon the work of reform. . . . The evils which were endured with patience so long as they were inevitable seem intolerable as soon as a hope can be entertained of escaping from them. The abuses which are removed seem to lay bare those which remain, and to render the sense of them more acute; the evil has decreased, it is true, but the perception of the evil is more keen. Feudalism in all its strength had not inspired as much aversion in the French as it did on the eve of its disappearance.[60]

In Book VIII of *The Republic*, Plato observed that 'in any form of government revolution always starts from the outbreak of internal dissension in the ruling class. The constitution cannot be upset so long as that class is of one mind, however small it may be.'[61]

These two observations can to some extent be combined. We shall see, not only that the dissension within the ruling class is a precondition for the expression of the discontent generated by 'rising expectations', but also that that feeling is to a considerable degree a *consequence* of the dissension within the ruling class.

However, this is not to deny the independent force of the phenomenon of rising expectations and its associated feeling of 'relative

[60] Alexis de Tocqueville, *On the State of Society in France Before the Revolution of 1789 (L'Ancien Régime et la Révolution)*, trans. Henry Reeve (London, 1856), pp. 322–3.
[61] Plato, *The Republic*, trans. F. M. Cornford (London, 1941), p. 262.

deprivation'. De Tocqueville's insight, elemental in its simplicity, has emerged strengthened from every later study of revolution.[62] At its most basic level, it warns us that the bare fact of misery, oppression, or social injustice is not enough to lead to a *perception* of injustice and a feeling of acute discontent. A people inured to slavery is incapable of making its own freedom, thought Machiavelli. Just so, groups which have experienced poverty or pariah status for generations should not be expected on that account to try to change a condition which they have come to accept as natural and inescapable. Something has to happen which, whether or not it corresponds to the objective reality, makes people think that things *can* be different, and which makes them act or react accordingly. Marx, who is often thought to have held that revolution is caused by simple want or oppression, clearly recognised the relative nature of discontent [3.2]; and Trotsky, as a good Marxist, drew the correct inference: 'In reality, the mere existence of privations is not enough to cause an insurrection; if it were, the masses would always be in revolt.'[63]

It was the clear fact of a general increase in prosperity in eighteenth-century France, as compared with the preceding period, that led de Tocqueville to make his assertion in such vigorous terms. Revolution here was so obviously a product of an improved rather than a deteriorating economic condition. And for France at least, de Tocqueville's findings have been reinforced by modern research.[64] But it needs only a few minor modifications, in directions indicated by de Tocqueville himself, to make his generalisation even stronger. One such has recently been proposed by the American sociologist James Davies. Davies suggests that

revolutions are most likely to occur when a prolonged period of objective economic and social development is followed by a short period of sharp

[62] And not simply studies of revolution. The concept of relative deprivation has been employed to account for collective behaviour of every sort, from nativistic movements and 'Cargo Cults', to medieval millennarianism and modern reform movements. For such an approach, see David Aberle, *The Peyote Religion of the Navaho* (Chicago, 1966), ch. 19. And see also W. G. Runciman, *Relative Deprivation and Social Justice* (London, 1966).

[63] Quoted in Brinton, *The Anatomy of Revolution*, p. 34.

[64] For a review of the evidence, concluding in favour of de Tocqueville, see Alexander Gerschenkron, 'Reflections on Economic Aspects of Revolutions', in *Internal War*, ed. H. Eckstein (Glencoe, 1964), pp. 180–204.

reversal. The all-important effect on the minds of people in a particular society is to produce, during the former period, an expectation of a continued ability to satisfy needs – which continue to rise – and during the latter, a mental state of anxiety and frustration when manifest reality breaks away from anticipated reality. The actual state of socioeconomic development is less significant than the expectation that past progress, now blocked, can and must continue in the future. . . . The crucial factor is the vague or specific fear that ground gained over a long period of time will be quickly lost.[65]

Revolutions, then, according to Davies, are made not by the destitute nor by the well-off, but by those who feel that their situation is improving less rapidly than they have come to expect. The revolutionary situation is made up of advance followed by retreat. Both terms, moreover, can be expressed in non-economic senses, in the form, for instance, of political authority or social prestige. Thus the 'retreat' might take the form of an economic recession following a period of prosperity, or the total failure of a sustained attempt at political reform. Put in this way, the hypothesis gains an admirable measure of support from past European Revolutions. The English Revolution of 1640, and the many other contemporaneous European Revolutions, broke out a decade or two after a long phase of economic growth had come to an end.[66] The French Revolution of 1789 occurred a decade after a period of economic improvement had given way to an economic recession, and two years after that recession had deteriorated into a crisis;[67] it also followed close on the heels of the monarchy's failure to overcome aristocratic opposition to serious measures of political reform. In this as in so many other ways the Russian case parallels the French closely. The Russian Revolution of 1905 took place after the depression of 1900 had interrupted the great surge of industrialisation that started in the 1880s; that of 1917, after the period of resumed growth was ended by the dislocation caused by the war effort.[68] And, just as the French Revolution was preluded

[65] James C. Davies, 'Toward a Theory of Revolution', *American Sociological Review*, vol. xxvii (1962), pp. 6, 8.
[66] See E. J. Hobsbawm, 'The Crisis of the Seventeenth Century', in T. H. Ashton (ed.), *Crisis in Europe 1560–1660* (London, 1965), pp. 5–58.
[67] Alfred Cobban, *A History of Modern France*, vol. i, p. 136.
[68] Gerschenkron, 'Reflections on Economic Aspects of Revolutions', pp. 192, 195.

by the failure of the reforming efforts of Crown ministers – especially Turgot and Necker – so the Russian Revolution of 1917 came after the failure of Witte and Stolypin to continue the programme of reforms against the intrigues of the court and the vested interests of the country.

These examples go a long way to validating de Tocqueville's hypothesis. But they do so by ignoring the differential effect of the process of amelioration on the different groups in the population. It might be better to amend de Tocqueville in a more general way. He is basically saying that men do not make radically new and sweeping demands, however miserable their conditions of life, until these conditions change in some significant way. The point is, those conditions do not have to change for the better, as he assumed; they may change for the worse, and yet still have the effect of precipitating radical demands. What matters is that something should happen to shake men out of their habitual patterns of action, their traditional ways of life with its traditional level of expectations. It may be the contact between a tribal society and a society of the Western industrial sort, in which case the result may be the development of reactive radical movements in the former, such as nativistic or 'cargo' cults.[69] Or it may be the effects of rapid commercial or industrial development, which have in the past thrown up such responses as the millenarian movements of the late Middle Ages in Europe, or the anarchist movement of southern Spain.[70] Or again, it may result from the draconian efforts at modernisation attempted from above by the ruling élites. Where these have failed, as in the last decades of Tsarist Russia, they can stimulate revolutionary demands among all classes in society; where they succeed, as in Germany and Japan in the late nineteenth century, they can create pockets of intense discontent, largely in the agrarian sector, which are highly susceptible to the nostalgic appeals of fascism.[71]

Whatever the cause of the general disturbance of traditional social life, and whether or not it can be agreed that the particular

[69] See, for instance, Peter Worsley, *The Trumpet Shall Sound* (London, 1957).
[70] See Norman Cohn, *The Pursuit of the Millennium* (2nd ed., London, 1970); E. J. Hobsbawm, *Primitive Rebels* (Manchester, 1959).
[71] For a general discussion of the political effects of different 'routes' to modern society, see Barrington Moore, Jr., *The Social Origins of Dictatorship and Democracy* (London, 1967), esp. pp. 433 ff.

process leads in the end to better conditions of life for a majority of the society, it is almost certainly the case that some groups suffer in the initial stages. The increasing prosperity of eighteenth-century France, it is true, seems to have been shared by all groups. The peasantry, in particular, were in a better position than they had ever been. Only the government was impoverished, and it was indeed its attempt to share in the general prosperity that precipitated the Revolution of 1789. But in many other cases the effect of rapid economic growth is to create a category of *nouveaux pauvres* to offset the *nouveaux riches*. Despite the abolition of serfdom in 1861, for instance, the Russian peasantry seem to have suffered a deterioration of condition as a result of the rapid industrialisation of the later nineteenth century. The expansion of the market economy in China in the early decades of this century seems to have affected its peasantry similarly.[72] Other deprived groups may be created: workers whose wages do not keep pace with prices in the usual inflationary conditions of economic growth; workers in industries which are bypassed by the new technology and so decline; the unemployed, in a society where institutions of support such as the manor and the extended family have been eroded by economic change, and where new institutions of social welfare have not yet developed. In addition, the initial phases of growth may well cause an overall decline in the standard of living, since the society must greatly increase its rate of savings for reinvestment, and consequently reduce the level of consumption.[73]

Revolutions then are fed by the discontents of both the losers and the gainers in a period of rapid economic and social change. The gainers want to go on gaining, and are impatient of any checks, human or natural, to their continued advance. They may also be driven by a desire to even up their rankings on the different social dimensions: for the economically advancing, this means gaining social and political power. The losers are fired not simply by their privations – which may be recent in origin and brutal in the manner of imposition – but also by their awareness of the success of other groups, who may have started on an equal or lower economic

[72] For Russia, see Gerschenkron, 'Reflections', pp. 191–3; for China, Barrington Moore, op. cit., pp. 218–22.

[73] For the general argument, with a host of examples, see Mancur Olsen, Jr, 'Rapid Growth as a Destabilising Force', *Journal of Economic History*, vol. XXIII (1963), pp. 529–52.

footing. In any case, they cannot help but be affected by the currents of change around them, with its promise of a better life, or at least a life under vastly changed conditions. They hear the echoes of distant conflicts in the capitals, and are often the recipients of emissaries in search of political allies, and with proposals for great reforms. The Russian peasant may not have been better off in economic terms after the ending of serfdom, but the freeing of his person, together with the other legal and administrative reforms of the time, could scarcely fail to raise his expectations with regard to the land. The Chinese peasant too suffered in the period of early capitalistic development. What turned this suffering into indignation was the concomitant decay of the gentry, the abandonment of their traditional obligations, and their conversion 'into landlord-usurers pure and simple'.[74] All groups, losers as well as gainers, are shaken out of the institutions which had previously fixed and restrained expectations: class, caste, family, village, occupation. They are placed in that situation analysed by Emile Durkheim as *anomie,* where the pursuit of boundless goals is frustrated only by the inability of available means to attain them [3.1].

De Tocqueville's observations on the conditions of revolution indicate the forces that sustain a revolutionary situation and perhaps a revolutionary movement. He allows us to see what groups will be involved when the struggle becomes open, the nature of their discontents and to some extent of their aspirations. But it is Plato who points to the effective causes of revolutions. Revolutions do not occur until divisions arise within the ruling class. No matter what the dissatisfactions of other groups in society, unless these ally with dissatisfied groups of the upper classes, there may be riots but no revolutions. Against the ruling instruments of a united dominant class, opposition, always present to a greater or lesser degree in society, is impotent. As long as the bureaucracy functions and the army remains loyal, the government need fear no challenge. Revolution becomes a reality when the competition for power between ruling groups effectively destroys the sovereignty of political authority. The common front against opposition from below is shattered, and with it the security against that opposition.

[74] Barrington Moore, op. cit., p. 220.

In the process of competition, individuals and whole groups of the upper classes are increasingly excluded from the centres of power. They may be individuals or groups who traditionally have taken a large part in the exercise of power, and are now being displaced by the promotion of 'new men' from below. They may include a significant number of new arrivals to the higher levels of society, who find that their new statuses carry far less power than had appeared from below, and who, by an infusion of new blood, give to old institutions a fresh impulse to struggle. These groups emerge in open opposition to the men and institutions that have excluded them. In doing so, they throw society into a revolutionary condition. They seize upon and exploit the discontents of other classes, encouraging and aiding their expression. They even invent and promulgate for these classes discontents and aspirations where none had existed before, and of which these classes may remain ignorant for a long time, during which their cause graces the manifestos and declarations of the warring upper classes. Of such a character may be the assertions of 'natural rights' or declarations of 'the rights of man'. The slogans, once formulated, can become deadly weapons against the very classes that propagate them in their particular conflict. But this is for the final phases of the revolutionary period. At the time such considerations, even if perceived, have to be ignored. The struggle at the top is too serious in its nature. From it, or so it seems at the time, will emerge the rulers of society. Such a fact has as its obverse the threat of complete political annihilation. What risk can be greater than the loss of this struggle?

Students of revolution have not, of course, failed to notice that among the conditions of revolution is a weak and divided ruling authority. Crane Brinton, writing of the antecedents to the English, American, French and Russian Revolutions, notes that 'what may be called the ruling class seems in all four of our societies to be divided and inept'.[75] Hannah Arendt declares:

Generally speaking, we may say that no revolution is even possible where the authority of the body politic is truly intact. . . . Revolutions always appear to succeed with amazing ease in their initial stage, and the reason is that the men who make them first only pick up the power of a

[75] Crane Brinton, *The Anatomy of Revolution*, p. 53.

regime in plain disintegration; they are the consequences but never the causes of the downfall of political authority.[76]

Sir Louis Namier remarks similarly:

... revolutions are not made; they occur. Discontent with government there always is; still, even when grievous and well-founded, it seldom engenders revolution till the moral bases of government have rotted away: the feeling of community between the masses and their rulers, and in the rulers a consciousness of their right and capacity to rule [3.7].

As a final example we may note Louis Gottschalk's finding that

the weakness of the conservative forces ... [is] the necessary immediate cause of revolution. Despite the universal demand for revolutionary change, despite intense hopefulness of success, unless those who wish to maintain the *status quo* are so weak that they cannot maintain themselves, there is little likelihood of a successful revolution.[77]

What de Tocqueville, as a contemporary witness, observed of the February Revolution of 1848, seems true of all revolutions: 'This time the public was not overthrowing the Government; it was allowing it to fall.' The July Monarchy fell 'before rather than beneath the blows of the victors, who were as astonished at their triumph as were the vanquished at their defeat'.[78]

It is one thing to see that revolutions are associated with a weak ruling class. It is quite another to say why that class is weak, and what relation this explanation bears to the causes of revolution. In most of the standard accounts, the inept and inefficient ruling classes appear simply as an item in the 'shopping-list' statement of the causes of revolution. Thus, Brinton lists as 'tentative uniformities' the following features of 'the old regimes' of societies that experience revolution: an economically advancing society, class antagonism, desertion of the intellectuals, a ruling class that has lost self-confidence, an inefficient government in financial difficulties, and the inept use of force against rebels. No attempt

[76] Arendt, *On Revolution*, p. 112.
[77] Louis Gottschalk, 'Causes of Revolution', *American Journal of Sociology*, vol. L (1944), p. 8.
[78] Alexis de Tocqueville, *The Recollections of Alexis de Tocqueville*, trans. Alexander Teixera de Mattos (London, 1948), pp. 41, 67.

is made to assign causal priority to any of these phenomena, or to link them in any connected pattern.[79] Where the attempt is made, as in Gottschalk's account, the weakness of the ruling class is assigned the status of an 'immediate' or precipitating cause, and distinguished clearly from other more fundamental 'remote' causes. The impression given is that a weak ruling class may well be a necessary condition of revolution, but that it is a subordinate one. It is mentioned for the sake of completion, a mere 'topping-up' of the account of more fundamental processes.

This is seriously to underestimate the phenomenon in the aetiology of revolution. The weak ruling class of revolutionary societies is not to be equated with the divisions within élites that produce *coups d'état* and palace revolutions. In the case of the latter there is the implicit premise that the victors will do nothing that will shake the control of the pre-existing institutions of political and economic power. The existence of this shared premise is indeed the reason why the game can go on for so long among the upper classes of some societies. Very different in character were the struggles within the ruling class of eighteenth-century France or nineteenth-century Russia. In these cases crucial sections of the traditional ruling class felt that they were fighting for their very survival as members of that class. The maintenance of their economic and social power seemed to hinge on securing a generous share in the exercise of that political power from which they were being increasingly excluded. Such a struggle could have no rules, no shared premise. Its reverberations were heard throughout society, reaching down to its lowest levels. It fed discontents to other classes, to a degree that threatened the suicide of the upper classes. When Lenin said that a revolution occurs 'when the upper class cannot and the lower class will not continue the old system' [3.3], he was concealing the most interesting part of the story. For it is clear from the history of past revolutions that the lower class 'will not' continue the old order *because*, and to a large extent *only when*, the upper class 'cannot'. The internecine struggles within the ruling class weakens it to the point where it cannot hold off the challenge of forces which it has itself largely created,

[79] Brinton, *Anatomy of Revolution*, pp. 264–6. A similar failing vitiates the more elaborate list of variables given by H. Eckstein in 'On the Etiology of Internal War', *History and Theory*, vol. IV (1965), pp. 133–63.

and which intend to go beyond anything any of its contending
parties aspired to. In this aspect, revolutions appear as the death-
rattle of aristocracies.

6 TWO EXAMPLES: THE CAUSES OF THE FRENCH AND RUSSIAN REVOLUTIONS

Two examples well illustrate this process: eighteenth-century
France and nineteenth-century Russia.

It is a promising start to find that a revolutionary, a reactionary,
and one who could claim to have learnt from both, agree substantially on the origins of the French Revolution. 'The patricians
began the Revolution,' said Chateaubriand, 'the plebeians finished
it.'[80] Marx wrote that 'the first blow dealt to the French monarchy
proceeded from the nobility, not from the peasants'.[81] Robespierre
makes the same point more elaborately:

> In states constituted as are nearly all the countries of Europe, [he
> wrote], there are three powers: the monarchy, the aristocracy and the
> people, and the people is powerless. Under such circumstances a
> revolution can break out only as the result of a gradual process. It begins
> with the nobles, the clergy, the wealthy, whom the people supports
> when its interests coincide with theirs in resistance to the dominant
> power, that of the monarchy. Thus it was that in France the judiciary,
> the nobles, the clergy, the rich, gave the original impulse to the revolu-
> tion. The people appeared on the scene only later. Those who gave the
> first impulse have long since repented, or at least wished to stop the
> revolution when they saw that the people might recover its sovereignty.
> But it was they who started it. Without their resistance, and their
> mistaken calculations, the nation would still be under the yoke of
> despotism.[82]

The eighteenth-century revolution in France, together with its
culmination, the events of 1789, was the last and the greatest of
the aristocratic *Frondes*. Monarchy and aristocracy had struggled

[80] Quoted G. Lefebvre, *The Coming of the French Revolution*, trans. R. R.
Palmer (Princeton, 1947), p. 3.

[81] Marx, 'The Indian Revolt', in Marx and Engels, *The First Indian War of
Independence* (London, 1960).

[82] Quoted Alfred Cobban, *A History of Modern France*, vol. I, p. 134.

with each other since the founding of the Capetian dynasty, with about equal fortune on either side. The seventeenth century, however, marked a turning-point in this long struggle. The two aristocratic *Frondes* of the mid-century interrupted the centralising efforts of Richelieu and Mazarin. They were suppressed, but their seriousness determined the monarchy to be ruthless in attempting to break the power of the aristocracy. Louis xiv and his minister Colbert curbed and cowed the nobles to an extent never before achieved by a French monarch.

The *parlements,* which together with some other bodies made up the sovereign courts of the realm, had played a leading part in the first *Fronde.* Their customary right to remonstrate before registering royal edicts made of them a potential source of political power in opposition to the Crown. Their leading officers, the *noblesse de la robe,* constituted an increasingly wealthy and influential section of the nobility. They were, in other words, ideally suited to provide the organisational focus of aristocratic opposition. Louis effectively emasculated them. They were strictly limited to their judicial functions, and remonstrance and registration were reduced to a formality.

The older sections of the nobility, the *noblesse d'épée,* was similarly stripped of political power. Two hierarchies were constructed by Louis, one of grandeur, the other of power. The highest and wealthiest nobles were brought to Versailles, where they displayed themselves, dazzling but impotent. The poorer nobles were either brought into the services of the Crown or, lacking the favours of the court, left to get even poorer in the provinces. La Bruyère put the position concisely: 'A nobleman, if he lives at home in his province, lives free but without substance; if he lives at court, he is taken care of, but enslaved.'[83]

But Louis was no leveller. He did not, and did not intend to, eliminate the distinctions of rank. The aristocracy was left a privileged stratum, keeping its economic independence through its possession of land or hereditary offices. It was almost bound, therefore, to try to restore its political fortunes after Louis had gone, and in this respect Louis bequeathed an ambivalent legacy to his monarchical successors. But for the eighteenth-century

[83] Quoted Franklin L. Ford, *Robe and Sword : The Regrouping of the French Aristocracy after Louis* xiv (New York, Harper Torchbook ed. 1965), p. vii.

53

aristocracy there was no ambivalence whatsoever. The reign of Louis XIV had gone immeasurably farther than any previous one in threatening their position within the state. Not only had the parlements been curbed, but the provincial Estates, for long the stronghold of the nobility, remained subordinated to the initiative and the scrutiny of royal commissioners. Most far-reaching of all were the measures which violated the traditional immunity of the nobility from ordinary taxation. There was no reason to feel confident that the bankrupt government left by Louis would not go much further in forcing the aristocracy to put its fortunes at the service of the state.

The lesson for the nobility was clear. No longer must it, as in the past, remain aloof from the central power, reacting in a costly and violent fashion only after its interests had been severely threatened. Security could only be achieved by the full exercise of political power. This was the message constantly reiterated by Boulanvilliers, by Fénelon, by Saint-Simon, and by the other writers for the nobility. A class for centuries content to seek exemption from the law now realised that its aim must be to make the law.

The political history of the eighteenth century is largely the record of the ensuing struggles, between the Crown and the nobility.[84] Two developments especially are noteworthy for their effects in creating a revolutionary situation. The first was the fusion of the two sections of the nobility, the nobility of the robe and of the sword, which had come together previously only in infrequent and uneasy alliance. The former was suspect on the grounds of its fairly recent origin and the fact that its members were, after all, the judicial representatives of the Crown; the latter because it had in the past tended to champion the Estates-General as against the parlements. Both suspicions had been stilled by the middle of the century. The nobility of the robe showed clearly that where the two clashed it put class interests before official ones. More significantly, the nobility of the sword soon came to see that the parlements were by far and away the most promising institutions from which to launch the aristocratic counter-offen-

[84] A detailed account of these is to be found in Felix Rocquain, *The Revolutionary Spirit Preceding the French Revolution*, trans. J. D. Hunting (London, 1894).

54

sive.[85] And it was in fact the parlements, especially the Paris parlement, that throughout the eighteenth century led the aristocratic campaign against the Crown.

Early in the century the parlements recovered fully the right to remonstrate before registering royal decrees. Led by the parlement of Paris, they soon showed that they were prepared to use that right to the fullest extent in the interests of their class. In fiscal matters, in the assertion of provincial autonomy, in defence of the Gallican and Jansenist interests against the Jesuits, they came into frequent and sometimes riotous conflict with the Crown. Particularly fierce were the struggles of 1725, 1730–2, 1751–4, 1771 and 1787–8.[86] These confrontations were often accompanied by wholesale exile of the parlementaires, arrests, royal intimidation, and acute popular disturbances.

This last leads us to a consideration of the second development. In their struggle with the Crown, the nobility deliberately and systematically stirred up public opinion against the monarchy. Once again, the nobility of the robe was in an ideal position to do this. As the trained and best-educated members of their class, they were its ablest propagandists. Their official positions gave them added advantages. In the manner of Sir Edward Coke and the English parliamentarians, they researched into, elaborated, invented and propagated the rights and prerogatives of the parlements. Often indeed their claims seemed to emulate those of the contemporary English Parliament. The founding of numerous provincial academies in the first half of the century was of great significance in this context. They provided centres for the provincial nobility to exchange ideas and to publish tracts and pamphlets lending their cause a respectable theoretical and historical flavour. The most imposing product of this activity, and the one which put the aristocratic thesis in its most attractive form, was the work of the President of the Bordeaux parlement, the Baron de Montesquieu: *The Spirit of the Laws.*[87]

The Crown was not without its own intellectual proponents, of course, especially the Physiocrats and occasionally Voltaire; and

[85] The process is fully documented in Ford, *Robe and Sword*.
[86] For details see Rocquain, *The Revolutionary Spirit*, pp. 20–3, 26–34, 51–71, 106–13, 161–84.
[87] For the activities of the provincial academies, and also of the aristocratic clubs and *salons*, see Ford, *Robe and Sword*, pp. 233–45.

55

something like a pamphlet war seems to have gone on in eighteenth-century France, similar to that of Tudor and Stuart England during another revolution. Moreover, the main philosophical currents of the time flowed in favour of the monarchy. The *philosophes,* whose very existence and activity depended on the continuing divisions at the top, were themselves very anxious to heal those divisions. They could see no future in a revived feudal and aristocratic constitution. The ideal authority seemed to be a reformed monarchy: enlightened by the philosophic literature, and with the power to put through schemes of rational reform against sectional interests. Thus the Crown was certainly not the weaker party in the struggle. In the 1770s indeed it seized the initiative, and by means of reformist fiscal policies sought to reveal the selfishness of the nobility [3.5].

Until the very eve of 1789, these policies had almost the opposite effect. They provoked crises which boosted the popularity of the nobility and lowered that of the monarchy. This underlined the fact that while the monarchy, since Louis xiv, was probably the strongest single force in society, its popular standing declined throughout the eighteenth century. The affair of the diamond necklace – which occasioned an orgy of virtuous indignation on the part of the Paris parlement – was simply the last straw. Perhaps it was the inherently weaker position of the nobility that made it fight with such desperation, and to employ such risky tactics in the struggle. No doubt, too, its social prestige and closeness to the local populations in the provinces gave it a clear advantage over the monarchy in securing popular favour. At any rate it is certain that for much of the century it was the nobility that made the running as far as popularity was concerned; and it was its example that spurred on other sections of the population.

The more refined ideas of the philosophes, which ultimately favoured monarchy, made difficult headway through the less educated layers of society. Their simpler ideas were appropriated by the nobility for its own use. How, asks George Rudé, did the ideas of the Enlightenment enter the popular consciousness? It was

not the philosophes themselves, nor the fashionable society and men of letters of the *salons,* that brought them down to street level and transformed abstract speculations into popular slogans and rallying calls for political action. This was partly the work of the pamphleteers of the Third Estate in 1788 and 1789; but, long before that, the ground had been well and truly prepared by the tracts and remonstrances published by the parlements, who, in their prolonged duel . . . with ministerial 'despotism', quoted freely, and almost indiscriminately, from the writings of the philosophes[88] [3.6].

It was not some radical pamphleteer, but the parlement of Rennes that in 1788 proclaimed: 'That man is born free, that originally men are equal, these are truths that have no need of proof'; and 'one of the first conditions of society is that particular wills should always yield to the general will'. Rudé continues: 'What was new in all this was that the parlements were not just writing political tracts, as the philosophes had done before them, but were deliberately setting out to influence public opinion and to marshall active public support in their struggles with the Crown.' And he adds that 'it was only when prodded into action by the parlements, the higher clergy and nobility that [the middle classes] began seriously to lay claim to social equality and a share in government'.[89]

The struggle reached a high and, as the event proved, a turning-point in the years 1787–9.[90] The Crown, now in desperate financial straits, had been making repeated attempts to tax the nobility. The reactions of the nobility were correspondingly more spectacular. In 1787 the parlement of Paris was exiled for rejecting the Crown's taxation proposals and demanding the calling of the Estates-General. It was reinstated following great popular excitement and the unanimous support of the provincial parlements. The dispute continued with increasing bitterness on both sides. In May 1788, secretly warned that force was to be used against it, the Paris parlement published a declaration of the fundamental laws of the kingdom, of which it announced itself to be the custodian. In it, it invoked the rights of man and of citizenship in support of its

[88] George Rudé, *Revolutionary Europe 1783–1815* (London, 1964), p. 75. The Grand Remonstrances of the Paris Parlement in 1753, asserting that the *parlements* were the guardians of the contract between king and people, sold more than 20,000 copies within a few weeks. Cobban, *History of Modern France*, vol. 1, p. 127.

[89] Rudé, *Revolutionary Europe*, pp. 75, 72.

[90] General accounts of the 'aristocratic revolt' are in Cobban, op. cit., vol. 1, pp. 126–33; Rudé, *Revolutionary Europe*, pp. 78–82; Lefebvre, *The Coming of the French Revolution*, pp. 28–37.

claims and those of the provincial bodies for the sharing of power with the monarch. In the same month the meeting of the Paris parlement was surrounded by troops, all parlements suspended and forty-seven new courts created to take their place.

This action of the government 'stirred up something like a nation-wide rebellion' against it.[91] The clergy reasserted their own right to immunity and backed the parlements. The dukes and peers of France associated themselves with the stand against the monarchy. In Paris and the provinces, both the middle and the lower classes, fired by the militant declarations of the parlements, joined in the hue and cry against the King's ministers. Riots broke out at Bordeaux, Dijon, Grenoble, Pau, Rennes and Toulouse. In some of these towns the nobility and the people took control by force; and in some places the provincial Estates were illegally convoked after lying dormant for over a century and a half. Most ominously for the government, the army proved unreliable. Staffed in many cities by members of the provincial nobility, it sometimes refused to fire, and fraternised with the riotous townsmen. Faced with this nation-wide revolt, the King capitulated. The Estates-General were summoned to meet the following year.

In the years following 1789 forces other than the aristocratic, as we know, were to express themselves, and to relegate the struggle within the ruling class to the scrap-heap.[92] But the Crown and the aristocracy jointly summoned up their own executioner. Their activities were replete with revolutionary precedents, not to be forgotten by other classes. The years 1787–9 concentrated and encapsulated these precedents for all to observe. The aristocratic class developed an organisation for political action, exchanging correspondence and passing instructions from town to town. Lefebvre notes that the Committee of Thirty, soon to take over the leadership of the Third Estate, seems to have originated as a centre of parliamentary resistance. In Brittany the nobility created committees in all the important cities, to which they dispatched delegates to stimulate action and give instructions. Successful appeals were made to the bourgeoisie, to artisans, even to peasant farmers and

[91] Rudé, op. cit., p. 80.
[92] The successive phases of that process, involving the bourgeoisie, the *sansculottes*, and the peasants, are superbly described in Lefebvre, op. cit., *passim*.

share-croppers. The troops were propagandised. As Lefebvre says,

the parlements especially taught the lesson, for their reiterated remonstrances, the attitude of the parlement of Paris after the royal session of
November 19, 1787, its declaration of fundamental laws, the inter-
dictions laid by some courts on collection of taxes, were to find equiva-
lents in the history of the Constituent Assembly; and indeed the
parlement of Paris went even further than the Constituent Assembly
in presuming to bring legal action against a minister, Calonne, who thus
became the first *émigré*.[93]

When a constitutional monarchist later asked the rhetorical
question, 'Who accustomed the people to illegal assemblies and to
resistance?', he could answer incontrovertibly, 'the parlements'.[94]

Russia at first glance presents evidence so strikingly in favour of
our thesis that detailed treatment would appear to be superfluous.
Nothing is so obvious, and more commented on, than the deep
divisions within the educated upper classes of the nineteenth and
early twentieth centuries. A whole section of the Russian gentry
cut themselves off spiritually, and often physically, from their
society. As a constituent part of the *intelligentsia*, they turned the
full weight of their position and their privileged westernised education against the existing order of state and society. There was a
sense indeed in which simply to be educated was to put oneself at
odds with the reactionary Tsarist autocracy which ruled Russia
until 1917. The intelligentsia, however, carried this opposition to
its ideological extreme. Alexander Herzen, who was a leading
member of the 'Moscow circles' of the 1830s and '40s and the
superb memoirist of this early period of the intelligentsia, summed
up their attitude: 'The leading characteristic of them all is a profound feeling of alienation from official Russia, from their environment, and at the same time an impulse to get out of it – and in
some a vehement desire to get rid of it.'[95] Isaiah Berlin echoes this
when he links the later Populists to a continuous tradition within the intelligentsia: ' . . . they looked on the government and
the social structure of their country as a moral and political

---

[93] Lefebvre, op. cit., p. 34.
[94] Quoted Cobban, op. cit., vol. I, p. 127.
[95] Alexander Herzen, *My Past and Thoughts*, vol. II, p. 415.

monstrosity – obsolete, barbarous, stupid and odious – and dedicated their lives to its total destruction.'[96]

But the alienation of the intelligentsia from the ruling structures is not the whole story of the division within the ruling class. The history of the ruling groups is more complicated.

Socially and intellectually the Russian intelligentsia evolved over a period of a century and a half, beginning in the middle of the eighteenth century. For much of this time it was dominated by members of the gentry.[97] Paradoxically, it was the state itself which brought about this development. Peter the Great repudiated all earlier criteria of gentry status, and made this status entirely dependent on state service. The Russian nobles were dragged from their boorish lives on their estates and forced to become bureaucrats. They were compulsorily educated: which meant that they acquired, with varying degrees of comprehension and completeness, the ideas of the contemporary Western European 'Enlightenment'. Hence, too, they acquired a new self-image, a new conception of their function in society. As the only educated members of a backward society, they had to be the bearers of Western civilisation to the unenlightened masses. Since they constituted something less than one per cent of the vast population, this enterprise was bound to take on, in some minds, the character of a religious mission. Herein lay the germs of the future intelligentsia [4.8].

For most of the eighteenth century the newly-educated gentry was identified with the state. It could hardly be otherwise, since the state was the only modernising agency in the society, and service in the state offered the most promising opportunities for the implementation of the new ideas. But towards the end of the century, the bureaucratic state and a section of the gentry began to draw apart. The main reason was the same as in France a little earlier: the continuing expansion of the central bureaucracy, which called for more specialised personnel, and increasingly demanded a life-long commitment to the bureaucracy as a career. The gentry

[96] 'Introduction to Franco Venturi, *Roots of Revolution* (London, 1960), p. xii.
[97] 'Gentry' is not a wholly satisfactory translation of the Russian *dvorianstvo*, but is probably the least misleading. Membership of the *dvorianstvo* depended on holding a specified rank in Peter the Great's Table of Ranks, i.e. on being in state service. No other attribute was of comparable importance. See Marc Raeff, *Origins of the Russian Intelligentsia : The Eighteenth Century Nobility* (New York, 1966), *passim*.

had no desire to escape service altogether, since wealth and standing depended so much on it. But after the death of Peter the Great many members had become used to spending only ten to fifteen years in service, after which, their fortunes made or sustained, they retired to their estates. Catherine the Great strengthened this tendency. Anxious to stop the pattern of aristocratic *coups* by which monarchs were imposed and deposed after Peter, she deliberately stimulated a corporate sentiment among the gentry, confirmed its absolute control over the serfs, and encouraged it to improve its estates and participate in local life. Members of the gentry were given an alternative mode of life to pursue, different from but no less 'enlightened' than service in the state bureaucracy, and equally different from the life of the pre-Petrine nobility. Some came to resent their total dependence on the autocratic state, and especially the fact that to keep up their positions they were now expected to remain in service for much longer. The alternative was exclusion from the Table of Ranks and consequent loss of status and fortune. The dilemmas of this situation of cross-pressure produced at least two figures who are among the progenitors of the nineteenth-century intelligentsia: Novikov and Radishchev. More characteristically, it produced a group of eccentric aristocrats, 'the result', as Herzen put it, 'of the combination of two elements so absolutely opposed to each other as the eighteenth century and Russian life'; and of which Herzen's own portrait of his father is as fine an example from real life as Tolstoy's portrait of the old Prince Bolkonsky, in *War and Peace*, is from the realm of fiction.[98]

The French Revolution widened the breach between state and gentry. Its effects seem to have been less to frighten the upper classes than to quicken the liberalising process begun by the Enlightenment, and to inspire some with a desire to emulate the French Third Estate. In the first half of his reign, Alexander I moved in sympathy with these currents among the nobility; but by the end this liberalism had all but disappeared and the autocratic system tightened up. In any case, it was the very reforms of the liberal era that were responsible for finally ousting the gentry from political power, and so precipitated the struggle between

[98] Herzen, *My Past and Thoughts*, vol. I, pp. 74–5. For a similar portrait of 'alienated nobility' at the end of the eighteenth century, see Kropotkin's remarks on his ancestors, *Memoirs of a Revolutionist* (London, 1906), p. 2.

Crown and gentry that made the Russian revolution a reality by the second half of the nineteenth century.

The architect of these reforms was Alexander's Minister, Michael Speransky, the son of a country priest whose antecedents were entirely bureaucratic, and who was specially marked out for the antipathy of the gentry. He was responsible for expanding and reorganising the bureaucracy, creating a structure that remained essentially the government of the country until 1905. The 'colleges' of Peter were converted into Ministries, which were increased in number. A Council of State was established, as the chief consultative body to the Tsar, and which for the first time made for the regular co-ordination of all the activities of the administration. The gentry opposed these reforms, just as it opposed the many others that Speransky planned but was unable to execute. In doing this, it showed that, just as in France, it was far from being always the standard-bearer of modernity. It opposed the autocracy because it feared its exclusion from power by the professional bureaucrats. In doing so, it often linked up with the liberal members of its class who opposed the autocracy on the grounds of constitutional and humanitarian principles. It was this coalition, still very feeble, that made possible the Decembrist revolt of 1825. And it was this coalition, vastly stronger, that was to emerge in the second half of the nineteenth century and finally overthrow Tsardom.

The Decembrist revolt marked the parting of the ways.[99] It was the last of the gentry-inspired palace revolutions of the eighteenth century. But in the seriousness of its political programme and the quality of its participants it also showed itself to be the first act of the Russian revolution. The intelligentsia in its most distinctive form can be dated from its occurrence. Men as widely differing as Herzen and Lenin came to regard the insurgents as the first martyrs of the revolution. Henceforward the Tsarist regime found itself engaged in a permanent war with some of the most brilliant and creative minds among its subjects.

In yet another way the Decembrist revolt marked a turning-point. Its failure turned the oppositional gentry away from the struggle within the political arena. The Decembrists had been intellectuals, but they were also primarily army officers, men of

[99] For an analysis, with documents, see Marc Raeff, *The Decembrist Movement* (New Jersey, 1966).

the world and of action. In spite of their opinions they had continued to serve the state. Their action, illegal as it was, in a sense was still an attempt to reform the state from within, rather than to overthrow it from without. They made no attempt to appeal for popular support. In this sense they continued the tradition of the educated eighteenth-century gentry who hoped to modernise Russia through the agency of an enlightened monarchy.

Their successors had no such hopes. After 1825 the intelligentsia totally renounced the state, and adopted an out-and-out revolutionary position. From the literary and philosophical circles of Herzen, Belinksy and Bakunin in the thirties and forties, through the Populists of the sixties and seventies, and down to the Marxists of the nineties and beyond, the common theme was the outright rejection of the whole social and political system. In consequence the intelligentsia made itself politically impotent. Its role in fact came to resemble that of the philosophes in eighteenth-century France, and it is this which should caution us against too easy analogies between the upper classes of France and Russia. For, to a far greater extent than the philosophic movement, the Russian intelligentsia drew upon the upper class, the gentry, which dominated it throughout the nineteenth century. And yet it is not basically these members of the gentry who provide the evidence for the division within the ruling class, on the analogy of the French parlementaires. The intelligentsia cut itself off from all the possible bases of power in Russian society, and was in no position to set up an effective counter to the power of the state. 'Foreigners at home, foreigners abroad' – as Herzen said – its members were in a state of political exile whether they actually left Russia or stayed at home. Their situation was aptly described by Belinsky in 1840:

What we have been taught has deprived us of religion; the conditions of life ... have failed to provide us with education and debarred us from all contact with knowledge; we are at odds with the reality around us and rightfully detest and despise it, as it rightfully detests and despises us. Where could we take refuge? On a deserted island which, for us, was our Circle.[100]

[100] Quoted E. Lampert, *Studies in Rebellion* (London, 1957), p. 43. For general studies of the Russian intelligentsia, see Richard Pipes (ed.), *The Russian Intelligentsia* (New York, 1961); France Venturi, *Roots of Revolution*.

Other sections of the gentry also renounced politics. Partly this was because Nicholas's reign completed the exclusion of the gentry from positions of power. The Decembrist rising had confirmed Nicholas's suspicions of the pretensions of the upper class. The arrest and conviction of the conspirators had affected practically all of the most prominent families of the realm. Nicholas therefore came to rely almost exclusively on the trained officials of his bureaucracy, and the reforms of his reign were mainly devoted to expanding and improving the bureaucratic machine of government, built up by Speranksy. Most notable and most effective of the innovations was the formation of the 'Third Section' of police spies. Throughout the nineteenth century the gentry, of course, nearly always had the option of becoming dedicated ministers and officials of the Tsar. But those who did so became completely dependent on the Tsar, and were separated from the rest of their class for whom state service was reduced to the minimum necessary to keep their status.

But the gentry, while not making their opposition explicit within the political sphere, did not, like the intelligentsia, part company with the whole social system. During the middle decades of the century they continued their opposition 'non-politically', away from the capital, at home on their estates. Here, in their 'nests of gentlefolk', they were able to resist the bureaucracy in innumerable ways, best illustrated in the literature of the times. Here they could use their positions to be defenders and patrons of the more radical opponents of Tsardom. They could also, like Tolstoy and Turgenev, themselves contribute as writers to the general intellectual opposition of their time, without necessarily bringing down the wrath of the bureaucracy upon themselves.[101] There were no spectacular confrontations with the government, on the lines of the clash between Crown and parlements in France. But there can be no question of the gentry's real ability to evade and obstruct the bureaucracy from a position that still kept them within the ruling circles of Russia. By the time of the 'great reforms' of the sixties, the Russian ruling class was deeply divided. It was an irony not unusual in Russian history that those very reforms,

[101] For the relation of gentry and writers, see R. Hingley, *Russian Writers and Society, 1825–1904* (London, 1967). And see also Monica Partridge, *Revolution and Nineteenth Century Russian Literature* (Nottingham, 1968).

initiated by the state, provided the institution that gave the gentry a base from which to launch its most powerful attack ever against the autocracy.

Whatever their other consequences, the reforms of Alexander II continued in the direction of the strengthening of the central administration. They left the bureaucratic structure still intact and offered no real concessions to the gentry.[102] But the debate over the emancipation of the serfs revived, after a generation, public discussion on political matters. And the creation of the *zemstvos* in 1864 provided the gentry, both conservative and liberal, with the institutional rallying-point that they had hitherto lacked. The *zemstvos* – elective authorities of local self-government – were hamstrung creations of the central bureaucracy, and successive measures of the government restricted their autonomy even beyond the original narrow conception. But as George Fischer says, 'the zemstvo was the most extensive and autonomous form of self-government in Russian history'.[103] Its importance lay in allowing the gentry an alternative focus for political activity to the central government. In the past the only method of exerting pressure had been at court, or through the threat of a *coup* carried out by the aristocratic Guards. Now the gentry could seek to share in the exercise of power by applying pressure from below, with all the support of professional and popular opinion that this implied. In the increasingly common phrase of the time, the demand came to be that 'the building should be crowned': that over and above the elective local councils there should now be an elected national assembly.

There is space here to indicate only very briefly how the opposition that crystallised around the zemstvos made possible the Revolution of 1905, that 'dress-rehearsal' wherein most of the forces that were to contend in 1917 displayed themselves. From the outset the gentry dominated the zemstvos, to be joined in the last decade of the century by many of the new professional intelligentsia brought into being by Russia's rapid industrialisation of

[102] For the significance of the reforms, see J. C. H. Keep, in the *New Cambridge Modern History*, vol. XI (ed. F. H. Hinsley), pp. 352–9.
[103] George Fischer, *Russian Liberalism: From Gentry to Intelligentsia* (Cambridge, Mass., 1958), p. 7. Fischer gives the best account of the *zemstvo* activities. Other good accounts are to be found in B. Pares, *History of Russia* (London, 1962 reprint), pp. 391 ff.; and Jacob Walkin, *The Rise of Democracy in Prerevolutionary Russia* (New York, 1962).

those years. Since many of the professional intelligentsia were themselves of gentry families or became landowners, their common cause against the central government was also the cause of a common class position. Pressure against the autocracy increased with the accession of Nicholas II in 1894, who took to heart the remark of Witte that autocracy and the zemstvos could not co-exist for any great length of time, and rebuked the zemstvo representatives for 'fostering senseless dreams of . . . sharing in the conduct of internal affairs'. Led by D. N. Shipov, described by Keep as 'a nobleman of impeccably conservative views', the chairmen of many zemstvo executives met and established a 'Bureau' to co-ordinate their political activities. Peter Struve, the ex-Marxist convert to liberalism, founded a newspaper *Liberation* to lead efforts to form a national organisation. Finally came the decisive step, in 1903, of the formation by the liberal gentry of a clandestine organisation, 'The Liberation League', which when formally constituted some months later adopted a programme calling for a constituent assembly elected by universal suffrage, extensive social reforms, and national self-determination. The National Congress of zemstvo leaders in the following year echoed these demands. The point had been reached where even the conservatives among the gentry were pressing for a national assembly, hoping to be able to exercise there the power that had been drained from the localities. The memorandum of the Congress to the Tsar provoked similarly worded memoranda from many quarters: the barristers and magistrates, the municipalities, and many assemblies of the nobility in the provinces [3.12]. As Kropotkin wrote, 'the zemstvo memorandum became thus a sort of ultimatum of the educated portion of that nation, which rapidly organised itself into a number of professional unions'.[104]

The full extent to which the Tsarist regime had lost the support of some of its wealthiest and most influential subjects was made clear in 1905, and more conclusively in 1917. In 1905 the Tsar found himself abandoned by almost all the professional classes and provincial gentry, while even large sections of the bureaucracy and the army showed themselves unreliable. The zemstvo liberals controlled the pace of events, at least in so far as they managed to impose their aims on nearly all the parties. The watchword put

[104] Kropotkin *Memoirs of a Revolutionist*, p. xxv.

forward everywhere by the strikers was the demand for a constituent assembly based on universal suffrage. And it was to a zemstvo deputation, headed by Prince Trubetskoy, that the Tsar made the promise to call a national assembly. The constitutionalism of the government was by 1907 fully revealed as a sham. The gentry pressed even harder, and the disaffection spread into the court and the bureaucracy. Rasputin was assassinated by Prince Yusopov, husband of the Tsar's niece, and Purishkevich, one of the extremist conservatives in the Duma. As Bernard Pares notes, 'they evidently hoped to save the dynasty'. Further, 'the Grand Dukes had come into line with the public, and visited the palace only to warn the sovereign'.[105] The disasters of the First World War completed the disintegration of the ruling class. It was the parties of the Duma, from the most conservative to the most liberal, who most vigorously assailed the government and demanded the granting of a full constitution. Walkin is right in remarking that 'whatever the part that propaganda, and the attitudes towards the state shaped by it, played in the emergence of mass riots [in 1917], the upper classes were its principal source'.[106] Protopopov, the Tsar's Minister, thus described the mood of the upper classes on the eve of 1917:

Even the very highest classes became *frondeurs* before the revolution; in the grand *salons* and clubs the policy of the government received harsh and unfriendly criticism. . . . Many Grand Dukes openly attended these meetings, and their presence gave a special authority in the eyes of the public to tales that were caricatures and to malicious exaggerations. A sense of the danger of this sport did not awaken till the last moment.[107]

In 1917, perhaps the most relevant feature of the Tsar's position was the loss of control over the army, and above all the disobedience of many of the senior officers. The generals offered their support to the Provisional Government, and agreed that Nicholas should abdicate. Once more, as in 1905, it was the upper classes who sank the monarchy. This time they were not able to keep control of events for long. But the revolutionaries who now stepped into the breach had played virtually no part in making it. The state's power

[105] Pares, *History of Russia*, p. 527.
[106] Walkin, *The Rise of Democracy*, p. 235.
[107] Quoted Leon Trotsky, *The History of the Russian Revolution*, 3 vols., translated by Max Eastman (London, Sphere Books ed., 1967), vol. 1, p. 77.

had been broken by a class which could claim to be far more revolutionary than they. As E. H. Carr says, 'the contribution of Lenin and the Bolsheviks to the overthrow of Tsarism was negligible . . . Bolshevism succeeded to a vacant throne'.[108]

This treatment of the revolutionary periods of France and Russia can serve, in conclusion, as illustration of two further distinctive characteristics of revolution. The first, already touched upon, is the insignificant part played by the professedly revolutionary groups in bringing about the revolution [3.10]. In nearly all cases the professional revolutionaries, after years or decades of theorising, organising, and plotting, are caught unprepared. They experience something like Auguste Blanqui's 'happy surprise' at the sudden turn of events, and leave their libraries, or hurry home from exile, or are liberated from prison. Since the collapse of the state has had so little to do with their own activities, they are even likely to be unduly gloomy about the prospects of revolution. De Tocqueville observed the perplexity of the 'leaders' of the February Revolution of 1848, sitting in their clubs and newspaper offices trying to organise the forces that had been unleashed with such apparent spontaneity. In 1871, the year of the Paris Commune, there was no leadership to the insurrection, and none for some time afterwards. The only possible insurrectionary authority was the Central Committee of the Federation of the National Guard, and they found themselves, quite without effort, master of the city. As Frank Jellinek says, 'the Committee sat in the Hôtel de Ville in the utmost perplexity. They never had the slightest idea that they might be called upon to act as a government.'[109] The best example of all is furnished by Lenin who, a matter of weeks before the February Revolution, was playing the role of elder prophet to a young Swiss audience, and reflecting that 'we, the old, may not live to see the decisive battles of the coming revolution'.[110]

---

[108] E. H. Carr, *A History of Soviet Russia*, vol. 1, *The Bolshevik Revolution* (London, 1960), p. 25.

[109] Frank Jellinek, *The Paris Commune of 1871* (London, 1937), p. 124.

[110] Lenin, 'Lecture on the 1905 Revolution', *Selected Works in Three Volumes*, vol. 1, p. 842. And cf. the comment of a leading participant in the February Revolution, S. Mstislavsky-Maslovsky: 'The Revolution surprised us – the party men of those days – sound asleep like the foolish virgins of the Gospel. Now, five years later, it seemed incredible that we could have failed to realise

Revolutionaries cannot by themselves make revolutions. They cannot usually even make effective propaganda for revolution. This role is reserved for those classes that are centrally placed in the power structure of society. Revolutionaries are marginal to that structure.

The second phenomenon to be noted is more remarkable. This is the great outburst of creativity in the intellectual and artistic spheres that has been associated with all the major European revolutions. There is no point in listing names here. One can perhaps simply refer to the 'cultural renaissances' of the period of the late sixteenth and early seventeenth century in England, of the eighteenth century in France, and of the nineteenth century in Russia. The parallel with the renaissances of Greece in the fifth century BC and Italy in the fifteenth century is especially striking. It is a plausible hypothesis that these cultural renaissances have all depended on similar conditions. What seems to have happened is that the revolutionary societies created *internally* the political conditions that the city-states of Greece and Italy created *externally*. The disunited ruling classes of the revolutionary societies brought about the dispersion and decentralisation of power that was achieved by the relative inability of the city-states to dominate each other during the specified periods. For Greece, this condition seems to have been given by the common struggle against Persia, and the balance of power and rivalry between Athens and Sparta during the fifth century. This state of affairs ended with the imposition of the Macedonian empire on the Greek states. Italy gained a similar relative autonomy of the city-states when the struggle between Pope and Emperor reached a temporary stalemate in the late fourteenth and fifteenth centuries. The independence of the states was largely lost when Spain conquered the peninsula for the Empire.

During the periods of stalemate, individuals can choose the most congenial despot, and they can leave him for another and

---

that the February wave was rising (not to speak of the oncoming storm). So many of us had spent years under the Tsarist regime preparing underground for those days with tense and eager faith, and when at last it came – the long-awaited and ardently desired revolution – we had nowhere to go.' Quoted in George Katkov, *Russia 1917 : The February Revolution* (London, 1967), p. xxvii.

perhaps rival despot, when the demands get too oppressive. The important thing seems to be the variety of centres of power in the same culture area, allowing writers and artists a choice of patrons and protectors. The wanderings of the Italian artists of the Renaissance are well known, and are perhaps best illustrated by Benvenuto Cellini as set down in his own *Autobiography*. In eighteenth-century France, Voltaire could enjoy the favour and protection now of the King, now of the parlements: and so keep something of his own integrity. The nineteenth-century Russian *intelligent* could even more readily rely on the protection of the disaffected gentry against the Tsarist bureaucracy; and if, like Chaadaev, he occasionally wrote flatteringly about the Tsar, he was simply maximising his chances of survival.

Nothing indeed better characterises a revolutionary society than the release of creative energies which accompanies the breakdown of the over-all consensus and authority patterns. The corollary of this breakdown of authority is that, so long as it lasts, it cannot prevent the new ideas from reaching every level of society. A striking testimony to this effect, which could stand for all revolutions, is offered by the French *avocat général* in 1770, when he acknowledged the futility of the state policy of suppressing the philosophic literature:

The philosophers have with one hand sought to shake the throne, with the other to upset the altars. Their purpose was to change public opinion on civil and religious institutions, and *the revolution has, so to speak, been effected*. History and poetry, romances and even dictionaries, have been infected with the poison of incredulity. Their writings are hardly published in the capital before they invade the provinces like a torrent. The contagion has spread even into workshops and cottages.[111]

If, as we have been arguing, revolution is the creation of the conditions of freedom, this passage indicates the point at which the revolution has become a reality in the society, and is a measure of the loss sustained when sovereignty is once more established out of the violence of civil war.

[111] Quoted Felix Rocquain, *The Revolutionary Spirit Preceding the French Revolution*, pp. 103–4.

7 THE COURSE OF REVOLUTIONS

David Hume says in one of his essays that whereas it is reasonable and possible to make generalisations about social processes *within* a society, it is far less easy to make generalisations about the behaviour of societies in relation to each other, since in the latter case too many inconstant factors are at play. Much the same sort of relationship seems to exist between generalisations as to the causes and as to the course of Revolutions. There seems to be a high degree of uniformity in the sociological patterns of all those societies which experienced the 'great Revolutions' of the past. The periods before the outbreak of violence, the periods of the various *anciens régimes,* exhibit the working out of long-term forces which are largely internal to the society, and which therefore can be interpreted and explained in terms of the general character of that society as it has been formed by its history. Once, however, the conflict becomes open and takes the form of civil war, so many contingent factors become operative that the search for uniformities yields less satisfying results. In particular, the struggle rapidly tends to go beyond the boundaries of the particular society, and its course therefore turns to an extraordinary extent on the interests and alliances of other societies. The civil war turns into an international war, with the various parties to the struggle appealing to different nations, and even to different groups within the same nation. Since the policies of these nations can vary remarkably over short periods of time, the outcomes of the internal revolutionary struggles will also vary in ways difficult to predict. How, for instance, could an observer in 1800 have been able to predict the foreign policies of Alexander I of Russia, with all this implied for the success or failure of the Napoleonic regime? How could a later observer be certain that the working-class movements of the capitalist countries would effectively hinder the aid being given by their governments to the 'White' Russians in the Russian Civil War: a factor that Lenin at least later regarded as crucial to the victory of the Bolsheviks?

Nevertheless, the courses of the 'great Revolutions' of the past do follow a certain basic though rather obvious uniformity, and the phenomenon deserves a brief treatment. We have seen that the classic Revolutions of the historians come at the end of the revolutions proper: the periods during which power has effectively become fragmented within the community, and in which new ideas of possible forms of order are established. This fact determines the stages through which most of these Revolutions have passed. Their course is marked by an open, concentrated, and accelerated struggle for power between all the groups that have been summoned up in the more protracted conflict before the outbreak of civil war. The final stage is reached when one or a combination of groups, with or without external support, is able to impose itself more or less firmly on a population exhausted by war and want.

Our task in dealing with this aspect of revolution is simplified by the fact that it has dominated the theoretical literature on the subject. Ever since the French Revolution had run its course, men were struck by what seemed the irresistible logic of events in its development, and had come to see this as the inherent logic of revolution as such. Partly this was due to the attitude of later revolutionaries themselves who, as we saw earlier, consciously aspired to imitate the course of the French Revolution. But more significant was the conviction that there was a sort of 'natural history' of revolution, a development as regular as the growth processes of organisms, and exhibiting the same orderly sequence of stages or phases. Knowing the particular species of an organism, we know enough about its general characteristics to be able to predict the direction and rate of its development. Revolution too was a 'species' of social life, with its own peculiar features of form and substance. Since all revolutions had similar causes and were composed of similar elements, their courses were bound to follow a basically uniform pattern. Peculiarly influential in this respect, and again on an organic analogy, was the conception of revolution as social 'pathology', as a disease or a fever of the body politic. Here, too, revolution could be expected to develop with a high degree of predictability, following the usual pathological sequence of symptoms, onset of illness, crisis, and restoration of health.

The conservative reaction to the French Revolution provided, in the writings of Burke, Gentz,[112] and de Maistre [5.2], some of the leading insights into the general course taken by Revolutions.

[112] See Friedrich Gentz, *The French and American Revolutions Compared*, trans. John Quincy Adams (1810) (Chicago, 1959).

But it was Hegel who, also reflecting on the French Revolution, gave the first important theoretical framework to the course of revolution. He saw at work a compelling process in which the Revolution, starting off with liberty as its aim, 'devoured its children' and crushed freedom in the name of necessity. For him this necessity followed by a dialectical progress from the attempt to establish freedom on the basis merely of an abstract understanding of the concept of freedom: as shown, for instance, in the writing of the philosophes and the *Declaration of the Rights of Man*. He acknowledged that with the French Revolution history had taken a decisive turn. Man had dared to subject the whole given social reality to the standards of reason, and had thereby taken an irreversible step forward. But to Hegel reason cannot govern reality unless reality has become rational in itself. The French Revolution had tried to build freedom with the materials merely of the theoretical components of freedom; it built upon a concrete reality, French society at the end of the eighteenth century, as yet unprepared for such a structure. As a necessary consequence, instead of establishing freedom it moved through violence and anarchy to despotism. The French Revolution showed

the freedom of the void which rises to a passion . . . when it turns to actual practice, it takes shape in religion and politics alike as the fanaticism of destruction – the destruction of the whole subsisting social order – as the elimination of individuals who are objects of suspicion to any social order, and the annihilation of any organisation which tries to rise anew from the ruins.[113]

Later writers remained indebted to this display of dialectical logic, although they usually changed the terms of expression. It was attractive because it had strong affinities with the cyclical view of revolution inherited from classical antiquity, it seemed to account for what had actually happened in the French Revolution, and it was apparently confirmed by the course of later Revolutions, especially those of 1848 and 1917. Marx in particular was always heavily influenced by Hegel's analysis of the French Revolution, and this can clearly be seen in his own accounts of the 1848

[113] Hegel, *The Philosophy of Right*, trans. T. M. Knox (Oxford, 1962), p. 22.

Revolutions [5.7]. In his case the terms of the dialectic were translated into the conflict of social classes, and the course of those Revolutions was seen as determined by the inherent inability of the current social order to satisfy the aspirations of all classes, particularly the proletariat.

The 1848 Revolutions themselves affected thinking about the course of revolutions. They seemed to give added reason for thinking that the cycle from freedom to despotism would perpetuate itself in all revolutions of the foreseeable future. For in making the social and economic content the heart of the revolutionary process, the Socialist parties of that year ensured that no Revolution from now on could ever hope to stop at mere constitution-making, but must press on in the attempt to overthrow the existing social and economic order and replace it with one that, in appearance at least, satisfied the economic demands of the vast majority of the population [5.8, 5.9]. Since the social resources available in most European societies were a long way from being able to satisfy those demands in practice, the attempt was bound to lead to dictatorship: either of the old popular Caesarian type, with its bread and circuses, or of the far more encompassing totalitarian type bred by the twentieth-century Revolutions.

Such gloomy thoughts afflicted most European liberals after 1848, and perhaps none so fruitfully as Jacob Burckhardt. It was he who, in an analysis of 'the crises of history', presented a sketch of the course of revolutions in the form in which it is now widespread [5.1]. The pattern is close to Hegel's, and undoubtedly owes something to the classical conception. But it goes much further in giving a detailed account of the 'natural history' of revolution, from the early stirrings of unrest in society, through the high point of terror and fanaticism, leading to a Thermidorean reaction, the *coup d'état* of the military 'saviour' of society, and finally restoration. Burckhardt regarded a social crisis – in which general category he placed revolution – as 'an expedient of nature, like a fever', and in this he again stands at the beginning of a host of later accounts. Where he differs from most of them, perhaps, is in seeing this fever as endemic in society, and especially modern society, since the French Revolution. The stage of restoration is for him also the stage of the recommencement of 'the spirit of change'. The re-imposed institutions are confronted by the generation which has been schooled by the crisis, and which has come to demand as a right what its fathers saw as an aim to be fought for. The overthrow of those institutions is hence simply a matter of time, after which the stages of the cycle will be repeated.

Burckhardt's sketch of the course of revolutions can be found substantially repeated in most of the well-known twentieth-century treatments of revolution. It is in Sorokin, Edwards, Brinton and Pettee. It is also in the accounts given by the students of social psychology and 'collective behaviour', such as Le Bon, Blumer, Hopper, and Smelser.[114] Thus Edwards notes the following stages in the causation and course of revolutions: 'preliminary symptoms of unrest', 'advanced symptoms of revolution', 'transfer of the allegiance of the intellectuals', elaboration of 'the social myth', 'development of the revolutionary mob', 'rule of the moderates', 'rise of the radicals', 'the Reign of Terror', and 'the return to normality'. Pettee offers us: 'social cramp', 'the crisis', 'dissolution', 'tentative trials of strength', 'the agony of the moderates', 'the show-down', 'the Terror', 'the Dictatorship', 'fatigue', 'post-revolutionary society'. Many of these writers draw upon the analogy with organic disease. Sorokin goes a little further and sees the principal characteristic of revolution as 'the biologisation of behaviour', a hair-raising process in which men lose all civilised habits and restraints and regress to a condition of primitive barbarity. Revolution to him is like a 'drunken debauch', to which follows a salutary headache (the reaction), leading once more to a sober state (an orderly rate of social evolution).

While the general agreement on the stages of revolution is impressive, the explanatory accounts given are usually less so. There is not much serious analysis of the 'causal mechanics' of the process, the forces that propel the revolution, with apparent irresistibility, from one stage to another. Sometimes we are simply referred to certain 'objective developmental tendencies', as in

[114] See P. Sorokin, *The Sociology of Revolution* (London, 1925); L. P. Edwards, *The Natural History of Revolution* (Chicago, 1927); Crane Brinton, *The Anatomy of Revolution*; Gustave le Bon, *The Psychology of Revolution* (London, 1913); H. Blumer, 'Collective Behaviour', in R. E. Park (ed.), *An Outline of the Principles of Sociology* (New York, 1939), pp. 221–80; Rex Hopper, 'The Revolutionary Process', *Social Forces*, vol. XXVIII (1950), pp. 270–9; Neil Smelser, *The Theory of Collective Behaviour* (London, 1962).

Borkenau's 'law of the twofold development of modern revolutions': "They begin as anarchistic movements against the existing bureaucratic State organisation, which they inevitably destroy; they continue by setting in its place another, in most cases stronger, bureaucratic organisation, which suppresses all free mass movements.'[115] Alternatively, the account is heavily informed by the organic growth analogy from natural history, and the sequence of stages is seen to follow 'naturally', almost as if guided by some sort of entelechy of the revolution. Thus, students of collective behaviour, such as Herbert Blumer and Rex Hopper, postulate a developmental sequence starting with a herdlike 'milling' of restless and discontented individuals (the mass), which turns into a stage of collective excitement (the crowd), then into a 'formal' stage involving the formulation of issues and the seizure of power, and finally into the 'institutional' stage where the revolutionary power is legalised and established as the political foundation of a new form of society.

Common to these accounts is that they commit the 'genetic fallacy'. No real explanation of the sequence of stages is given. There is simply a description, in temporal order, of a series of events occurring over a certain period of time. The illusion of an explanation is created by references to 'the dialectic of revolution', 'the inherent logic of revolution', or to some ill-defined psychological properties of crowds and masses. But what links up the stages of a revolution into the widely-observed uniformities remains mysterious. An identical weakness of logic was largely responsible for discrediting nineteenth-century theories of social evolution, with their fondness for postulating stages of human development without explaining how societies moved from one stage to another.[116] The sceptical attitude commonly held towards theories of revolution no doubt stems partly from seeing the parallel.

But the explanation of the sequence is, after all, not so very mysterious. Let us remove first the contingent factors from the development of the Revolution. Let us discount the vagaries of foreign politics, the volatile nature of international alliances, the

---

[115] F. Borkenau, 'State and Revolution in the Paris Commune, The Russian Revolution, and the Spanish Civil War', p. 67.

[116] For a summary of the objections to such theories, see Ernest Gellner *Thought and Change* (London, 1964), ch. 1.

accidents of personality. What remains is a situation as old as politics itself: the struggle between warring groups to seize control of the state and impose their will on the rest of the population. Engels once chided the anarchists for wanting revolution and yet not admitting this basic fact about it. 'Have these gentlemen ever seen a revolution? A revolution is certainly the most authoritarian thing there is; it is the act whereby one part of the population imposes its will upon the other part by means of rifles, bayonets and canon....'[117]

At this point, the Revolution is best assimilated to war: in Clausewitz's famous definition, the continuation of ordinary politics 'by other means'. Like war, the Revolution continues ordinary politics, but with a concentration of time that necessitates a speeding up of tempo and an open appeal to means that are usually employed only sparingly, or at least covertly.[118] It is normal in Western societies for groups to struggle for power. It is normal, too, for force to be used or threatened in that struggle. But generally the group that takes possession of the state, and so secures a monopoly of the use of the most powerful instruments of violence, can prevent the expression of force on the part of other groups. Its ideology becomes the dominant ideology: as Marx put it, the ruling ideas of an age are the ideas of the ruling class. Other groups have to justify their claims in terms of these ideas, and this usually means that their demands do not basically threaten the power or legitimacy of the ruling group. But there comes the time when, as we have seen, competition for power within the ruling group undermines its legitimacy and weakens its over-all control of the society. The claims of other groups are revived or fashioned anew. The upper classes themselves are often the instructors in the arts of violent agitation, in dramatic appeals to 'the nation', in discovering and exploiting mass discontents. The restraints of 'ordinary politics', as once defined by the ruling group, drop away. Finally comes some incident, some manoeuvre, which highlights and

---

[117] Engels, 'On Authority', in Marx and Engels *Selected Works*, vol. 1, p. 639.
[118] The relationship of 'revolutionary' to 'ordinary' politics is similar to the relation of 'battles' to 'war', in Hobbes' admirable expression of it: 'For "war" consisteth not in battle only, or the act of fighting; but in a tract of time wherein the will to contend by battle is sufficiently known; ... not in actual fighting, but in the known disposition thereto all the time there is no assurance to the contrary.' *Leviathan*, ch. 13.

intensifies the conflict, transforming it into open civil war. Then comes the series of events commonly designated 'the Revolution'.

The 'logic of revolutionary stages' is the logic of this basic situation. It is the logic of attempting to teach freedom by the sword, in a situation where to be defeated in the struggle is to lose everything, including life; and so where every party is prepared to resort to the most extreme measures. The notion of legitimacy has disappeared, buried beneath rival ideologies each claiming to embody the substance of the Revolution, and each therefore trying to halt the course of events at the appropriate moment. But lacking legitimacy each party that gains dominance rests demonstrably on force, to which it has to appeal as a matter of daily existence [5.4]. It is easily toppled by any party that can secure superior force: something true enough of the periods of ordinary politics, but now made vastly easier to accomplish in the shifting fortunes of civil war. The temporary victory of one party throws into an equally temporary alliance all its opponents, divergent and contradictory as their aims may be. Since circumstances make it unlikely that the ruling party can deliver more than a fraction of what it promises, the easiest strategy for its opponents is to outbid it in appeals to the people, and to attempt to harness the force of the popular organisations that have come into being. Usually, too, it is easy to win over important sections of the army, either of the officers or of the men. The troops will frequently be involved in wars in defence of the revolution, in conditions where ordinary military discipline is weak, and the provision of supplies and equipment poor and uncertain.

The Revolution therefore tends to follow a leftward movement. Moderate policies based on moderate means give way successively to more extremist policies based on extremist means. Each party tries to secure a more popular base by appealing over the heads of the current office-holders. The process can culminate, as it did so remarkably in the French Revolution, in the attempt to achieve the 'despotism of liberty' by means of a 'Reign of Terror'. Here the rigours of a popular dictatorship are justified by an appeal to the continuing danger from the many suppressed enemies of the Revolution, the more to be feared because of their collaboration with foreign enemies. The wars will also worsen an already disturbed economic condition, thus entailing perhaps strict rationing and the provision of other welfare services. This adds to the harshness of the dictatorship, which comes to treat all criticism as treason, and to insist on unquestioning compliance with its decrees.

But the movement towards extremism carries within it the forces that halt it. In attempting to force people to be free, the dictatorship daily adds recruits to an opposition made up of all the defeated parties of the earlier stages of the Revolution. The removal of one layer of enemies simply exposes another layer to fill the same role, until the dictatorship is left defenceless. Finally it is overthrown in a 'Thermidorean reaction', sometimes with the aid of a military commander who then or later seizes power himself. The institution of a dictatorship based openly on the army reveals what the ideologies of the preceding phases have attempted to cover: that the condition of rule is the winning over of the allegiance of the military, or, at least, not provoking its active resistance.[119] Henceforward the Revolution assumes even more strictly the character of a military struggle, carried out usually on an international front. In some cases, as with the Bolsheviks, the dictatorship manages to survive the international civil war; in others, as with the Cromwellian Protectorate and with Napoleon's Empire, it gives way to a 'Restoration' regime. Such a regime contains formal elements of the pre-Revolutionary order; but it differs fundamentally from it in at least one important respect. It is the heir to the regeneration and reaffirmation of sovereignty that is the main accomplishment of the various Revolutionary regimes, and which its predecessor of the *ancien régime* so fatally lacked.

The contradictions contained within the logic of the revolutionary situation are well illustrated by Cromwell. Cromwell is repeatedly charged with hypocrisy; but the hypocrisy arises out of his position, not his personality. His New Model Army had fought with Parliament against the threat of royal tyranny. The victorious Parliament, dominated by Presbyterians, was now attempting to exercise a tyranny more severe than the monarch's. Cromwell's control of the army allowed him to play the role of arbiter, enforcing tolerance in the midst of selfish and competing despotisms. 'What's for their good, not what pleases them,' was his declared

[119] There is a good analysis of the problem in C. K. Chorley, *Armies and the Art of Revolution* (London, 1943), pp. 254–60.

intention in 1647. He was 'not wedded and glued to forms of government', and in the interests of toleration he was prepared to rely on a frankly dictatorial instrument. Christopher Hill writes that 'through the Major-Generals he enforced a greater degree of religious toleration than any Parliament elected on a propertied franchise could approve of'.[120] And yet his rule came to be detested by almost every group in the country. After his death his name was linked for a century and a half with military dictatorship and the hated institutions of the standing army.

'''Tis against the will of the nation,' Calamy said of the Protectorate; 'there will be nine in ten against you.' 'But what,' Cromwell replied, 'if I should disarm the nine and put a sword in the tenth man's hand? Would not that do the business?' The only 'business' this could do, as was the case with all similar enterprises subsequently, was to lend strength to the theory of the revolutionary cycle, conceived in liberty and ending in despotism. Gardiner, the historian of the English Revolution, put the point simply at the very outset of his great work: 'It is never possible for men of the sword to rear the temple of recovered freedom. Honestly as both military and political leaders desired to establish popular government, they found themselves in a vicious circle from which there was no escape.'[121]

8 CONCLUSION: NEW VARIETIES OF REVOLUTION

It is tempting to conclude this essay with an examination of the prospects of revolution in the contemporary world. This century has seen not only the Russian Revolutions of 1905 and 1917, but the Central European Revolutions of 1918, the Chinese Revolutions of 1911 and 1949, the Mexican Revolution of 1911, the Cuban Revolution of 1959, and a host of national and social movements in Eastern Europe, Africa, Asia and Latin America, which have termed their successes 'Revolutions'. Moreover, in the 'May

---

[120] Christopher Hill, *Oliver Cromwell* (London, 1958); and for all quotations from Cromwell.

[121] S. R. Gardiner, *History of the Great Civil War* (London, 1893), vol. I, p. I.

events' of 1968 in France it has seen that rare phenomenon, a serious challenge from the Left, in peacetime, to the authority of the state in an advanced industrial society. There is not therefore any lack of material for the study of the problem in what has so often been called 'the century of revolution'.

Nevertheless, and perhaps fortunately, I must resist the temptation. Partly this is for reasons of space; but, even more, the scope of this introduction as I have conceived it precludes detailed treatment of twentieth-century developments. I have looked at the concept, causes, and course of revolution as it emerged and was experienced in Europe between the eighteenth and the twentieth centuries. All three aspects were shaped by certain features common to the history of European societies up to the eighteenth century: the experience of feudalism, the attempt by the Crown to destroy the independent power of the aristocracy, and a long drawn-out aristocratic resistance to this attempt. Together with this went certain other general developments such as the growth of urban and commercial centres, and commercial and professional middle classes, to offset the wealth and power of the landed classes. Once this situation had changed significantly in any direction, the phenomenon of revolution itself underwent change.

Thus, while the concept of revolution as the dissolution of sovereignty could persist into a society now largely urban, industrial, and bureaucratic, it was unlikely that the general factors causing revolution would recur in any simple way, or that the classic course would be followed. The necessary pre-condition of revolution is still the breakdown of consensus among the ruling groups; but the consequences of that breakdown in a society mainly characterised by large-scale industrial and governmental bureaucracies are bound to be very different from one in a society with large autonomous areas of political and economic power. Particularly, it seems improbable that modern industrial societies would exhibit the sort of slow, long-term distintegration of centralised power that was so distinctive a feature of earlier revolutionary situations, and lent them their characteristic flavour. The exigencies of bureaucratic organisation are against it, even where those organisations have uncertain or divided leadership. Indeed, most modern bureaucracies seem quite capable of dispensing with a head altogether, and could be content to go on responding in

81

ritualistic ways to stimuli from the environment, an increasing number of which they themselves inspire either directly or indirectly.

So far as the course of revolutions is concerned, this has been affected even more decisively by the developments of this century. I have already pointed out how the classic sequence of stages, as established by the great French Revolution, was constantly subject to complication by the intervention of foreign states. In this century the fact of intervention can no longer be considered merely as a complicating factor distorting the pure logic of the revolutionary sequence. Indeed, it now is and must be the dominating consideration in all conceptions of revolutionary strategy. All revolution is now, in a way never before so, world revolution [6.6]. Whether in promoting or in preventing revolution, the hand of one or another of the great industrial powers of the world is generally at work: supporting, intimidating, intervening. And while this is true for all industrial societies as well, nowhere is it more obvious than in the revolutions of the 'Third World'. To the fact of historical traditions and social structures remote from those of Europe, societies of the 'Third World' must add the experience of dependence on the industrial powers of the West and the constant threat of intervention by these powers. No wonder that it is in these societies that revolution, unquestionably taken over from Europe, shows the greatest deviation in cause and course from the European pattern of the past.

I hope I have said enough to justify the restricted treatment of this essay. Twentieth-century developments in the theory and practice of revolution need and deserve another volume. A leading theme in such a volume would have to be a study of the distinctive type of colonial or nationalist revolution, starting perhaps with the American Revolution of the eighteenth century, and showing how the idea of revolution and that of nationalism came to be fused in the various struggles for political independence among the subjects of dynastic and colonial empires. Clearly such a theme requires separate and detailed treatment. What might be stressed again at this point is that the concepts of the social sciences, 'bureaucracy' and 'feudalism', for instance, no less than 'revolution', are historically conditioned and must be analysed with respect for the historical context. The life of a concept, the creation of particular men at a particular time, persists far beyond any distinctive content that may originally have inspired it. The sociologist needs the historian to caution him against the pointless attempt to build up a battery of concepts, universal in scope but empty and valueless in dealing with the concrete, historical reality.

With this disclaimer, then, some concluding remarks can serve partly as recapitulation, and partly as comment on the state of the revolutionary idea today.

I have been concerned to elucidate the historical significance of revolution. I have seen it as a concept whose modern form was a creation of the eighteenth century. The French Revolution stamped its content decisively upon this concept. During the nineteenth and twentieth centuries, Europe and some other parts of the world both re-acted to, and to an extent, re-enacted, the course and consequences of that revolution. Similar conditions produced similar events. But never exactly. Later revolutions occurred within the context and with the consciousness of earlier revolutions. This was bound to affect their outcomes. We can see this especially clearly in the case of Russia, where the revolution was pushed to a conclusion by men who were steeped in the theory and practice of past European revolutions, and who were obsessed with the need to avoid their common fate. That they were not able to do so to a very great extent is an impressive testimony to the power of objective circumstances over the intentions of individuals: a lesson repeatedly taught by revolutions. Still, there were differences, of varying degrees of importance, in all revolutions subsequent to the French. This was recognised not only by the actors but by all the major theorists of revolution, even while they were struck by the similarities. The question therefore arises whether circumstances have changed so much by the mid-twentieth century that the whole nature of revolution, as I have analysed it, has been transformed to the point where its earlier significance is now superseded.

The revolution we looked at was a phenomenon of transitional societies.[122] It occurred in societies undergoing the transformation from being largely peasant or agrarian based, to being largely

---

[122] For some excellent remarks on the theme of this and the next paragraph, see Harvey Wheeler, *Democracy in a Revolutionary Era: The Political Order Today* (New York, 1968), pp. 90–1.

urban and commercially or industrially based. If we allow the vagueness, we may call it a revolution of 'modernisation': equivalent roughly to Marx's category of 'bourgeois' revolutions. The social groupings involved in it were the peasants, the land-owners, the urban artisans, and the urban professional and commercial middle classes. The first two classes provided the spark and much of the fuel for the revolution. Afterwards, if they did not actually disappear, they either fused with the other classes or their activities became subordinate to and dependent on those of the urban classes.

The new sort of society, of the commercial or industrial type, developed slowly and unevenly following the revolution. Even today, in a society such as France, there are pockets of 'pre-revolutionary' sentiments and activities. But certain common features emerged which prevented a recurrence of revolutions of the classic type. This was not simply because new social groups now occupied the centre of the stage: Marx, after all, expected the classes of industrial society to engage in a revolutionary struggle at least as severe as that of the earlier revolutions. Nor was it because the working classes were 'bought off' and turned away from revolutionary aspirations by an increasingly higher standard of living. Apart from the fact that there were working-class groups whose conditions worsened as a result of industrialisation, past experience suggested that revolutionary demands would grow, not weaken, as the situation improved and expectations rose.

Far more important was the new political framework within which aspirations were conceived and demands made. The earlier revolutions occurred in societies where the state was weak or discredited, and at any rate regarded by all the educated classes as utterly backward in comparison with nearly every other element of society. Whole areas of life were quite untouched by it, and there were influential social groups which had the prestige and wealth to hold on to a considerable degree of political autonomy. The effects of the 'great Revolutions' in almost every case were to strengthen the power of the state and to eliminate the remaining autonomous sectors. From then on, as both Marx and de Tocqueville noted, all attempts to change society either assumed the agency of the state in effecting the changes, or, despite initial intentions, ended up by relying on the state and expanding its scope and power [6.1]. Occasionally, as with Germany and the Habsburg

Empire in 1918, defeat in a long drawn-out war weakened the state temporarily to the point where there was a power vacuum, in which the revolutionary parties postured briefly. But they seemed quite incapable of tackling the structure and power of the modern state as such, and they were crushed as soon as the state recovered its confidence. The revolutionary parties of the Left, in any case, were as dazzled by the potentialities of the new state as the conservative parties of the Right. The programmes and strategy of the working-class parties, even where, as with the German Social-Democratic party, they remained formally revolutionary, were shaped to a predominant extent by the day-to-day bargaining with the institutions of the state, which imposed their own forms of procedure on the parties. Increasingly, as Michels so brilliantly demonstrated, the structure of the left-wing parties came to mirror the structure of the state, so in practice nullifying the democratic intentions of the parties, and ensuring that even if they did make a successful bid for power, they would simply substitute the rule of another bureaucratic élite for the existing one [5.15].

The rapid expansion of bureaucracy, both private and public, linked to larger, professional standing armies, offered the most serious obstacle to a recurrence of large-scale revolution. Max Weber, the great theorist of bureaucracy, saw this development as crucial in reducing revolutions now merely to the scope of *coups d'état* [6.4]. Bureaucracy was indispensable to modern societies. Revolutionary parties could no more do without it than any other, and any seizure of power by them would simply amount to putting new political figureheads at the top of a largely autonomous bureaucratic organization. The revolutions of the past had depended for their depth and intensity on the gradual but massive disintegration of political power. Such a condition now appeared highly improbable, since continuing bureaucratic functioning was seen as a technical necessity of contemporary societies, a premise of its very survival. One of the most difficult problems confronting modern revolutionaries has therefore been seen as that of finding sufficient non-bureaucratic 'space' in society in which to elaborate a new set of values and a new sort of social organisation.[123] Modern industrial-bureaucratic societies tolerate, and indeed encourage, many

[123] See Barrington Moore, Jr, 'Revolution in America?' *New York Review of Books*, 30 January 1969, pp. 6–11.

varieties of 'sub-culture'. But, consciously or unconsciously, the whole weight of their systems is thrown against the development of a revolutionary 'counter-culture'.

Revolutionary theorists of this century, in so far as they have dealt with industrial societies at all, have been driven to find their revolutionary material in those social groups least implicated in bureaucratic activities. Even the Marxists, while still affirming that the proletariat must ultimately be the basis of any serious revolutionary movement, have admitted that the working-class movement has to a large extent been 'incorporated' in the regular framework of capitalist politics, and for the time being at least is indifferent to revolution. Instead they have placed their hopes on the students, the intellectuals, the independent professional groups, even sometimes the forces of the 'Third World', as all being in a certain degree free of the dominant influences of contemporary capitalist societies, and able perhaps to give a revolutionary lead to the proletariat [6.10]. The events of May 1968 in France lent some support to this view. But they also showed that this constellation of forces was an insufficient agent of revolution; that the groups had aims so diffuse that they were unlikely ever to move decisively against the main centres of power; and that, in any case, as so often before, they were able to act only because the French Government had temporarily lost its nerve, and on recovering it was able to dispel them with conspicuously little effort.[124] It would be absurd to deny that revolution of some sort could occur in industrial societies. Many types of breakdown, admittedly of a largely technological kind, can be envisaged as providing the opportunity for radical political action. But the evidence suggests that whatever action is engaged in will have to have an entirely different strategy and character from that of traditional revolutions.

There remain the societies of the 'Third World'. As Europe and North America industrialised, it was natural to expect that revolutions of the type they experienced would occur in other societies making the similar transition from peasant-agrarian to industrial-urban bases. But it was here that the historical nature of revolution showed itself most dramatically. For the revolutions of the non-

---

[124] See the discussion on May 1968 by E. J. Hobsbawm, 'Birthday Party', *New York Review of Books*, 22 May 1969, pp. 4–11.

European world took place almost entirely in the shadow of the European revolutions and the societies they had given birth to. Partly this meant that 'Third World' revolutions, like the later European ones, were affected by the course and consequences of the earliest European revolutions. In this sense, as the latest revolutionary societies, they represented the extreme end of the continuum which began with the English and French Revolutions of the seventeenth and eighteenth centuries, and were therefore bound to differ most in character from those earlier models.

But the more important distorting factor was the fact of a European presence itself within the societies of the 'Third World'. European and American colonialism in the nineteenth and twentieth centuries meant that the industrial societies became implicated politically and economically in Asia, Africa, Latin America and the Middle East. From this followed profound economic and social changes that were mainly responsible for producing revolutionary situations in the 'Third World', so that the revolutions, when they came, were not only directed against the industrial powers, but also indirectly inspired by them. The revolutionary groups were faced with the prospect of fighting not only their internal opponents, but, allied with them and presenting a far more serious problem, a foreign power backed by the resources of an industrial society. This was bound to affect their aims and strategy to a predominant extent, and so to make the causes, course and consequences of 'Third World' revolutions very different from earlier European ones. The one exception might appear to be the American 'Revolution' of the eighteenth century that established the independence of the British North American colonies. But apart from the fact that such a colonial 'revolution' was in any case of a different type from the internal revolutions of Europe, the conditions of the 'Third World' are so very different from those of the eighteenth-century colonies that the analogy can only be superficial.

A likelier model for the 'Third World' is the Russian Revolution. It is already becoming common to see this Revolution as the first 'revolution of backward countries', with the guiding ideas and impulses coming from outside, from the West, and carried by an educated Westernised élite far removed in culture from the rest of the population[125] [6.8, 6.9]. This conception is all the more plausible for having been held, in its main outlines, by the Russian revolutionaries themselves, Lenin and especially Trotsky. The latter, in his 'law of combined and uneven development', gave a striking summary of the peculiarities of Russia's social and economic development, when compared with the West [5.12]. He observed in particular the part played by the West itself in this development, and considered that this fact must affect decisively the character of the revolution in Russia, as well as in all other societies which exhibited the characteristics of uneven development. It was this conception that determined the elimination of the middle class as the possible agent of even a 'bourgeois' revolution in Russia, and the entrusting of this task to a combination of the forces of the proletariat and the peasantry. Once that revolution had been made, moreover, there could be no stopping at this stage. Merely to safeguard that revolution, the proletariat would have to press on to the socialist revolution, breaking with the wealthier peasantry and relying upon the proletariat of the advanced West to secure itself against the intervention of the capitalist states [5.13].

The Russian Revolution stands half-way between the European revolutions and the revolutions of the 'Third World', such as those of China and Cuba. On the one side Trotsky's enunciation of the 'law of combined and uneven development' and his conception of the 'permanent revolution' points towards the peculiar conditions of 'Third World' societies. But on the other side, the Russian Revolution also had a great deal in common with the earlier revolutions of the West. Perhaps the most significant feature here was the time-scale over which the revolutionary situation in Russia developed, as well as the point in history at which the evolution was taking place. The Russian Revolution was a process beginning, as we have seen, at the end of the eighteenth century, and extending throughout the nineteenth. Given such a lengthy course, it was able to exhibit many of the characteristics typical of the European revolutions which also developed as a slow, gigantic process of breakdown. Moreover, despite the self-deprecating declarations of many of the educated Russians themselves, the

[125] See especially Theodore H. von Laue, *Why Lenin? Why Stalin? A Reappraisal of the Russian Revolution 1900–30* (Philadelphia, 1964).

Russian intelligentsia was very far from being a simple copy of the educated classes of the West. The Russian Revolution was not, as Arnold Toynbee and others have held, an act of mimesis. The intelligentsia evolved a distinctive culture of its own, which indeed at several points, notably in literature, reached higher than anything being produced in the West at the time, and which itself added an invaluable element to the culture of the West. Here again Russia stood half-way, a part of Europe as creator, and a part of the Europeanised creation that increasingly became the fate of the rest of the world.

With the changing nature of revolutionary conditions went an equally profound change in conceptions of revolutionary strategy. Already, in a famous preface of 1895, Engels had declared that revolution in the old style, with street fighting and barricades, had become obsolete through the developments of military technology, of communications, and the planning of cities on the principles of counter-insurgency. He advised the socialist parties of Europe to concentrate instead on the struggle by electoral means [6.5]. The Russian Revolution was still decided by the struggle for power within the major cities; but it was the last great Revolution to be successful with this strategy. In any case, both Lenin and Trotsky recognised the crucial role of the peasantry, who formed the vast majority of the army, and much that was distinctive in their theory and strategy was a response to this.

As the revolutionary idea moved out of Europe, the strategic role of the cities and the urban classes receded. The peasantry, and the struggle in the countryside, took their place. In left-wing theorising the proletariat always remained a nominally important revolutionary agent, but in practice all revolutionary energies became concentrated on the organisation of the peasants and the guerrilla warfare of the countryside. Mao Tse-tung shocked Moscow and many of his colleagues in the Chinese Communist party – just as Lenin had done on an earlier occasion – by elevating the peasantry to a primary position in the revolutionary struggle [6.7]. This, and the elaboration of the technique of guerrilla warfare as the main form of the 'international civil war', was no more than a sensible recognition of the facts of colonial and quasi-colonial societies. Similarly, current revolutionary theory has insisted even more on the special conditions of 'Third World'

89

societies, and the obsolescence of the city as the focus of revolutionary activity. 'The city,' said Fidel Castro, 'is a cemetery of revolutionaries and resources'; and Ché Guevara and Régis Debray have generalised from the experience of the Cuban Revolution to produce a revolutionary strategy for Latin America based entirely on the building up of a mobile guerrilla army.[126] In this conception, not only is the traditional appeal to the urban classes scorned, but the peasantry itself is regarded with suspicion, as too vulnerable to the counter-measures of the government. The experience even of China and Vietnam as the model of 'Third World' revolutions is rejected; for those countries could turn their revolutions into acts of national liberation, and so exploit normally passive forces. In the situation of Latin America, the enforced strategy of contemporary revolutionary movements of the 'Third World' is seen at its clearest and bleakest: a moving armed band, unable to depend even upon its natural ally, the peasantry, renouncing the leadership of the party organisation of the cities, confronting not only the massively-equipped national armed forces, but the forces of world powers with vested interests in the *status quo*. Revolutions have always at some stage drawn in international forces; but never so soon as now, never with such consequence that the success of revolution depends on defeating half the military might of the world.

[126] Régis Debray, *Revolution in the Revolution?*, trans. Bobbye Ortiz (Harmondsworth, 1968). For the more practical manual, see Ché Guevara, *Guerrilla Warfare* (Harmondsworth, 1969).

Readings

I The Content of the Revolutionary Idea

1.1 ON THE MEANING OF THE WORD 'REVOLUTIONARY'

From the Marquis de Condorcet, 'Sur Le Sens Du Mot Révolutionnaire',
Oeuvres (1847–9), vol. XII, pp. 615–24, translated by Sarah Lutman.

Condorcet (1743–94) wrote this piece in 1793. He was soon to be claimed by the French Revolution, a fact which gives a special poignancy to this affirmation of revolution as an act of liberation, and the justification of special 'revolutionary' measures to safeguard the revolutionary state.

From *revolution* we have derived revolutionary, and the general meaning of this word expresses everything which appertains to a revolution.

But we have made it our own, in that one of the states, which was oppressed for a long time by despotism, has made in a few years, the only republic where liberty has been based entirely on equal rights. Thus the word revolutionary can only be applied to revolutions which have liberty as their object.

We say a man is revolutionary when he is bound to the principles of revolution, when he acts for it and is prepared to sacrifice himself to maintain it.

A revolutionary spirit is one which is fit to produce and to direct a revolution made in the interests of liberty.

A revolutionary law is one whose object is to maintain this revolution and to accelerate or to regulate its progress.

A revolutionary measure is one which can ensure the success of the revolution.

We understand therefore that these laws and measures are not of the kind which are suitable for a peaceful society; they are characteristically appropriate only to a revolutionary period, however useless or unjust in another. . . .

When a country recovers its liberty, when this revolution is a fact, but is not yet completed, there naturally exist a large number of men who wish to produce a revolution in reverse – *a counter-revolution*, and who, merged with the mass of citizens, could become dangerous if they were allowed to act together, and to gather to them all those who share their ideas but are restrained by fear or idleness. Here, therefore, is a danger against which one is justified in defending oneself; thus, all actions, however insignificant, which increase this danger, may become subject to a repressive law, and all actions which forestall them, can legitimately be required of the citizens.

The social pact has for its object the equal and total enjoyment of human rights. It is founded on the mutual guarantee of these rights. But this guarantee ceases with respect to those who wish to dissolve it. Consequently, when it is established that such people exist in a society, one has the right to find means to discover them, and when they are discovered, one need only be restrained by the limits of the natural right of defence. The same applies if a more precious right is threatened; if, in order to preserve it, one has to sacrifice the exercise of a less important right. For such a right ceases to exist, because it would be nothing more, to him who claimed it, than the freedom to violate in others a more precious right.

In the fire of London, in 1666, the fire was not cut off, because the law forbade the demolition of houses. Furniture and goods belonging to absentees were allowed to burn, because it was forbidden to break in doors. Let us not imitate this example. . . .

Let us not imagine that we can justify all excesses by 'necessity, the excuse of tyrants'. But let us also beware of slandering the friends of liberty by judging the laws they have adopted, and the measures that they propose, merely by rules which are true, ultimately, only for peaceful times.

If zeal, even for the most just of causes, sometimes becomes culpable, let us remember that moderation is not always wisdom.

Let us make revolutionary laws, but to accelerate the time when we would have no more need of them. Let us adopt revolutionary measures, not to prolong or make bloody the revolution, but to complete it and to hasten its end.

Alteration in the meaning of words indicates an alteration in the things themselves.

Aristocracy signifies government by wise men. Old men governed by their authority and experience, poor and small tribes. A small number of rich men governed with arrogance these tribes transformed into opulent and populous towns. From that time aristocracy became the exact synonym for tyranny.

1.2 THE CONTENT OF REVOLUTION IS SOCIAL, NOT POLITICAL

From Karl Marx, 'Critical Notes on "The King of Prussia and Social Reform"', in Writings of the Young Marx on Philosophy and Society, edited and translated by L. D. Easton and K. H. Guddat (New York, 1967), pp. 356–7.

In this early work (1844), and in the following three extracts, Marx defines and elaborates his concept of revolution as a social act in which the proletariat is the agency of human emancipation. See also 'Introduction' p. 32–7. The 'Critical Notes . . .' were written in response to an article by Arnold Ruge, who signed himself 'A Prussian' and is so referred to in the text. Marx remarks on the insufficiency of the concept of a purely political revolution in the case of the worker, in the degraded conditions in which he lives.

The *community* from which the worker is *isolated* is a community of a very different order and extent than the *political* community. This community, from which *his own labour* separates him, is *life* itself, physical and spiritual life, human morality, human activity, human enjoyment, *human* existence. *Human existence* is the *real community* of man. As the disastrous isolation from this existence is more final, intolerable, terrible, and contradictory than isolation from the political community, so is the ending of this isolation. And even a partial reaction, a *revolt* against it, means all the more, as *man* is more than *citizen* and *human life* more than *political life*.

95

Hence, however *partial* the *industrial* revolt may be, it conceals within itself a *universal* soul: no matter how universal a *political* revolt may be, it conceals a *narrow-minded* spirit under the *most colossal* form.

The 'Prussian' worthily closes his article with the following phrase: 'A *social revolution without a political soul* (i.e. without organising insight from the standpoint of the whole) is impossible.'

We have seen that a *social* revolution involves the standpoint of the *whole* because it is a protest of man against dehumanised life even if it occurs in only *one* factory district, because it proceeds from the *standpoint* of the *single actual individual,* because the *community* against whose separation from himself the individual reacts is the *true* community of man, *human* existence. The *political soul* of a revolution, on the other hand, consists in the *tendency* of politically uninfluential classes to end their *isolation* from the *state* and from *power.* Its standpoint is that of the state, an *abstract* whole, which exists only through the separation from actual life and which is *unthinkable* without the *organised* antithesis between the universal idea and the individual existence of man. Hence a revolution of the *political soul* also organises, in accordance with the *narrow* and *split* nature of this soul, a ruling group in society at the expense of society.

We would like to confide to the 'Prussian' what a '*social revolution* with a *political* soul' is; at the same time we also suggest to him that he has not raised himself above the narrow political standpoint even in *phraseology.*

A '*social*' revolution with a *political* soul is either a compounded absurdity if the 'Prussian' means by 'social' revolution a 'social' revolution in *contrast* to a political one and nevertheless attributes to this social revolution a political rather than a social soul. Or a '*social revolution with a political soul*' is nothing but a *paraphrase* of what used to be called a '*political revolution*' or a '*revolution pure and simple*'. Any revolution breaks up the *old society;* to that extent it is *social.* Any revolution overthrows the *old ruling power;* to that extent it is *political.*

The 'Prussian' may choose between the *paraphrase* and the *absurdity!* But though it is paraphrastic or senseless to speak of a *social revolution* with a *political soul,* it is sensible to talk about a *political revolution* with a *social* soul. *Revolution* in general – the *overthrow* of the existing ruling power and the *dissolution* of the old conditions – is a *political act*. Without *revolution,* however, *socialism* cannot come about. It requires this *political act* so far as it needs *overthrow* and *dissolution*. But where its *organising activity* begins, where its *own aim* and *spirit* emerge, there socialism throws the *political* hull away.

1.3 REVOLUTION THE RE-INTEGRATION OF SOCIAL AND POLITICAL MAN

From Karl Marx, 'On the Jewish Question' (1843), in
Karl Marx: Early Writings, *edited and translated by*
T. B. Bottomore (London, 1963), pp. 27–31.

Marx sees the French Revolution as having bifurcated man into an abstract rational creature for public purposes, and an egoistic creature in his private economic and social life. A real revolution will re-integrate the two spheres, so that the rational and moral life of the abstract 'citizen' will characterise the everyday activities of the private individual.

Political emancipation is at the same time the *dissolution* of the old society, upon which the sovereign power, the alienated political life of the people, rests. Political revolution is a revolution of civil society. What was the nature of the old society? It can be characterised in one word: *feudalism.* The old civil society had a *directly political* character; that is, the elements of civil life such as property, the family, and types of occupations had been raised, in the form of lordship, caste and guilds, to elements of political life. They determined, in this form, the relation of the individual to the *state as a whole*; that is, his *political* situation, or in other words, his separation and exclusion from the other elements of society. For this organisation of national life did not constitute property and labour as social elements; it rather succeeded in *separating* them from the body of the state, and made them *distinct* societies within society. Nevertheless, at least in the feudal sense, the vital functions and conditions of civil society remained political. They excluded the individual from the body of the state, and transformed the *particular* relation which existed between his corporation and the state into a general relation between the individual and social life, just as they transformed his specific civil activity and situation into a general activity and situation. As a result of this organisation, the state as a whole and its consciousness, will and activity – the general political power – also necessarily appeared as the *private* affair of a ruler and his servants, separated from the people.

The political revolution which overthrew this power of the ruler, which made state affairs the affairs of the people, and the political state a matter of *general* concern, i.e. a real state, necessarily shattered everything – estates, corporations, guilds, privileges – which expressed the separation of the people from community life. The political revolution therefore *abolished* the *political character of civil society*. It dissolved civil society into its basic elements, on the one hand *individuals*, and on the other hand the *material and cultural elements* which formed the life experience and the civil situation of these individuals. It set free the political spirit which had, so to speak, been dissolved, fragmented and lost in the various culs-de-sacs of feudal society; it reassembled these scattered fragments, liberated the political spirit from its connection with civil life and made of it the community sphere, the *general* concern of the people, in principle independent of these particular elements of civil life. A *specific* activity and situation in life no longer had any but an individual significance. They no longer constituted the general relation between the individual and the state as a whole. Public affairs as such became the general affair of each individual, and political functions became general functions.

But the consummation of the idealism of the state was at the same time the consummation of the materialism of civil society. The bonds which had restrained the egoistic spirit of civil society were removed along with the political yoke. Political emancipation was at the same time an emancipation of civil society from politics and from even the *semblance* of a general content.

Feudal society was dissolved into its basic element, *man*; but into *egoistic* man who was its real foundation.

Man in this aspect, the member of civil society, is now the foundation and presupposition of the *political* state. He is recognised as such in the rights of man.

But the liberty of egoistic man, and the recognition of this liberty, is rather the recognition of the *frenzied* movement of the cultural and material elements which form the content of his life.

Thus man was not liberated from religion; he received religious liberty. He was not liberated from property; he received the liberty to own property. He was not liberated from the egoism of business; he received the liberty to engage in business.

The *formation of the political state,* and the dissolution of civil society into independent *individuals* whose relations are regulated by *law,* as the relations between men in the corporations and guilds were regulated by *privilege,* are accomplished by *one and the same act.* Man as a member of civil society – *non-political* man – necessarily appears as the *natural* man. The rights of man appear as natural rights because *conscious* activity is concentrated upon political *action. Egoistic* man is the *passive, given* result of the dissolution of society, an object of *direct apprehension* and consequently a *natural* object. The *political revolution* dissolves civil society into its elements without *revolutionising* these elements themselves or subjecting them to criticism. This revolution regards civil society, the sphere of human needs, labour, private interests and civil law, as the *basis of its own existence,* as a self-subsistent *precondition,* and thus as its *natural basis.* Finally, man as a member of civil society is identified with *authentic man, man* as distinct from citizen, because he is man in his sensuous, individual and *immediate* existence, whereas *political* man is only abstract, artificial man, man as an *allegorical, moral* person. Thus man as he really is, is seen only in the form of *egoistic* man, and man in his *true* nature only in the form of the *abstract citizen.*

The abstract notion of political man is well formulated by Rousseau:

Whoever dares undertake to establish a people's institutions must feel himself capable of *changing,* as it were, *human nature* itself, of *transforming* each individual who, in isolation, is a complete but solitary whole, into a *part* of something greater than himself, from which in a sense, he derives his life and his being; ... of substituting a limited and moral existence for the physical and independent life. .... His task, in short, is to take from *a man his own powers,* and to give him in exchange alien powers which he can only employ with the help of other men.

Every emancipation is a *restoration* of the human world and of human relationships to *man himself.*

Political emancipation is a reduction of man, on the one hand to a member of civil society, an *independent* and *egoistic* individual, and on the other hand, to a *citizen,* to a moral person.

Human emancipation will only be complete when the real, individual man has absorbed into himself the abstract citizen; when as an individual man, in his everyday life, in his work, and in his relationships, he has become a *species-being;* and when he has recognised and organised his own powers (*forces propres*) as *social* powers so that he no longer separates this social power from himself as *political* power.

1.4 REVOLUTION THE EMANCIPATION OF HUMANITY THROUGH THE PROLETARIAT

From Karl Marx, 'Contribution to the Critique of Hegel's Philosophy of Right' (1843–4), in Karl Marx: Early Writings, edited and translated by T. B. Bottomore (London, 1963), pp. 55–9.

The peculiarly backward condition of Germany, according to Marx, makes it incapable of making a bourgeois political revolution on the model of the French. But this condition also paradoxically allows it to jump the political stage and, through the material agency of the proletariat, bring about the revolution of human emancipation which is the programme of German social philosophy. This comment on German social conditions allowed such Russian Marxists as Lenin and Trotsky to draw, in a more sociological form, similar inferences from the backward condition of Russia.

It is not *radical* revolution, *universal human* emancipation, which is a Utopian dream for Germany, but rather a partial, *merely* political revolution which leaves the pillars of the building standing. What is the basis of a partial, merely political revolution? Simply this: a *section of civil society* emancipates itself and attains universal domination; a determinate class undertakes, from its *particular situation,* a general emancipation of society.

This class emancipates society as a whole, but only on condition that the whole of society is in the same situation as this class; for example, that it possesses or can easily acquire money or culture.

No class in civil society can play this part unless it can arouse, in itself and in the masses, a moment of enthusiasm in which it associates and mingles with society at large, identifies itself with it, and is felt and recognised as the *general representative* of this society. Its aims and interests must genuinely be the aims and interests of society itself, of which it becomes in reality the social head and heart. It is only in the name of general interests that a particular class can claim general supremacy. In order to attain this liberating position, and the political direction of all spheres of society, revolutionary energy and consciousness of its own power do not suffice. For a *popular revolution* and the *emancipation of a particular class* of civil society to coincide, for *one* class to represent the whole of society, another class must concentrate in itself all the evils of society, a particular class must embody and represent a general obstacle and limitation. A particular social sphere must be regarded as the *notorious crime* of the whole society, so that emancipation from this sphere appears as a general emancipation. For *one* class to be the liberating class *par excellence*, it is necessary that another class should be openly the oppressing class. The negative significance of the French nobility and clergy produced the positive significance of the bourgeoisie, the class which stood next to them and opposed them.

But in Germany every class lacks the logic, insight, courage and clarity which would make it a negative representative of society. Moreover, there is also lacking in every class the generosity of spirit which identifies itself, if only for a moment, with the popular mind; that genius which pushes material force to political power, that revolutionary daring which throws at its adversary the defiant phrase: *I am nothing and I should be everything*. The essence of German morality and honour, in classes as in individuals, is a *modest egoism* which displays, and allows others to display, its own narrowness. The relation between the different spheres of German society is, therefore, not dramatic, but epic. Each of these spheres begins to be aware of itself and to establish itself beside the others, not from the moment when it is oppressed, but from the moment that circumstances, without any action of its own, have created a new sphere which it can in turn oppress. Even the *moral sentiment of the German middle class* has no other basis than the consciousness of being the representative of the narrow and limited mediocrity of all the other classes. It is not only the German kings, therefore, who ascend their thrones *mal à propos*. Each sphere of civil society suffers a defeat before gaining the victory; it erects its own barrier before having destroyed the barrier which opposes it; it displays the narrowness of its views before having displayed their generosity, and thus every opportunity of playing an important role has passed before it properly existed, and each class, at the very moment when it begins its struggle against the class above it, remains involved in a struggle against the class beneath. For this reason, the princes are in conflict with the monarch, the bureaucracy with the nobility, the bourgeoisie with all of them, while the proletariat is already beginning its struggle with the bourgeoisie. The middle class hardly dares to conceive the idea of emancipation from its own point of view before the development of social conditions, and the progress of political theory, show that this point of view is already antiquated, or at least disputable.

In France it is enough to be something in order to desire to be everything. In Germany no one has the right to be anything without first renouncing everything. In France partial emancipation is a basis for complete emancipation. In Germany complete emancipation is a *conditio sine qua non* for any partial emancipation. In France it is the reality, in Germany the impossibility, of a progressive emancipation which must give birth to complete liberty. In France every class of the population is *politically idealistic* and considers itself first of all, not as a particular class, but as the representative of the general needs of society. The role of liberator can, therefore, pass successively in a dramatic movement to different classes in the population, until it finally reaches the class which achieves social freedom; no longer assuming certain conditions external to man, which are none the less created by human society, but organising all the conditions of human life on the basis of social freedom. In Germany, on the contrary, where practical life is as little intellectual as intellectual life is practical, no class of civil society feels the need for, or the ability to achieve, a general emancipation, until it is forced to it by its *immediate* situation, by *material* necessity and by its *fetters themselves*.

Where is there, then, a *real* possibility of emancipation in Germany?

This is our reply. A class must be formed which has *radical chains*, a class in civil society which is not a class of civil society, a class which is the dissolution of all classes, a sphere of society which has a universal character because its sufferings are universal, and which does not claim a *particular redress* because the wrong which is done to it is not a *particular wrong* but *wrong in general*. There must be formed a sphere of society which claims no *traditional* status but only a human status, a sphere which is not opposed to particular consequences but is totally opposed to the assumptions of the German political system; a sphere, finally, which cannot emancipate itself without emancipating itself from all the other spheres of society, without, therefore, emancipating all these other spheres, which is, in short, a *total loss* of humanity and which can only redeem itself by a *total redemption of humanity*. This dissolution of society, as a particular class, is the *proletariat*.

The proletariat is only beginning to form itself in Germany, as a result of the industrial movement. For what constitutes the proletariat is not *naturally existing* poverty, but poverty *artificially produced*, is not the mass of people mechanically oppressed by the weight of society, but the mass resulting from the *disintegration* of society and above all from the disintegration of the middle class. Needless to say, however, the numbers of the proletariat are also increased by the victims of natural poverty and of Christian-Germanic serfdom.

When the proletariat announces the *dissolution of the existing social order*, it only declares the *secret of its* own existence, for it *is* the *effective* dissolution of this order. When the proletariat demands the *negation of private property* it only lays down as a *principle for society* what society has already made a principle *for the proletariat*, and what the latter already involuntarily embodies as the negative result of society. Thus the proletarian has the same right, in relation to the new world which is coming into being, as the *German king* has in relation to the existing world when he calls the people *his* people or a horse *his* horse. In calling the people his private property the king simply declares that the owner of private property is king.

Just as philosophy finds its *material* weapons in the proletariat, so the proletariat finds its *intellectual* weapons in philosophy. And once the lightning of thought has penetrated deeply into this virgin soil of the people, the *Germans* will emancipate themselves and become *men*.

Let us sum up these results. The emancipation of Germany is only possible *in practice* if one adopts the point of view of that theory according to which man is the highest being for man. Germany will not be able to emancipate itself from the *Middle Ages* unless it emancipates itself at the same time from the *partial* victories over the Middle Ages. In Germany *no* type of enslavement can be abolished unless *all* enslavement is destroyed. Germany, which likes to get to the bottom of things, can only make a revolution which upsets *the whole order* of things. The *emancipation of Germany* will be an *emancipation of man*. *Philosophy* is the *head* of this emancipation and the *proletariat* is its *heart*. Philosophy can only be realised by the abolition of the proletariat, and the proletariat can only be abolished by the realisation of philosophy.

1.5 REVOLUTION THE DISSOLUTION OF ALL CLASSES AND ABOLITION OF THE DIVISION OF LABOUR

From Karl Marx and Friedrich Engels, The German Ideology (1846), edited by R. Pascal (New York, 1963 ed.), pp. 68–9, 204.

Finally, from the conception of history we have sketched, we obtain these conclusions: (1) In the development of productive forces there comes a stage at which productive forces and means of intercourse are called into existence, which, under the existing relationships, only cause mischief, and which are no longer productive but destructive forces (machinery and money); and connected with this a class is called forth, which has to bear all the burdens of society without enjoying its advantages, which, ousted from society, is forced into the most decided antagonism to all other classes; a class which forms the majority of all members of society, and from which emanates the consciousness of the necessity of a fundamental revolution, the communist consciousness, which may, of course, arise among the other classes too through the contemplation of the situation of this class. (2) The conditions under which definite productive forces can be applied, are the conditions of the rule of a definite class of society, whose social power, deriving from its property, has its practical-idealistic expression in each case in the form of the State; and, therefore, every revolutionary struggle is directed against a class, which till then has been in power. (3) In all revolutions up till now, the mode of activity always remained unscathed and it was only a question of a different distribution of this activity, a new distribution of labour to other persons, whilst the communistic revolution is directed against the preceding *mode* of activity, does away with *labour*, and abolishes the rule of all classes with the classes themselves, because it is carried through by the class which no longer counts as a class in society, is not recognised as a class, and is in itself the expression of the dissolution of all classes, nationalities, etc., within present society; and (4) Both for the production on a mass scale of this communist consciousness, and for the success of the cause itself, the alteration of men on a mass scale is necessary, an alteration which can only take place in a practical movement, a *revolution*; this revolution is necessary, therefore, not only because the ruling class cannot be overthrown in any other way, but also because the class *overthrowing* it can only in a revolution succeed in ridding itself of all the muck of ages and become fitted to found society anew. . . . In revolutionary activity, change of self coincides with change of circumstances.

1.6 GOVERNMENT AND REVOLUTION ARE INCOMPATIBLE

From Pierre-Joseph Proudhon (1809–65), Confessions of a
Revolutionary *(1849), translated by George Woodcock, in*
A Hundred Years of Revolution *(London, 1948), pp. 237–8.*

*See 'Introduction', pp. 14–16. Proudhon is attacking an article by de
Girardin in which the latter upholds the idea of the 'revolution from
above' as against 'the revolution from below'.*

It pleases this ingenious journalist to call the revolution by
initiative, by intelligence, by progress and ideas, *revolution from
above*; it pleases him to call the revolution by insurrection and
despair, *revolution from below*. It is just the contrary that is true.

From above, in the mind of the author I quote, means evidently
power; *from below*, means the people. On one side the action of
governments, on the other the initiative of the masses.

Thus we must know which of these two initiatives, that of the
government or that of the people, is the more intelligent, the more
progressive, the more pacific.

But the revolution from above is, inevitably, revolution by the
good pleasure of a prince, by the despotism of a minister, by the
fumblings of an assembly, by the violence of a club; it is revolution
by dictatorship and despotism.

Thus it was practised by Louis xiv, Robespierre, Napoleon,
Charles x; thus it was desired by Messieurs Guizot, Louis Blanc,
Léon Faucher. The whites, the blues, the reds, all are in agreement
on this point.

Revolution by the initiative of the masses, is revolution by the
concurrence of the citizens, by the experience of the workers, by
progress and the diffusion of light, revolution by liberty. Condorcet, Turgot, Danton, sought revolution from below, the true
democracy. One of the men who revolutionised most, and who
governed least, was Saint Louis. France, in the time of Saint
Louis, had created herself; she had produced, as a vine pushes
forth its buds, her lords and vassals: when the king published his
famous decree, he was no more than the registrar of the public
wishes.

Socialism surrendered fully to the illusion of Jacobinism; the divine Plato, more than two thousand years ago, was a sad example of this. Saint-Simon, Fourier, Owen, Cabet, Louis Blanc, all partisans of the organisation of work by the State, by capital, by whatsoever authority, call, like M. de Girardin, for the revolution *from above*. Instead of teaching the people to organise themselves, instead of appealing to their experience and reason, they ask for power over them. In what way did they differ from despots? They also are utopists, like all despots.

A government can never be revolutionary, and that for the very simple reason that it is a government. Society alone, the mass penetrated by intelligence, can revolutionise itself, because it alone can rationally display its spontaneity, analyse and explain the mystery of its destiny and its origin, change its faith and philosophy; because, finally, it alone is capable of struggling against its author, and producing its own fruit. Governments are the scourges of God, established to *discipline* the world; and you want them to destroy themselves, to create liberty, to make revolutions!

This cannot happen. All revolutions, from the consecration of the first king up to the declaration of the Rights of Man, have been accomplished by the spontaneity of the people; if sometimes the rulers have followed the popular initiative, it has been because they have been forced and constrained to it. Almost always, they have hindered, repressed and struck; never, of their own volition, have they revolutionised anything. Their role is not to aid progress, but to restrain it. Even if, which is a contradiction, they possessed revolutionary science, social science, they could not apply it; they would not have the right to do so. It would be necessary for them beforehand to pass their science on to the people, for them to obtain the consent of the citizens: that is to misunderstand the nature of authority and power.

1.7 REVOLUTION THE DIRECT INTER-FERENCE OF THE MASSES IN HISTORIC EVENTS

From Leon Trotsky (1879–1940), The History of the Russian Revolution, 3 vols. (1929–30), translated by Max Eastman (London, Sphere Books ed. 1967), vol. 1, pp. 15–17.

The most indubitable feature of a revolution is the direct inter-ference of the masses in historic events. In ordinary times the state, be it monarchical or democratic, elevates itself above the nation, and history is made by specialists in that line of business – kings, ministers, bureaucrats, parliamentarians, journalists. But at those crucial moments when the old order becomes no longer endurable to the masses, they break over the barriers excluding them from the political arena, sweep aside their traditional representatives, and create by their own interference the initial groundwork for a new regime. Whether this is good or bad we leave to the judgement of moralists. We ourselves will take the facts as they are given by the objective course of development. The history of a revolution is for us first of all a history of the forcible entrance of the masses into the realm of rulership over their own destiny.

In a society that is seized by revolution classes are in conflict. It is perfectly clear, however, that the changes introduced between the beginning and the end of a revolution in the economic bases of the society and its social substratum of classes are not sufficient to explain the course of the revolution itself, which can overthrow in a short interval age-old institutions, create new ones, and again overthrow them. The dynamic of revolutionary events is *directly* determined by swift, intense and passionate changes in the psy-chology of classes which have already formed themselves before the revolution.

The point is that society does not change its institutions as need arises, the way a mechanic changes his instruments. On the contrary, society actually takes the institutions which hang upon it as given once for all. For decades the oppositional criticism is nothing more than a safety-valve for mass dissatisfaction, a con-dition of the stability of the social structure. Such in principle, for example, was the significance acquired by the social-democratic criticism. Entirely exceptional conditions, independent of the will of persons or parties, are necessary in order to tear off from discontent the fetters of conservatism, and bring the masses to insurrection.

The swift changes of mass views and moods in an epoch of revolution thus derive, not from the flexibility and mobility of man's mind, but just the opposite, from its deep conservatism. The chronic lag of ideas and relations behind new objective conditions, right up to the moment when the latter crash over people in the form of a catastrophe, is what creates in a period of revolution that leaping movement of ideas and passions which seems to the police mind a mere result of the activities of 'demagogues'.

The masses go into a revolution not with a prepared plan of social reconstruction, but with a sharp feeling that they cannot endure the old regime. Only the guiding layers of a class have a political programme, and even this still requires the test of events, and the approval of the masses. The fundamental political process of the revolution thus consists in the gradual comprehension by a class of the problems arising from the social crisis – the active orientation of the masses by a method of successive approximations. The different stages of a revolutionary process, certified by a change of parties in which the more extreme always supersedes the less, express the growing pressure to the left of the masses – so long as the swing of the movement does not run into objective obstacles. When it does, there begins a reaction: disappointments of the different layers of the revolutionary class, growth of indifferentism, and therewith a strengthening of the position of the counter-revolutionary forces. Such, at least, is the general outline of the old revolutions.

Only on the basis of a study of political processes in the masses themselves, can we understand the role of parties and leaders, whom we least of all are inclined to ignore. They constitute not an independent, but nevertheless a very important, element in the process. Without a guiding organisation the energy of the masses would dissipate like steam not enclosed in a piston-box. But nevertheless what moves things is not the piston or the box, but the steam.

1.8 REVOLUTION AS TRAGIC ACTION

From Raymond Williams, Modern Tragedy *(London, 1966), pp. 65–7.*

Williams argues that revolution, like tragedy, should be seen as part of a whole action in which the concealed disorder of the old regime is revealed and resolved in the act of revolution.

As we have reduced tragedy to the death of the hero, so we have reduced revolution to its crisis of violence and disorder. In simple observation, these are often the most evident effects, but in the whole action they are both preceded and succeeded, and much of their meaning depends on this fact of continuity. Thus it is strange that from our whole modern history revolution should be selected as the example of violence and disorder: revolution, that is, as the critical conflict and resolution of forces. To limit violence and disorder to the decisive conflict is to make nonsense of that conflict itself. The violence and disorder are in the whole action, of which what we commonly call revolution is the crisis.

The essential point is that violence and disorder are institutions as well as acts. When a revolutionary change has been lived through, we can usually see this quite clearly. The old institutions, now dead, take on their real quality as systematic violence and disorder; in that quality, the source of the revolutionary action is seen. But while such institutions are still effective, they can seem, to an extraordinary extent, both settled and innocent. Indeed they constitute, commonly, an order, against which the very protest, of the injured and oppressed, seems the source of disturbance and violence. Here, most urgently, in our own time, we need to return the idea of revolution, in its ordinary sense of the crisis of a society, to its necessary context as part of a whole action, within which alone it can be understood.

Order and disorder are relative terms, although each is experienced as an absolute. We are aware of this relativism, through history and comparative studies: intellectually aware, though that is often not much use to us, under the pressure of fear or interest or in the simple immediacy of our local and actual world. In the ideas of both tragedy and revolution, this dimension and yet also these difficulties are at once encountered. I have already argued that the relation between tragedy and order is dynamic. The tragic action is rooted in a disorder, which indeed, at a particular stage, can seem to have its own stability. But the whole body of real forces is engaged by the action, often in such a way that the underlying disorder becomes apparent and terrible in overtly tragic ways. From the whole experience of this disorder, and through its specific action, order is recreated. The process of this action is at times remarkably similar to the real action of revolution.

Yet revolution, at least in its feudal form as rebellion, is often, in many valued tragedies, the disorder itself. The restoration of 'lawful' authority is there literally the restoration of order. But the essential consideration lies deeper than this, below the false consciousness of feudal attitudes to rebellion. It is not difficult to see that the feudal definitions of lawful authority and rebellion are, at the political level, at worst timeserving, at best partisan. The majesty of kings is usually the political façade of successful usurpers and their descendants. What challenges it, as an action, is of the same human kind as what established it.

1.9 REVOLUTION AS RELIGION

Revolutions are often seen as secularised lineal descendants of religions, retaining many characteristics of the latter. In the following two extracts, a contemporary émigré and a later student of the great French Revolution both point to the parallel with earlier religious movements.

1.9.1. *From the* Memoirs of Mallet du Pan, *in* Nations and Empires, *eds. R. C. Bridges et. al. (London, 1969), pp. 83-4. Written in 1794-5.*

That which changes not . . . is the essence of the revolutionary doctrine. All who in France choose the Republic are infected with it; it bears sway in administrations, sections, clubs; the popular societies of every city, town and village – those mighty resorts of the lower orders – harbour and foster it. This anti-social theory serves as a creed to the partisans of Revolution. This is what is ignored by that throng of futile writers and ignorant reasoners who labour

III

in Germany to mislead both sovereigns and people, by invariably representing the French Revolution as merely local, the result of causes peculiar to France, and prolonged only by the necessity of resisting foreign warfare. Nothing can be more false than these assertions. The revolutionary system is applicable to all nations; it is based on philosophical maxims which suit all climates and oppose every government. Its authors show no more favour to that of England, than to an Eastern government; their doctrines corrupt republics and monarchies alike. We both have seen, and do see, their emissaries tutor the inhabitants of the neutral states, of Genoa, Switzerland and Sweden, precisely as they would the subjects of the belligerent powers. The three Assemblies which have subverted France, and particularly that one which now exists, have regarded this system with blind enthusiasm. The fanaticism of irreligion, equality and propagandism, is to the full as inflamed with zeal as any religious fanaticism, and employs means a thousand times more atrocious.

This formidable sect has affinity with the English Presbyterians, the German *illuminati*, and all the disciples of modern philosophy throughout Europe. These all regard France as the metropolis of their doctrine, and the centre of union. Hitherto, all religions have tended to subdue the passions: this creed excites them all, and sets them free from restraint. In the north and south alike, in every region, rank, and country, it enlists the unsuccessfully ambitious, men ruined or discredited, men of letters, each of whom conceives himself alone capable of governing malcontents, visionaries, enthusiasts, and the lower classes of people. It develops and propagates itself like Islamism, by arms, and by opinion; in one hand it holds the sabre, in the other the rights of man. One of the principal motives which induced its founders to commence a war with the powers, was the hope of accelerating the spread of revolutionary principles, by the conquest and corruption of nations and soldiers. The Convention and the Jacobin club have organized their missions of proselytism at home and abroad, as systematically as the Jesuits have organised theirs in America and China.

1.9.2. *From Alexis de Tocqueville (1805-59)*, On the State of Society in France Before the Revolution of 1789 (L'Ancien Régime et la Révolution), *translated by Henry Reeve (London, 1856), pp. 17-23.*

All mere civil and political revolutions have had some country for their birthplace, and have remained circumscribed within its limits. The French Revolution, however, had no territorial boundary – far from it; one of its effects has been to efface as it were all ancient frontiers from the map of Europe. It united or it divided mankind in spite of laws, traditions, characters, and languages, turning fellow-countrymen into enemies, and foreigners into brothers; or rather, it formed an intellectual country common to men of every nation, but independent of all separate nationalities.

We should search all the annals of history in vain for a political revolution of the same character; that character is only to be found in certain religious revolutions. And accordingly it is to them that the French Revolution must be compared, if any light is to be thrown upon it by analogy.

Schiller remarks, with truth, in his 'History of the Thirty Years' War', that the great Reformation of the sixteenth century had the effect of bringing together nations which scarcely knew each other, and of closely uniting them by new sympathies. Thus it was that Frenchmen warred against Frenchmen, while Englishmen came to their assistance; men born on the most distant shores of the Baltic penetrated into the very heart of Germany in order to defend Germans of whose existence they had never heard until then. International wars assumed something of the character of civil wars, whilst in every civil war foreigners were engaged. The former interests of every nation were forgotten in behalf of new interests; territorial questions were succeeded by questions of principle. The rules of diplomacy were involved in inextricable confusion, greatly to the horror and amazement of the politicians of the time. The very same thing happened in Europe after 1789.

The French Revolution was then a political revolution, which in its operation and its aspect resembled a religious one. It had every peculiar and characteristic feature of a religious movement; it not only spread to foreign countries, but it was carried thither by preaching and by propaganda. It is impossible to conceive a stranger spectacle than that of a political revolution which inspires proselytism, which its adherents preach to foreigners with as much ardour and passion as they have shown in enacting it at home. Of all the new and strange things displayed to the world by the French Revolution, this assuredly is the newest. On penetrating deeper into this matter, we shall most likely discover that this similarity of effects must be produced by a latent similarity of causes.

The general character of most religions is, that they deal with man by himself, without taking into consideration whatever the laws, the traditions, and the customs of each country may have added to his original nature. Their principal aim is to regulate the relations of man towards God, and the rights and duties of men towards each other, independently of the various forms of society. The rules of conduct which they inculcate apply less to the man of any particular country or period than to man as a son, a father, a servant, a master or a neighbour. Being thus based on human nature itself, they are applicable to all men, and at all times, and in all places. It is owing to this cause that religious revolutions have so often spread over such vast spheres of action, and have seldom been confined, like political revolutions, to the territory of a single nation, or even of a single race. If we investigate this subject still more closely, we shall find that the more any religion has possessed the abstract and general character to which I refer, the wider has it spread, in spite of all differences of laws, of climate, and of races. . . .

The French Revolution proceeded, as far as this world is concerned, in precisely the same manner that religious revolutions proceed with regard to the next; it looked upon the citizen in the abstract, irrespective of any particular society, just as most religions looked upon man in general independently of time or country. It did not endeavour merely to define what were the especial rights of a French citizen, but what were the universal duties and rights of all men in political matters.

It was by thus recurring to that which was least peculiar and, we might almost say, most *natural* in the principles of society and of government that the French Revolution was rendered intelligible to all men, and could be imitated in a hundred different places.

As it affected to tend more towards the regeneration of mankind than even towards the reform of France, it roused passions such as the most violent political revolutions had never before excited. It inspired a spirit of proselytism and created the propaganda. This gave to it that aspect of a religious revolution which so terrified its contemporaries, or rather, we should say, it became a kind of new religion in itself – a religion, imperfect it is true, without a God, without a worship, without a future life, but which nevertheless, like Islam, poured forth its soldiers, its apostles, and its martyrs over the face of the earth.

1.10 THE REVOLUTIONARY CATECHISM

From Robert Payne, Zero: The Story of Terrorism *(London, 1951), pp. 7–14.*

Written in 1869, the Catechism appears to have been the joint work of the anarchist Mikhail Bakunin (1814–76) and the nihilist S. G. Nechaev (1847–83). Its extremism marks it clearly as a product of the revolutionary intelligentsia of nineteenth-century Russia; but it is also the clearest expression of the extent to which the principle of revolutionism, having entered the European consciousness, had intensified as it diffused outwards.

See also 'Introduction', p. 5–6.

THE REVOLUTIONARY CATECHISM
The Duties of the Revolutionary towards himself
1. Every revolutionary must be a dedicated man. He should have no personal affairs, no business, no emotions, no attachments, no property and no name. All these must be wholly absorbed in the single thought and the single passion for revolution.
2. The revolutionary knows that in the very depths of his being he has broken all ties with society, both in word and deed. He breaks all ties with the civilised world, its laws, its customs, its morality, all those conventions generally accepted by the world. He is their implacable enemy, and if he has intercourse with the world, it is only for the purpose of destroying it.
3. The revolutionary despises all dogmas and all sciences, leaving them for future generations. He knows only one science:

the science of destruction. For this reason, but only for this reason, he will study physics, mechanics, chemistry and perhaps medicine. With the same end in view he will dedicate himself day and night to the science of life: he will study men, their characteristics, the roles they play, all the phenomena of modern society in all its forms. The object is perpetually the same: the quickest and surest way of destroying the whole filthy order.

4. The revolutionary despises public opinion, he despises the present social morality and hates all its manifestations. The revolutionary defines as moral only that which assists the revolution, and defines as immoral and criminal that which stands in his way.

5. The revolutionary is wholly dedicated. He must show no mercy to the State or towards the civilized classes of society; nor does he ask for mercy for himself. Between him and society there is waged a mortal war, declared or concealed, a relentless and irreconcilable fight to the death. He must accustom himself to torture.

6. Tyrannical towards himself, the revolutionary must be tyrannical towards others. All the emotions that move human beings, all the soft and enervating feelings of kinship, love, friendship, gratitude and honour, must give way to a cold and single-minded passion for revolution. For him there exists only one pleasure, one consolation, one reward, one satisfaction – the success of the revolution. Night and day he must have but one thought, but one aim – merciless destruction. Coldly, relentlessly, he pursues his aim, and he must be prepared to perish himself, as he must be prepared to destroy with his own hands those who stand in his way.

7. The nature of the true revolutionary is to exclude all sensitivity and all romantic enthusiasm; he must exclude equally all thoughts of hatred and vengeance. The revolutionary passion, practised at every moment of the day until it has become a habit, is to be employed coldly, with calculation. At all times the revolutionary must obey, not his personal impulses, but those which serve the cause of the revolution.

The Duties of the Revolutionary towards his Revolutionary Comrades
8. The revolutionary can have no friendship or affection except for those who have proved by their actions that they, like him, are agents of the revolution. His degree of friendship, devotion and

obligation towards a revolutionary comrade must be determined only by the comrade's degree of usefulness to the cause of total revolutionary destruction. . . .

11. When a comrade is in danger, it may be necessary to determine whether he is expendable. The decision must not be arrived at on the basis of sentiment; only the eventual success of the revolution has any importance at this juncture. The revolutionaries must therefore make an equation between the revolutionary usefulness of the comrade who is in danger and the number of comrades who may become expendable in the effort to save him. The actual equation must be examined, and action must be taken solely in accordance with the solution of the equation.

The Duties of the Revolutionary towards Society

12. The new member, having given proof of his loyalty not by words, but by deeds, can be received into the society only by the unanimous agreement of all the members.

13. The revolutionary enters the world of the state, of the classes and of so-called civilisation, and he lives in this world only because he has faith in its quick and complete destruction. He no longer remains a revolutionary if he keeps faith with anything in this world. *He should not hesitate to destroy any position, any place, or any man in this world.* He must hate everyone and everything with an equal hatred. All the worse for him if he has in the world relationships with parents, friends or lovers; *he is no longer a revolutionary if he is swayed by these relationships.*

14. Since the final aim is implacable destruction, the revolutionary can and sometimes must live within society, while pretending to be completely other than he is. A revolutionary must penetrate everywhere; he must enter high society as well as the middle classes; he must penetrate the shops, the churches, the palaces of the aristocracy, the official, military and literary worlds; he must be found among the members of the Third Division and even in the Imperial Palace.

15. In the foul society we live in, it is necessary to divide people into several categories; the first category comprises those who must be condemned to death without delay. Comrades must make the registers of the condemned according to the relative gravity of their crimes, always remembering what is useful for the success of the

revolution; and when the registers have been compiled, the executions should be so arranged that those who are first on the register should actually be executed before the others.

16. When a list of those who are condemned to death is made, he who makes it must in no way allow himself to be influenced by considerations of hatred; nor can the hatred evoked among others but be of advantage to the revolution, if it causes a ferment among the people. Whenever a man is murdered, our duty is to concern ourselves only with the question – in what way has his death profited the revolution? So we must first destroy these people whose existence is most inimical to the revolutionary organization; their violent and sudden death will put fear into the heart of the government, break its will, and deprive it of its most energetic and intelligent agents.

17. The second group composes those to whom we concede life provisionally in order that, by a series of monstrous acts, they may drive the people into inevitable revolt.

18. The third group consists of animals in high positions remarkable neither for their intelligence nor their energy, but who have wealth, connections, influence and power as a result of their position. These we must exploit in every conceivable manner; we must blackmail them, ferret out their dirty secrets, and make them our slaves. In this way their power, their position, their influence, and their wealth become an inexhaustible treasure, and a precious asset in our adventure.

19. The fourth group is composed of various ambitious people in the service of the state; and liberals of varying shades of opinion. The revolutionaries will pretend to be blindly conspiring with them, obediently following their aims. But we shall do this only the more successfully in order to bring them under our power, *so as to reveal their secrets and completely compromise them*. Thereupon, no path of retreat will be open to them, and they can be used to create disorder within the state.

20. The fifth group comprises doctrinaires, conspirators, and revolutionaries; those who orate away at meetings, or on paper. They must be constantly driven into ambiguous positions; they must be compelled to come out into the open and assume real and dangerous tasks. The majority of these will disappear, but of the rest we shall make genuine revolutionaries.

21. The sixth group is extremely important. These are women and we shall divide them into three classes. First, completely frivolous women, unintelligent and without the least signs of sensitivity – these are to be used in exactly the same way as the third and fourth groups among men. Second, women who are ardent, capable, and devoted to the revolution, but who do not belong to us because they have not reached the stage of complete understanding of revolutionary action; we shall use them as we use the fifth group among men. Finally, there are the women who are completely with us: those who are wholly with us and have accepted our program in its entirety. These we are to regard as the most precious of our treasures, and without them nothing can be done.

The Duties of the Revolutionary Association towards the People
22. The purpose of our society is the entire emancipation and happiness of the people, namely the labourers. We are convinced that this happiness and emancipation can only come about as a result of an all-destroying popular revolt. The society will use all its resources to increase and intensify the evils and miseries of the people, believing that at last their patience will be exhausted and they can be incited to a revolutionary *levée-en-masse*.

23. By a popular revolution, the society does not mean a revolution which follows the classic patterns of the West, a pattern which finds itself completely restrained by the existence of property and the traditional social orders of so-called civilisation and morality; and so the western concept of revolution has hitherto meant only the exchanging of one form of political organisation for another, thus creating the so-called revolutionary state. The only revolution which can do any good to the people is that which destroys, from top to bottom, every idea of the state, overthrowing all traditions, social orders, and classes in Russia.

24. With this end in view, the society has no intention of imposing on the people from above any other organisation. The future organisation will no doubt spring up from the movement and life of the people, but this is a matter for future generations to decide. Our task is terrible, total, inexorable, and universal destruction!

25. It follows that in drawing closer towards the people, we must unite, above all, with those elements of the people who have never

ceased to protest since the foundations of the State of Muscovy, not only in words, but in deeds, against everything directly or indirectly connected with the state; against the nobility, against the bureaucracy, against priests, and every kind of tradesman; against all the exploiters of the people. We must unite with the adventurous bands of robbers, who are the only true revolutionaries of Russia.

26. To concentrate the people into a single force wholly destructive and wholly invincible – this is our aim, our conspiracy, and our task!

2 The Organisation of State and Party in the Revolution

2.1 THE COUNCIL SYSTEM AND THE EUROPEAN REVOLUTIONARY TRADITION: THE CASE OF THE HUNGARIAN REVOLUTION OF 1956

From Hannah Arendt, The Origins of Totalitarianism *(2nd ed., New York, 1958), pp. 496–500.*

For 2.1–2.6, see 'Introduction', pp. 18–24.

The Hungarian people, young and old, knew that they were 'living amidst lies' and asked, unanimously and in all manifestos, for something the Russia intelligentsia apparently had even forgotten how to dream of, namely, for freedom of thought. It would probably be erroneous to conclude from this unanimity that the same concern for freedom of thought which gave rise to the rebellion among the intellectuals also turned the rebellion into a revolution of the whole people, an uprising which spread like wildfire until no one was left outside its ranks except the members of the political police – the only Hungarians prepared to defend the regime. A similar error would be to conclude from the initiative taken by members of the Communist Party that the revolution was primarily an inner-party affair, a revolt of 'true' against 'false' communists. The facts speak an altogether different language. What are the facts?

An unarmed and essentially harmless student demonstration

grew from a few thousand suddenly and spontaneously into a huge crowd which took it upon itself to carry out one of the students' demands, the overturning of Stalin's statue in one of the public squares in Budapest. The following day, some students went to the Radio Building to persuade the station to broadcast the sixteen points of their manifesto. A large crowd immediately gathered, as if from nowhere, and when the AVH, the political police guarding the building, tried to disperse the crowd with a few shots, the revolution broke out. The masses attacked the police and acquired their first weapons. The workers, hearing of the situation, left the factories and joined the crowd. The army, called to defend the regime and help the armed police, sided with the revolution and armed the people. What had started as a student demonstration had become an armed uprising in less than twenty-four hours.

From this moment onward, no programmes, points or manifestos played any role; what carried the revolution was the sheer momentum of acting-together of the whole people whose demands were so obvious that they hardly needed elaborate formulation: Russian troops should leave the territory and free elections should determine a new government. The question was no longer how much freedom to permit to action, speech and thought, but how to institutionalise a freedom which was already an accomplished fact. For if we leave aside the outside interventions of Russian troops – first of those stationed in the country and then of regular battalions coming from Russia in full battle preparation – we may well say that never a revolution achieved its aims so quickly, so completely and with so few losses. The amazing thing about the Hungarian revolution is that there was no civil war. For the Hungarian army disintegrated in hours and the dictatorship was stripped of all power in a couple of days. No group, no class in the nation opposed the will of the people once it had become known and its voice had been heard in the market-place. For the members of the AVH, who remained loyal to the end, formed neither group nor class, the lower echelons having been recruited from the dregs of the population: criminals, Nazi agents, highly compromised members of the Hungarian fascist party, the higher ranks being composed of Moscow agents, Hungarians with Russian citizenship under the orders of NKVD officers.

The swift disintegration of the whole power structure – party, army and governmental offices – and the absence of internal strife in the developments that followed are all the more remarkable when we consider that the uprising was clearly started by communists, who, however, did not retain the initiative, and still never became the object of wrath and vengeance for non-communists nor turned themselves against the people. The striking absence of ideological dispute, the concomitant lack of fanaticism and the ensuing atmosphere of fraternity, which came into being with the first demonstration in the streets and lasted until the bitter end, can be explained only on the assumption that ideological indoctrination had disintegrated even more swiftly than the political structure. It was as though ideology, of whatever shade and brand, had simply been wiped out of existence and memory the moment the people, intellectuals and workers, communists and non-communists, found themselves together in the streets fighting for freedom. In this respect, the change in reality brought about by the revolution had much the same effect on the minds of the Hungarian people as the sudden breakdown of the Nazi world had on the minds of the German people.

Important as these aspects are, they tell us more about the nature of the regime the Hungarian revolution rebelled against than about the revolution itself. In its positive significance, the outstanding feature of the uprising was that no chaos resulted from the actions of people without leadership and without a previously formulated programme. First, there was no looting, no trespassing of property, among a multitude whose standard of life had been miserable and whose hunger for merchandise notorious. There were no crimes against life either, for the few instances of public hanging of AVH officers were conducted with remarkable restraint and discrimination. Instead of the mob rule which might have been expected, there appeared immediately, almost simultaneously with the uprising itself, the Revolutionary and Workers' Councils, that is, the same organisation which for more than a hundred years now has emerged whenever the people have been permitted for a few days, or a few weeks or months, to follow their own political devices without a government (or a party programme) imposed from above.

For these councils made their first appearance in the revolution which swept Europe in 1848; they reappeared in the revolt of the

Paris Commune in 1871, existed for a few weeks during the first Russian revolution of 1905, to reappear in full force in the October revolution in Russia and the November revolutions in Germany and Austria after the First World War. Until now, they have always been defeated, but by no means only by the 'counter-revolution'. The Bolshevik regime destroyed their power even under Lenin and attested to their popularity by stealing their name (*soviet* being the Russian word for council). In Russia, the Supreme Soviet is needed to conceal the fact that the true seat of power is in the party apparatus and to present to the outside world the façade of a non-existent parliament. In addition, it serves as a kind of honour system; membership, acquired through nomination by the party, is bestowed for outstanding achievement in all professions and walks of life. Members of the Russian soviets neither rule nor govern; they do not legislate and have no political rights whatsoever, not even the privilege to execute party orders. They are not supposed to act at all; they are chosen in recognition of non-political achievements – for their contribution to the 'building of socialism'. When Soviet-Russian tanks crushed the revolution in Hungary, they actually destroyed the only free and acting *soviets* in existence anywhere in the world. And in Germany again, it was not the 'reaction', but the Social Democrats who liquidated the Soldiers' and Workers' Councils in 1919.

In the case of the Hungarian revolution, even more markedly than in the case of earlier ones, the establishment of the Councils represented 'the first practical step to restore order and to reorganise the Hungarian economy on a socialist basis, but without rigid Party control or the apparatus of terror'. The councils thus were charged with two tasks, one political, the other economic, and though it would be wrong to believe that the dividing line between them was unblurred, we may assume that the Revolutionary Councils fulfilled mainly political functions while the Workers' Councils were supposed to handle economic life. . . .

In order to understand the council system, it is well to remember that it is as old as the party system itself; as such, it represents the only alternative to it, that is, the only alternative of democratic electoral representation to the one presented by the Continental multi-party system with its insistence on class interests on the one hand and ideology, or *Weltanschauung,* on the other. But while the historical origin of the party system lies in Parliament with its factions, the councils were born exclusively out of the actions and spontaneous demands of the people, and they were not deduced from an ideology nor foreseen, let alone preconceived, by any theory about the best form of government. Wherever they appeared, they were met with utmost hostility from the party-bureaucracies and their leaders from right to left and with the unanimous neglect of political theorists and political scientists. The point is that the councils have always been undoubtedly democratic, but in a sense never seen before and never thought about. And since nobody, neither statesman nor political scientists nor parties, has ever paid any serious attention to this new and wholly untried form of organisation, its stubborn re-emergence for more than a century could not be more spontaneous and less influenced by outside interest or theory.

Under modern conditions, the councils are the only democratic alternative we know to the party system, and the principles on which they are based stand in sharp opposition to the principles of the party system in many respects. Thus, the men elected for the councils are chosen at the bottom, and not selected by the party machinery and proposed to the electorate either as individuals with alternative choices or as a slate of candidates. The choice, moreover, of the voter is not prompted by a programme or a platform or an ideology, but exclusively by his estimation of a man, in whose personal integrity, courage and judgement he is supposed to have enough confidence to entrust him with his representation. The elected, therefore, is not bound by anything except trust in his personal qualities, and his pride is 'to have been elected by the workers, and not by the government' or a party, that is, by his peers and from neither above nor below.

Once such a body of trusted men is elected, it will of course again develop differences of opinion which in turn may lead into the formation of 'parties'. But these groups of men holding the same opinion within the councils would not be parties, strictly speaking; they would constitute those factions from which the parliamentary parties originally developed. The election of a candidate would not depend upon his adherence to a given faction, but still on his personal power of persuasion with which he could present his point of view. In other words, the councils would control the parties, they would not be their representatives. The strength of any given faction would not depend upon its bureaucratic apparatus and not even upon the appeal of its programme or *Weltanschauung,* but on the number of trusted and trustworthy men it holds in its ranks. This development manifested itself clearly in the initial stages of the Russian revolution, and the chief reason why Lenin felt he had to emasculate the *soviets* was that the Social Revolutionaries counted more men trusted by the people than the Bolsheviks; the power of the Communist Party, which had been responsible for the revolution, was endangered by the council system which had grown out of the revolution.

Remarkable, finally, is the great inherent flexibility of the system, which seems to need no special conditions for its establishment except the coming together and acting together of a certain number of people on a non-temporary basis. In Hungary, we have seen the simultaneous setting-up of all kinds of councils, each of them corresponding to a previously existing group in which people habitually lived together or met regularly and knew each other. Thus neighbourhood councils emerged from sheer living together and grew into country and other territorial councils; revolutionary councils grew out of fighting together; councils of writers and artists, one is tempted to think, were born in the *cafés,* students' and youths' councils at the university, military councils in the army, councils of civil servants in the ministries, workers' councils in the factories, and so on. The formation of a council in each disparate group turned a merely haphazard togetherness into a political institution.

2.2 THE POPULAR CLUBS OF THE GREAT FRENCH REVOLUTION

From Peter Kropotkin, The Great French Revolution, 1789–93, *translated by N. F. Dryhurst (London, 1909), pp. 363–5.*

Everywhere and always a revolution is made by minorities. Even among those deeply interested in the Revolution it is only a minority that devotes itself entirely to it. This was also the case in France in 1793.

As soon as royalty was overthrown a gigantic movement was set on foot throughout the provinces against the revolutionists who had dared to fling down the head of a King as a defiance to all the reactionaries of Europe. In the manor-house, the drawing-room, the confessional, the cry was: 'What scoundrels to have dared to do that! Now they will stop at nothing: they are going to rob us of our wealth, or else guillotine us!' And so the plots of the counter-revolutionists redoubled in vigour.

The church, every court of Europe, the English middle classes, all took part in the work of intrigue, propaganda and corruption for organising the counter-revolution.

The maritime towns, especially such as Nantes, Bordeaux and Marseilles, where there were many rich merchants, Lyons, the manufacturer of luxury, Rouen, the centre of trade and industry, became powerful centres of reaction. Whole regions were influenced by priests and *émigrés* who had returned under false names, and also by English and Orléanist gold, as well as by emissaries from Italy, Spain and Russia.

The party of the 'Gironde' served as the rallying-point for this mass of reaction, for the royalists knew perfectly well that the Girondins, in spite of their apparent republicanism, were really their allies, and that they were compelled to be so *by the logic of their party*, which is always much more powerful than the party label. And the people, on its side, understood the situation perfectly. It knew that so long as the Girondins remained in the Convention no real revolutionary measure would be possible, and that the war carried on so feebly by these sybarites of the Revolution would be prolonged indefinitely to the utter exhaustion of France. Accordingly, therefore, as the necessity for 'purifying the Convention' by the elimination of the Girondins became more and more evident, the people on its side tried to organise itself for the local struggles which were imminent in every large city and every small town and village.

We have already remarked that the Directories of the departments were mostly counter-revolutionary. The Directories of the districts were equally so. But the municipalities, established by the law of 1789, were much more democratic. It is true that when they were first constituted in the summer of 1789, they mercilessly repressed the peasant revolts. But, as the Revolution developed, the municipalities, elected by the people often in the midst of insurrectionary disturbances and under the supervision of the Popular Societies, gradually became more revolutionary.

In Paris, previous to 10 August, the council of the Commune had been composed of middle-class democrats. But during the night of 10 August, a new revolutionary Commune was elected by the forty-eight sections, and although the Convention, at the instance of the Girondins, had dissolved this Commune, the new Commune elected on 2 December 1792, with its procurator, Chaumette, its deputy-procurator, Hébert, and its mayor, Pache (who was appointed somewhat later), was a frankly revolutionary body.

An elected body of officials invested with powers so extensive and so diverse as those entrusted to the council of the Paris Commune would have certainly inclined by degrees towards a moderate policy. But the people of Paris had, in the sections, centres for revolutionary action. These sections, however, according as they arrogated to themselves various political powers, such as the right of distributing cards of citizenship to show that the recipient was not a royalist conspirator, the appointing of volunteers to fight in La Vendée, and so on – these very sections, whose Committee of Public Welfare and the Committee of General Safety were working to make them political organs, in their turn soon inclined to officialism and conservatism. In 1795, they became, in fact, the rallying-point for the middle-class reaction.

This is why a network of Popular Societies and Fraternal Societies, as well as Revolutionary Committees, was constituted side by side with the Commune and the sections to become, after the expulsion of the Girondins in the Year II of the Republic, a real power for action. All these groups federated with each other, either for momentary purposes or for continuous action, and they endeavoured to put themselves in touch with the thirty-six thousand communes of France. For this purpose they organised a special correspondence-bureau.

A new, freely constituted organisation thus came into existence. And when we study these groupings – these 'free understandings', we should say now – we see before us the realisation of what the modern anarchist groups in France are advocating without even knowing that their grandfathers had already put it into practice during so tragic a moment of the Revolution as was the early part of 1793.

2.3 THE PARIS COMMUNE, 1871

From Karl Marx, 'The Civil War in France' (1871), in Karl Marx and Friedrich Engels, Selected Works in Two Volumes (Moscow, 1962), vol. 1, pp. 516–22.

On the dawn of 18 March, Paris arose to the thunderburst of 'Vive la Commune!' What is the Commune, that sphinx so tantalising to the bourgeois mind?

The proletarians of Paris [said the Central Committee in its manifesto of the 18th March] amidst the failures and treasons of the ruling classes, have understood that the hour has struck for them to save the situation by taking into their own hands the direction of public affairs. . . . They have understood that it is their imperious duty and their absolute right to render themselves masters of their own destinies, by seizing upon the governmental power.

But the working class cannot simply lay hold of the ready-made state machinery, and wield it for its own purposes.

The centralised state power, with its ubiquitous organs of standing army, police, bureaucracy, clergy, and judicature – organs wrought after the plan of a systematic and hierarchic division of labour – originates from the days of absolute monarchy, serving nascent middle-class society as a mighty weapon in its struggles against feudalism. Still, its development remained clogged by all manner of medieval rubbish, seigniorial rights, local privileges, municipal and guild monopolies and provincial constitutions. The gigantic broom of the French Revolution of the eighteenth century swept away all these relics of bygone times, thus clearing simultaneously the social soil of its last hindrances to the superstructure of the modern State edifice raised under the First Empire, itself the offspring of the coalition wars of old semi-feudal Europe against modern France. During the subsequent *régimes* the Government, placed under parliamentary control – that is, under the direct control of the propertied classes – became not only a hotbed of

huge national debts and crushing taxes; with its irresistible allure-
ments of place, pelf and patronage, it became not only the bone of
contention between the rival factions and adventurers of the ruling
classes; but its political character changed simultaneously with the
economic changes of society. At the same pace at which the progress of modern industry developed, widened, intensified the class
antagonism between capital and labour, the State power assumed
more and more the character of the national power of capital over
labour, of a public force organised for social enslavement, of an
engine of class despotism. After every revolution marking a progressive phase in the class struggle, the purely repressive character
of the State power stands out in bolder and bolder relief. The
Revolution of 1830, resulting in the transfer of government from
the landlords to the capitalists, transferred it from the more remote
to the more direct antagonists of the working men. The bourgeois
Republicans, who, in the name of the Revolution of February, took
the State power, used it for the June massacres, in order to convince
the working class that 'social' republic meant the republic ensuring
their social subjection, and in order to convince the royalist bulk
of the bourgeois and landlord class that they might safely leave the
cares and emoluments of government to the bourgeois 'Republicans'. However, after their one heroic exploit of June, the bourgeois Republicans had, from the front, to fall back to the rear of
the 'Party of Order' – a combination formed by all the rival
fractions and factions of the appropriating class in their now openly
declared antagonism to the producing classes. The proper form of
their joint-stock Government was the *Parliamentary Republic*,
with Louis Bonaparte for its President. Theirs was a regime of
avowed class terrorism and deliberate insult toward the 'vile
multitude'. If the Parliamentary Republic, as M. Thiers said,
'divided them (the different fractions of the ruling class) least', it
opened an abyss between that class and the whole body of society
outside their spare ranks. The restraints by which their own divisions had under former regimes still checked the State power, were
removed by their union; and in view of the threatening upheaval
of the proletariat, they now used that State power mercilessly and
ostentatiously as the national war-engine of capital against labour.
In their uninterrupted crusade against the producing masses they
were, however, bound not only to invest the executive with con-

tinually increased powers of repression, but at the same time to divest their own parliamentary stronghold – the National Assembly – one by one, of all its own means of defence against the Executive. The Executive, in the person of Louis Bonaparte, turned them out. The natural offspring of the 'Party-of-Order' Republic was the Second Empire.

The empire, with the *coup d'état* for its certificate of birth, universal suffrage for its sanction, and the sword for its sceptre, professed to rest upon the peasantry, the large mass of producers not directly involved in the struggle of capital and labour. It professed to save the working class by breaking down Parliamentarism, and, with it, the undisguised subserviency of Government to the propertied classes. It professed to save the propertied classes by upholding their economic supremacy over the working class; and, finally, it professed to unite all classes by reviving for all the chimera of national glory. In reality, it was the only form of government possible at a time when the bourgeoisie had already lost, and the working class had not yet acquired, the faculty of ruling the nation. It was acclaimed throughout the world as the saviour of society. Under its sway, bourgeois society, freed from political cares, attained a development unexpected even by itself. Its industry and commerce expanded to colossal dimensions; financial swindling celebrated cosmopolitan orgies; the misery of the masses was set off by a shameless display of gorgeous, meretricious and debased luxury. The State power, apparently soaring high above society, was at the same time itself the greatest scandal of that society and the very hotbed of all its corruptions. Its own rottenness, and the rottenness of the society it had saved, were laid bare by the bayonet of Prussia, herself eagerly bent upon transferring the supreme seat of that regime from Paris to Berlin. Imperialism is, at the same time, the most prostitute and the ultimate form of the State power which nascent middle-class society had commenced to elaborate as a means of its own emancipation from feudalism, and which full-grown bourgeois society had finally transformed into a means for the enslavement of labour by capital.

The direct antithesis to the empire was the Commune. The cry of 'social republic', with which the revolution of February was ushered in by the Paris proletariat, did but express a vague aspiration after a Republic that was not only to supersede the monarchical form of class-rule, but class-rule itself. The Commune was the positive form of that Republic.

Paris, the central seat of the old governmental power, and, at the same time, the social stronghold of the French working class, had risen in arms against the attempt of Thiers and the Rurals to restore and perpetuate that old governmental power bequeathed to them by the empire. Paris could resist only because, in consequence of the siege, it had got rid of the army, and replaced it by a National Guard, the bulk of which consisted of working men. This fact was now to be transformed into an institution. The first decree of the Commune, therefore, was the suppression of the standing army, and the substitution for it of the armed people.

The Commune was formed of the municipal councillors, chosen by universal suffrage in the various wards of the town, responsible and revocable at short terms. The majority of its members were naturally working men, or acknowledged representatives of the working class. The Commune was to be a working, not a parliamentary body, executive and legislative at the same time. Instead of continuing to be the agent of the Central Government, the police was at once stripped of its political attributes, and turned into the responsible and at all times revocable agent of the Commune. So were the officials of all other branches of the Administration. From the members of the Commune downwards, the public service had to be done at *workmen's wages*. The vested interests and the representation allowances of the high dignitaries of State disappeared along with the high dignitaries themselves. Public functions ceased to be the private property of the tools of the Central Government. Not only municipal administration, but the whole initiative hitherto exercised by the State was laid into the hands of the Commune. . . .

The Paris Commune was, of course, to serve as a model to all the great industrial centres of France. The communal regime once established in Paris and the secondary centres, the old centralised Government would in the provinces, too, have to give way to the self-government of the producers. In a rough sketch of national organisation which the Commune had no time to develop, it states clearly that the Commune was to be the political form of even the smallest country hamlet, and that in the rural districts the standing army was to be replaced by a national militia, with an extremely short term of service. The rural communes of every district were to administer their common affairs by an assembly of delegates in the central town, and these district assemblies were again to send deputies to the National Delegation in Paris, each delegate to be at any time revocable and bound by the *mandat impératif* (formal instructions) of his constituents. The few but important functions which still would remain for a central government were not to be suppressed, as has been intentionally misstated, but were to be discharged by Communal, and therefore strictly responsible agents. The unity of the nation was not to be broken, but, on the contrary, to be organised by the Communal Constitution and to become a reality by the destruction of the State power which claimed to be the embodiment of that unity independent of, and superior to, the nation itself, from which it was but a parasitic excrescence. While the merely repressive organs of the old governmental power were to be amputated, its legitimate functions were to be wrested from an authority usurping preeminence over society itself, and restored to the responsible agents of society. Instead of deciding once in three or six years which member of the ruling class was to misrepresent the people in Parliament, universal suffrage was to serve the people, constituted in Communes, as individual suffrage serves every other employer in the search for the workmen and managers in his business. And it is well known that companies, like individuals, in matters of real business generally know how to put the right man in the right place, and, if they for once make a mistake, to redress it promptly. On the other hand, nothing could be more foreign to the spirit of the Commune than to supersede universal suffrage by hierarchic investiture.

It is generally the fate of completely new historical creations to be mistaken for the counterpart of older and even defunct forms of social life, to which they may bear a certain likeness. Thus, this new Commune, which breaks the modern State power, has been mistaken for a reproduction of the medieval Communes, which first preceded, and afterwards became the substratum of, that very State power. The Communal Constitution has been mistaken for an attempt to break up into a federation of small states, as dreamt of by Montesquieu and the Girondins, that unity of great nations which, if originally brought about by political force, has now become a powerful coefficient of social production. The antagonism

133

of the Commune against the State power has been mistaken for an exaggerated form of the ancient struggle against over-centralisation. Peculiar historical circumstances may have prevented the classical development, as in France, of the bourgeois form of government, and may have allowed, as in England, the completion of the great central State organs by corrupt vestries, jobbing councillors, and ferocious poor-law guardians in the towns, and virtually hereditary magistrates in the counties. The Communal Constitution would have restored to the social body all the forces hitherto absorbed by the State parasite feeding upon, and clogging the free movement of, society. By this one act it would have initiated the regeneration of France. The provincial French middle class saw in the Commune an attempt to restore the sway their order had held over the country under Louis Philippe, and, which, under Louis Napoleon, was supplanted by the pretended rule of the country over the towns. In reality, the Communal Constitution brought the rural producers under the intellectual lead of the central towns of their districts, and these secured to them, in the working men, the natural trustees of their interests. The very existence of the Commune involved, as a matter of course, local municipal liberty, but no longer as a check upon the, now superseded, State power. . . .

The Commune made that catchword of bourgeois revolutions, cheap government, a reality, by destroying the two greatest sources of expenditure – the standing army and State functionarism. Its very existence presupposed the non-existence of monarchy, which, in Europe at least, is the normal incumbrance and indispensable cloak of class-rule. It supplied the Republic with the basis of really democratic institutions. But neither cheap Government nor the 'true Republic' was its ultimate aim; they were its mere concomitants.

The multiplicity of interpretations to which the Commune has been subjected, and the multiplicity of interests which construed it in their favour, show that it was a thoroughly expansive political form, while all previous forms of government had been emphatically repressive. Its true secret was this. It was essentially a working-class government, the produce of the struggle of the producing against the appropriating class, the political form at last discovered under which to work out the economic emancipation of labour.

2.4 THE 'WITHERING AWAY' OF THE STATE

From Friedrich Engels, Anti-Dühring *(Moscow, 1959), pp. 386–7.*

Marx left his followers with little guidance as to the place of the state in the proletarian revolution. There was the essay on the Paris Commune, and a passing reference to the 'dictatorship of the proletariat' in his Critique of the Gotha Programme *(1875). It was Engels who, in this work of 1878, committed himself to the assertion that the state would 'wither away', and so allowed later Marxists to steal the clothes of the anarchists while still holding on to their own.*

Whilst the capitalist mode of production more and more completely transforms the great majority of the population into proletarians, it creates the power which, under penalty of its own destruction, is forced to accomplish this revolution. Whilst it forces on more and more the transformation of the vast means of production, already socialised, into state property, it shows itself the way to accomplishing this revolution. *The proletariat seizes political power and turns the means of production in the first instance into state property.*

But, in doing this, it abolishes itself as proletariat, abolishes all class distinctions and class antagonisms, abolishes also the state as state. Society thus far, based upon class antagonisms, had need of the state, that is, of an organisation of the particular class, which was *pro tempore* the exploiting class, for the maintenance of its external conditions of production, and, therefore, especially, for the purpose of forcibly keeping the exploited classes in the condition of oppression corresponding with the given mode of production (slavery, serfdom, wage-labour). The state was the official representative of society as a whole; the gathering of it together into a visible embodiment. But it was this only in so far as it was the state of that class which itself represented, for the time being, society as a whole: in ancient times, the state of slave-owning citizens; in the Middle Ages, the feudal lords; in our time, the bourgeoisie. When at last it becomes the real representative of the whole of society, it renders itself unnecessary. As soon as there is no longer any social class to be held in subjection; as soon as class rule, and the individual struggle for existence based upon our present anarchy in production, with the collisions and excesses arising from these, are removed, nothing more remains to be repressed, and a special repressive force, a state, is no longer necessary. The first act by virtue of which the state really constitutes itself the representative of the whole of society – the taking possession of the means of production in the name of society – that is, at the same time, its last independent act as a state. State interference in social relations becomes, in one domain after another, superfluous, and then withers away of itself; the government of persons is replaced by the administration of things, and by the conduct of processes of production. The state is not 'abolished'. *It withers away*. This gives the measure of the value of the phrase 'a free people's state', both as to its justifiable use at times by agitators, and as to its ultimate scientific insufficiency; and also of the demands of the so-called anarchists for the abolition of the state out of hand.

2.5 THE SOVIET

From Leon Trotsky, 'The Soviet and the Revolution' (1905), in Our Revolution *(New York, 1918), pp. 151–61.*

The history of the Soviet is a history of fifty days. The Soviet was constituted on 13 October; its session was interrupted by a military detachment of the government on 3 December. Between those two dates the Soviet lived and struggled.

What was the substance of this institution? What enabled it in this short period to take an honourable place in the history of the Russian proletariat, in the history of the Russian Revolution?

The Soviet organised the masses, conducted political strikes, led political demonstrations, tried to arm the working men. But other revolutionary organisations did the same things. The substance of the Soviet was its effort to become *an organ of public authority*. The proletariat on one hand, the reactionary press on the other, have called the Soviet 'a labour government'; this only reflects the fact that the Soviet was in reality *an embryo of a revolutionary govern-*

ment. In so far as the Soviet was in actual possession of authoritative power, it made use of it; in so far as the power was in the hands of the military and bureaucratic monarchy, the Soviet fought to obtain it. Prior to the Soviet, there had been revolutionary organisations among the industrial working men, mostly of a Social-Democratic nature. But those were organisations *among* the proletariat; their immediate aim was to *influence the masses*. The Soviet is an organisation of the proletariat; its aim is to fight for *revolutionary power*.

At the same time, the Soviet was *an organised expression of the will of the proletariat as a class*. In its fight for power the Soviet applied such methods as were naturally determined by the character of the proletariat as a class: its part in production; its numerical strength; its social homogeneity. In its fight for power the Soviet has combined the direction of all the social activities of the working class, including decisions as to conflicts between individual representatives of capital and labour. This combination was by no means an artificial tactical attempt: it was a natural consequence of the situation of a class which, consciously developing and broadening its fight for its immediate interests, had been compelled by the logic of events to assume a leading position in the revolutionary struggle for power.

The main weapon of the Soviet was a political strike of the masses. The power of the strike lies in disorganising the power of the government. The greater the 'anarchy' created by a strike, the nearer its victory. This is true only where 'anarchy' is not being created by anarchic actions. The class that puts into motion, day in and day out, the industrial apparatus and the governmental apparatus; the class that is able, by a sudden stoppage of work, to paralyse both industry and government, must be organised enough not to fall the first victim of the very 'anarchy' it has created. The more effective the disorganisation of government caused by a strike, the more the strike organisation is compelled to assume governmental functions.

The Council of Workmen's Delegates introduces a free press. It organises street patrols to secure the safety of the citizens. It takes over, to a greater or less extent, the post office, the telegraph, and the railroads. It makes an effort to introduce the eight-hour workday. Paralysing the autocratic government by a strike, it brings its own democratic order into the life of the working city population.

After 9 January the revolution had shown its power over the minds of the working masses. On 14 June, through the revolt of the Potemkin Tavritchesky, it had shown that it was able to become a material force. In the October strike it had shown that it could disorganise the enemy, paralyse his will, and utterly humiliate him. By organising Councils of Workmen's Deputies all over the country, *it showed that it was able to create authoritative power*. Revolutionary authority can be based only on active revolutionary force. Whatever our view on the further developments of the Russian revolution, it is a fact that so far no social class besides the proletariat has manifested readiness to uphold a revolutionary authoritative power. The first act of the revolution was an encounter in the streets of the *proletariat* with the monarchy; the first serious victory of the revolution was achieved through the *class-weapon of the proletariat,* the political strike; the first nucleus of a revolutionary government was *a proletarian representation.* The Soviet is the first democratic power in modern Russian history. The Soviet is the organised power of the masses themselves over their component parts. This is a true, unadulterated democracy, without a two-chamber system, without a professional bureaucracy, with the right of the voters to recall their deputy any moment and to substitute another for him. Through its members, through deputies elected by the working men, the Soviet directs all the social activities of the proletariat as a whole and of its various parts; it outlines the steps to be taken by the proletariat, it gives them a slogan and a banner. This art of directing the activities of the masses on the basis of organised self-government, is here applied for the first time on Russian soil. Absolutism ruled the masses, but it did not direct them. It put mechanical barriers against the living creative forces of the masses, and within those barriers it kept the restless elements of the nation in an iron bond of oppression. The only mass absolutism ever directed was the army. But that was not directing, it was merely commanding. In recent years, even the directing of this atomised and hypnotised military mass has been slipping out of the hands of absolutism. Liberalism never had power enough to command the masses, or initiative enough to direct them. Its attitude towards mass movements, even if they helped liberalism directly, was the same as towards awe-inspiring natural phenomena – earthquakes or volcanic eruptions. The proletariat appeared on the battlefield of the revolution as a self-reliant aggregate, totally independent from bourgeois liberalism. . . .

The fifty-day period was the period of the greatest power of the revolution. *The Soviet was its organ in the fight for public authority.* The class character of the Soviet was determined by the class differentiation of the city population and by the political antagonism between the proletariat and the capitalistic bourgeoisie. This antagonism manifested itself even in the historically limited field of a struggle against absolutism. After the October strike, the capitalistic bourgeoisie consciously blocked the progress of the revolution, the petty middle class turned out to be a nonentity, incapable of playing an independent role. The real leader of the urban revolution was the proletariat. Its class organisation was the organ of the revolution in its struggle for power.

The struggle for power, for public authority – this is the central aim of the revolution. The fifty days of the Soviet's life and its bloody finale have shown that urban Russia is too narrow a basis for such a struggle, and that even within the limits of the urban revolution, a local organisation cannot be the central leading body. For a national task the proletariat required an organisation on a national scale. The St Petersburg Soviet was a local organisation, yet the need of a central organisation was so great that it had to assume leadership on a national scale. It did what it could, still it remained primarily the *St Petersburg* Council of Workmen's Deputies. The urgency of an all-Russian labour congress, which undoubtedly would have authority to form a central leading organ, was emphasised even at the time of the first Soviet. The December collapse made its realisation impossible. The idea remained, an inheritance of the Fifty Days.

The idea of a Soviet has become ingrained in the consciousness of the working men as the first prerequisite to revolutionary action of the masses. Experience has shown that a Soviet is not possible or desirable under all circumstances. The objective meaning of the Soviet organisation is to create conditions for disorganising the government, for 'anarchy', in other words for a revolutionary conflict. The present lull in the revolutionary movement, the mad triumph of reaction, make the existence of an open, elective, authoritative organisation of the masses impossible. There is no doubt, however, that *the first new wave of the revolution will lead to the creation of Soviets all over the country*. An All-Russian Soviet, organised by an All-Russian Labour Congress, will assume leadership of the local elective organisations of the proletariat. Names, of course, are of no importance; neither are details of organisation; the main thing is: a centralised democratic leadership in the struggle of the proletariat for a popular government. History does not repeat itself, and the new Soviet will not have again to go through the experience of the Fifty Days. These, however, will furnish it with a complete programme of action.

This programme is perfectly clear. To establish revolutionary co-operation with the army, the peasantry, and the plebeian lower strata of the urban bourgeoisie. To abolish absolutism. To destroy the material organisation of absolutism by reconstructing and partly dismissing the army. To break up the entire bureaucratic apparatus. To introduce an eight-hour workday. To arm the population, starting with the proletariat. To turn the Soviets into organs of revolutionary self-government in the cities. To create Councils of Peasants' Delegates (Peasants' Committees) as local organs of the agrarian revolution. To organise elections to the Constituent Assembly and to conduct a pre-election campaign for a definite programme on the part of the representatives of the people.

2.6 ON THE SOVIET AS THE FORM OF THE REVOLUTIONARY STATE

From V. I. Lenin (1870–1924), Selected Works in Three Volumes *(Moscow, n.d.), vol.* ii, *pp. 57–8, 64–6, 435–6. Written in 1917.*

The main feature of our revolution, a feature that most imperatively demands thoughtful attention, is the *dual power* which arose in the very first days after the triumph of the revolution.

This dual power is evident in the existence of *two* governments: one is the main, the real, the actual government of the bourgeoisie, the 'Provisional Government' of Lvov and Co., which holds all the organs of power in its hands; the other is a supplementary and parallel government, a 'controlling' government in the shape of the Petrograd Soviet of Workers' and Soldiers' Deputies, which holds no organs of state power, but directly rests on the support of an obvious and indisputable majority of the people, on the armed workers and soldiers.

The class origin and the class significance of this dual power is the following: the Russian revolution of March 1917 not only swept away the whole tsarist monarchy, not only transferred the entire power to the bourgeoisie, but also *came close to establishing* a revolutionary-democratic dictatorship of the proletariat and peasants. The Petrograd and the other, the local, Soviets of Workers' and Soldiers' Deputies constitute precisely such a dictatorship (that is, a power resting not on law but directly on the force of armed masses of the population), a dictatorship precisely of the above-mentioned classes. . . .

The Soviets of Workers', Soldiers', Peasants' and other Deputies are not understood; not only in the sense that their class character, their part in the *Russian* revolution, is not clear to the majority. They are not understood also in the sense that they constitute a new form, or rather a new *type of state*.

The most perfect, the most advanced type of bourgeois state is the *parliamentary democratic republic*: power is vested in parliament; the state machine, the apparatus and organ of administration, is of the customary kind: the standing army, the police and the bureaucracy – which in practice is never replaced, is privileged and stands *above* the people.

Since the end of the nineteenth century, however, revolutionary epochs have advanced a *higher* type of democratic state, a state which in certain respects, as Engels put it, ceases to be a state, is 'no longer a state in the proper sense of the word'. This state is of the type of the Paris Commune, one in which a standing army and police divorced from the people are *replaced* by the directly armed people themselves. It is *this feature* that constituted the very essence of the Commune, which has been so belied and slandered by the bourgeois writers, and to which has been erroneously ascribed, among other things, the intention of immediately 'introducing' socialism.

This is the type of state which the Russian revolution *began* to create in 1905 and in 1917. A Republic of Soviets of Workers', Soldiers', Peasants' and other Deputies, united in an All-Russian Constituent Assembly of people's representatives or in a Council of Soviets, etc., is what is *already being realised* in our country now, at this juncture. It is being realised by the initiative of many millions of people who, of their own accord, are creating a democracy *in their own way*, without waiting until the Cadet professors draft their legislative bills for a parliamentary bourgeois republic, or until the pedants and routine-worshippers of petty-bourgeois 'Social-Democracy', like Mr Plekhanov or Kautsky, renounce their distortions of the Marxist teaching on the state.

Marxism differs from anarchism in that it recognises the *need* for a state and for state power in the period of revolution in general, and in the period of transition from capitalism to socialism in particular.

Marxism differs from the petty-bourgeois, opportunist 'Social-Democratism' of Plekhanov, Kautsky and Co. in that it recognises that what is required during these two periods is *not* a state of the customary parliamentary bourgeois republican type, but a state of the Paris Commune type.

The main distinctions between a state of the latter type and the old state are as follows.

It is extremely easy (as history proves) to revert from a parliamentary bourgeois republic, to a monarchy, for all the machinery of repression – the army, the police, and the bureaucracy – is left intact. The Commune and the Soviets of Workers', Soldiers', Peasants' and other Deputies *smash* and remove that machinery.

The parliamentary bourgeois republic hampers and stifles the independent political life of the *people*, their direct participation in the *democratic* organisation of the life of the state from top to bottom. The opposite is the case with the Soviets of Workers' and Soldiers' Deputies.

The latter reproduce the type of state which was being evolved by the Paris Commune and which Marx described as 'the political form at last discovered under which to work out the economic emancipation of labour'.

The usual objection is that the Russian people are not yet prepared for the 'introduction' of the Commune. This was the argument of the serf-owners when they claimed that the peasants were not prepared for freedom. The Commune, i.e. the Soviets of Workers' and Peasants' Deputies, does not 'introduce', does not intend to 'introduce', and must not introduce *any* reforms which have not absolutely matured both in economic reality and in the consciousness of the overwhelming majority of the people. The deeper the economic collapse and the crisis produced by the war, the more urgent becomes the need for the most perfect political form, which will *facilitate* the healing of the terrible wounds inflicted on mankind by the war. The less the organisational experience of the Russian people, the more resolutely must we *proceed* to organisational development by the *people themselves,* and not merely by the bourgeois politicians and 'well-placed' bureaucrats. . . .

The Soviets are a new state apparatus which, in the first place, provides an armed force of workers and peasants; and this force is not divorced from the people, as was the old standing army, but is very closely bound up with the people. From the military point of view this force is incomparably more powerful than previous forces; from the revolutionary point of view, it cannot be replaced by anything else. Secondly, this apparatus provides a bond with the people, with the majority of the people, so intimate, so indissoluble, so readily controllable and renewable, that nothing even remotely like it existed in the previous state apparatus. Thirdly, this apparatus, by virtue of the fact that its personnel is elected and subject to recall at the people's will without any bureaucratic formalities, is far more democratic than any previous apparatus. Fourthly, it provides a close contact with the most varied professions, therefore facilitating the adoption of the most varied and most radical reforms without bureaucracy. Fifthly, it provides a form of organisation of the vanguard, i.e. of the most class-conscious, most energetic and most progressive section of the *oppressed* classes, the workers and peasants, and so constitutes an apparatus by means of which the vanguard of the oppressed classes can elevate, train, educate, and lead *the entire vast mass* of these classes, which has up to now stood completely outside of political life and history. Sixthly, it makes it possible to combine the advantages of the parliamentary system with the advantages of immediate and direct democracy, i.e. to vest in the people's elected representatives both legislative *and executive* functions. Compared with the bourgeois parliamentary system, this is an advance in democracy's development which is of world-wide, historic significance.

2.7 PARLIAMENTARY AND REVOLUTION-ARY SOCIALISM COMPARED

From Georges Sorel (1847–1922), Reflections on Violence (1908), translated by T. E. Hulme and J. Roth (New York, Collier Books ed., 1961), pp. 115–18.

Sorel argues that parliamentary socialism has compromised with the state to such an extent that only syndicalism can accomplish a revolution.

If by chance our Parliamentary Socialists get possession of the reins of Government, they will prove to be worthy successors of the Inquisition, of the Old Régime, and of Robespierre; political courts will be at work on a large scale, and we may even suppose that the *unfortunate* law of 1848, which abolished the death penalty in political matters, will be repealed. Thanks to this *reform*, we might again see the State triumphing by the hand of the executioner.

Proletarian acts of violence have no resemblance to these proscriptions; they are purely and simply acts of war; they have the value of military demonstrations, and serve to mark the separation of classes. Everything in war is carried on without hatred and without the spirit of revenge: in war the vanquished are not killed; non-combatants are not made to bear the consequences of the disappointments which the armies may have experienced on the fields of battle; force is then displayed according to its own nature, without ever professing to borrow anything from the judicial proceedings which society sets up against criminals.

The more Syndicalism develops, by abandoning the old superstitions which come to it from the Old Régime and from the Church – through the men of letters, professors of philosophy, and historians of the Revolution – the more will social conflicts assume the character of a simple struggle, similar to those of armies on campaign. We cannot censure too severely those who teach the people that they ought to carry out the highly idealistic decrees of a progressive justice. Their efforts will only result in the maintenance of those ideas about the State which provoked the bloody acts of '93, whilst the idea of a class war, on the contrary, tends to refine the conception of violence.

Syndicalism in France is engaged on an antimilitarist propaganda, which shows clearly the immense distance which separates it from Parliamentary Socialism in its conception of the nature of the State. Many newspapers believe that all this is merely an exaggerated humanitarian movement, provoked by the articles of Hervé; this is a great error. We should be misconceiving the nature of the movement if we supposed that it was merely a protest against harshness of discipline, against the length of military service, or against the presence, in the higher ranks, of officers hostile to the existing institutions of the country; these are the reasons which led many middle-class people to applaud declamations against the army at the time of the Dreyfus case, but they are not the Syndicalists' reasons.

The army is the clearest and the most tangible of all possible manifestations of the State, and the one which is most firmly connected with its origins and traditions. Syndicalists do not propose to reform the State, as the men of the eighteenth century did; they want to destroy it, because they wish to realise this idea of Marx's that the Socialist revolution ought not to culminate in the replacement of one governing authority by another minority. The Syndicalists outline their doctrine still more clearly when they give it a more ideological aspect, and declare themselves antipatriotic – following the example of the *Communist Manifesto*.

It is impossible that there should be the slightest understanding between Syndicalists and official Socialists on this question; the latter, of course, speak of breaking up everything, but they attack men in power rather than power itself; they hope to possess the State forces, and they are aware that on the day when they control the Government they will have need of an army; they will carry on foreign politics, and consequently they in their turn will have to praise the feeling of devotion to the fatherland.

Parliamentary Socialists perceive that antipatriotism is deeply rooted in the minds of Socialist workmen, and they make great efforts to reconcile the irreconcilable; they are anxious not to oppose too strongly ideas to which the proletariat has become attached, but at the same time they cannot abandon their cherished State, which promises them so many delights. . . .

Thus it cannot any longer be contested that there is an absolute opposition between revolutionary Syndicalism and the State; this opposition takes in France the particularly harsh form of anti-patriotism, because the politicians have devoted all their knowledge and ability to the task of spreading confusion in people's minds about the essence of Socialism. On the plane of patriotism there can be no compromises and half-way positions; it is therefore on this plane that the Syndicalists have been forced to take their stand when middle-class people of every description employed all their powers of seduction to corrupt Socialism and to alienate the workers from the revolutionary idea. They have been led to deny the idea of patriotism by one of those necessities which are met with at all times in the course of history, and which philosophers have sometimes great difficulty in explaining – because the choice is imposed by external conditions, and not freely made for reasons drawn from the nature of things. This character of historical necessity gives to the existing anti-patriotic movement a strength which it would be useless to attempt to dissimulate by means of sophistries.

We have the right to conclude from the preceding analysis that Syndicalist violence, perpetrated in the course of strikes by pro-letarians who desire the overthrow of the State, must not be confused with those acts of savagery which the superstition of the State suggested to the revolutionaries of 1793, when they had power in their hands and were able to oppress the conquered – following the principles which they had received from the Church and from the Monarchy. We have the right to hope that a Socialist revolution carried out by pure Syndicalists would not be defiled by the abominations which sullied the middle-class revolutions.

2.8 MASS PARTIES INHERENTLY CONSERVATIVE, NOT REVOLUTIONARY

From Robert Michels, Political Parties (1915), translated by Eden and Cedar Paul (New York, Collier Books ed., 1962), pp. 334–7.

Basing his argument on an analysis of the German Social Democratic Party, Michels argues that it is not mere opportunism, but the nature of mass party organisation as such that prevents socialist parties from being truly revolutionary agents.

The analysis here made shows clearly that the internal policy of the party organisations is today absolutely conservative, or is on the way to become such. Yet it might happen that the external policy of these conservative organisms would be bold and revolutionary; that the anti-democratic centralisation of power in the hands of a few leaders is no more than a tactical method adopted to effect the speedier overthrow of the adversary; that the oligarchs fulfil the purely provisional function of educating the masses for the revolution, and that organisation is after all no more than a means employed in the service of an amplified Blanquist conception.

This development would conflict with the nature of party, with the endeavour to organise the masses upon the vastest scale imaginable. As the organisation increases in size, the struggle for great principles becomes impossible. It may be noticed that in the democratic parties of today the great conflicts of view are fought out to an ever-diminishing extent in the field of ideas and with the weapons of pure theory, that they therefore degenerate more and more into personal struggles and invectives, to be settled finally upon considerations of a purely superficial character. The efforts made to cover internal dissensions with a pious veil are the inevitable outcome of organisation based upon bureaucratic principles, for, since the chief aim of such an organisation is to enroll the greatest possible number of members, every struggle on behalf of ideas within the limits of the organisation is necessarily regarded as an obstacle to the realisation of its ends, an obstacle, therefore, which must be avoided in every possible way. This tendency is reinforced by the new parliamentary character of the political party. 'Party organisation' signifies the aspiration for the greatest number of members. 'Parliamentarism' signifies the aspiration for the greatest number of votes. The principal fields of party activity are electoral agitation and direct agitation to secure new members. What, in fact, is the modern political party? It is the methodical organisation of the electoral masses. The Socialist Party, as a political aggregate endeavouring simultaneously to recruit members and to recruit votes, finds here its vital interests, for every decline in membership and every loss in voting strength diminishes its political prestige. Consequently great respect must be paid, not only to new members, but also to possible adherents, to those who in Germany are termed *mitläufer*, in Italy *simpatizzanti*, in Holland *geestverwanten*, and in England *sympathisers*. To avoid alarming these individuals, who are still outside the ideal worlds of socialism or democracy, the pursuit of a policy based on strict principle is shunned, while the consideration is ignored whether the numerical increase of the organization thus effected is not likely to be gained at the expense of its quality.

The last link in the long chain of phenomena which confer a profoundly conservative character upon the intimate essence of the political party (even upon that party which boasts itself revolutionary) is found in the relationships between party and state. Generated to overthrow the centralised power of the state, starting from the idea that the working class need merely secure a sufficiently vast and solid organisation in order to triumph over the organisation of the state, the party of the workers has ended by acquiring a vigorous centralisation of its own, based upon the same cardinal principles of authority and discipline which characterise the organisation of the state. It thus becomes a governmental party, that is to say, a party which, organised itself like a government on the small scale, hopes some day to assume the reins of government upon the large scale. The revolutionary political party is a state within the state, pursuing the avowed aim of destroying the existing state in order to substitute for it a social order of a fundamentally different character. To attain this essentially political end, the party avails itself of the socialist organisation, whose sole justification is found precisely in its patient but systematic preparation for the destruction of the organisation of the state in its existing form. The subversive party organises the *framework* of the social revolution. For this reason it continually endeavours to strengthen its positions, to extend its bureaucratic mechanism, to store up its energies and its funds.

Every new official, every new secretary, engaged by the party is in theory a new agent of the revolution; in the same way every new section is a new battalion; and every additional thousand francs furnished by the members' subscriptions, by the profits of the socialist press, or by the generous donations of sympathetic benefactors, constitute fresh additions to the war-chest for the struggle against the enemy. In the long run, however, the directors of this revolutionary body existing within the authoritarian state, sustained by the same means as that state and inspired by the like spirit of discipline, cannot fail to perceive that the party organisation, whatever advances it may make in the future, will never succeed in becoming more than an ineffective and miniature copy of the state organisation. For this reason, in all ordinary circumstances, and as far as prevision is humanly possible, every attempt of the party to measure its forces with those of its antagonists is foredoomed to disastrous failure. The logical consequence of these considerations is in direct conflict with the hopes entertained by the founders of the party. Instead of gaining revolutionary energy as the force and solidity of its structure has increased, the precise opposite has occurred; there has resulted, *pari passu* with its growth, a continued increase in the prudence, the timidity even, which inspires its policy. The party, continually threatened by the state upon which its existence depends, carefully avoids (once it has attained to maturity) everything which might irritate the state to excess. The party doctrines are, whenever requisite, attenuated and deformed in accordance with the external needs of the organisation. Organisation becomes the vital essence of the party. During the first years of its existence, the party did not fail to make a parade of its revolutionary character, not only in respect of its ultimate ends, but also in respect of the means employed for their attainment – although not always in love with these means. But as soon as it attained to political maturity, the party did not hesitate to modify its original profession of faith and to affirm itself revolutionary only 'in the best sense of the word', that is to say, no longer on lines which interest the police, but only in theory and on paper.

This same party, which at one time did not hesitate, when the triumphant guns of the bourgeois governors of Paris were still smoking, to proclaim with enthusiasm its solidarity with the communards, now announces to the whole world that it repudiates anti-militarist propaganda in any form which may bring its adherents into conflict with the penal code, and that it will not assume any responsibility for the consequences that may result from such a conflict. A sense of responsibility is suddenly becoming active in the Socialist Party. Consequently it reacts with all the authority at its disposal against the revolutionary currents which exist within its own organisation, and which it has hitherto regarded with an indulgent eye. In the name of the grave responsibilities attaching to its position it now disavows anti-militarism, repudiates the general strike, and denies all the logical audacities of its past.

2.9 REVOLUTION, DEMOCRACY, AND THE 'DICTATORSHIP OF THE PROLETARIAT'

From Rosa Luxemburg (1870–1919), 'The Russian Revolution', in The Russian Revolution and Leninism or Marxism?, *with an introduction by Bertram D. Wolfe (Ann Arbor paperback ed., 1961), pp. 59–62, 68–72.*

In these notes, written in a German prison in 1918, Rosa Luxemburg welcomed the Russian Revolution, but was fiercely critical of the Bolsheviks' attitude to democracy.

From the special inadequacy of the Constituent Assembly which came together in October, Trotsky draws a general conclusion concerning the inadequacy of any popular representation whatsoever which might come from universal popular elections during the revolution.

Thanks to the open and direct struggle for governmental power [he writes] the labouring masses acquire in the shortest time an accumulation of political experience, and the climb rapidly from step to step in their political development. The bigger the country and the more rudimentary its technical apparatus, the less is the cumbersome mechanism of democratic institutions able to keep pace with this development.

Here we find the 'mechanism of democratic institutions' as such called in question. To this we must at once object that in such an estimate of representative institutions there lies a somewhat rigid and schematic conception which is expressly contradicted by the historical experience of every revolutionary epoch. According to Trotsky's theory, every elected assembly reflects once and for all only the mental composition, political maturity and mood of its electorate just at the moment when the latter goes to the polling place. According to that, a democratic body is the reflection of the masses at the end of the electoral period, much as the heavens of Herschel always show us the heavenly bodies not as they are when we are looking at them but as they were at the moment they sent out their light-messages to the earth from the measureless distances of space. Any living mental connection between the representatives, once they have been elected, and the electorate, any permanent interaction between one and the other, is hereby denied.

Yet how all historical experience contradicts this! Experience demonstrates quite the contrary: namely, that the living fluid of the popular mood continuously flows around the representative bodies, penetrates them, guides them. How else would it be possible to witness, as we do at times in every bourgeois parliament, the amusing capers of the 'people's representatives', who are suddenly inspired by a new 'spirit' and give forth quite unexpected sounds; or to find the most dried-out mummies at times comporting themselves like youngsters and the most diverse little *Scheidemaennchen* suddenly finding revolutionary tones in their breasts – whenever there is rumbling in factories and workshops and on the streets?

And is this ever-living influence of the mood and degree of political ripeness of the masses upon the elected bodies to be renounced in favour of a rigid scheme of party emblems and tickets in the very midst of revolution? Quite the contrary! It is precisely the revolution which creates by its glowing heat that delicate, vibrant, sensitive political atmosphere in which the waves of popular feeling, the pulse of popular life, work for the moment on the representative bodies in most wonderful fashion. It is on this very fact, to be sure, that the well-known moving scenes depend which invariably present themselves in the first stages of every revolution, scenes in which old reactionaries or extreme moderates, who have issued out of a parliamentary election by limited suffrage under the old regime, suddenly become the heroic and stormy spokesmen of the uprising. The classic example is provided by the famous 'Long parliament' in England, which was elected and assembled in 1642 and remained at its post for seven whole years and reflected in its internal life all alterations and displacements of popular feeling, of political ripeness, of class differentiation, of the progress of the revolution to its highest point, from the initial devout skirmishes with the Crown under a Speaker who remained on his knees, to the abolition of the House of Lords, the execution of Charles and the proclamation of the republic.

And was not the same wonderful transformation repeated in the French Estates General, in the censorship-subjected parliament of Louis Philippe, and even – and this last, most striking example was very close to Trotsky – even in the Fourth Russian Duma which, elected in the Year of Grace 1909 under the most rigid rule of the counter-revolution, suddenly felt the glowing heat of the impending overturn and became the point of departure for the revolution?

All this shows that 'the cumbersome mechanism of democratic institutions' possesses a powerful corrective – namely, the living movements of the masses, their unending pressure. And the more democratic the institutions, the livelier and stronger the pulse-beat of the political life of the masses, the more direct and complete is their influence – despite rigid party banners, outgrown tickets (electoral lists) etc. To be sure, every democratic institution has its limits and shortcomings, things which it doubtless shares with all other human institutions. But the remedy which Trotsky and Lenin have found, the elimination of democracy as such, is worse than the disease it is supposed to cure; for it stops up the very living source from which alone can come the correction of all the innate shortcomings of social institutions. That source is the active, untrammelled, energetic political life of the broadest masses of the people. . . .

Lenin says: the bourgeois state is an instrument of oppression of the working class; the socialist state, of the bourgeoisie. To a certain extent, he says, it is only the capitalist state stood on its head. This simplified view misses the most essential thing: bourgeois class rule has no need of the political training and education of the entire mass of the people, at least not beyond certain narrow limits. But for the proletarian dictatorship that is the life element, the very air without which it is not able to exist. . . .

It is the very giant tasks which the Bolsheviks have undertaken with courage and determination that demand the most intensive political training of the masses and accumulation of experience.

Freedom only for the supporters of the government, only for the members of one party – however numerous they may be – is no freedom at all. Freedom is always and exclusively freedom for the one who thinks differently. Not because of any fanatical concept of 'justice' but because all that is instructive, wholesome and purifying in political freedom depends on this essential characteristic, and its effectiveness vanishes when 'freedom' becomes a special privilege.

The Bolsheviks themselves will not want, with hand on heart, to deny that, step by step, they have to feel out the ground, try out, experiment, test now one way now another, and that a good many of their measures do not represent priceless pearls of wisdom. Thus it must and will be with all of us when we get to the same point – even if the same difficult circumstances may not prevail everywhere.

The tacit assumption underlying the Lenin-Trotsky theory of the dictatorship is this: that the socialist transformation is something for which a ready-made formula lies completed in the pocket of the revolutionary party, which needs only to be carried out energetically in practice. This is, unfortunately – or perhaps fortunately – not the case. Far from being a sum of ready-made prescriptions which have only to be applied, the practical realisation of socialism as an economic, social and juridical system is something which lies completely hidden in the mists of the future. What we possess in our programme is nothing but a few main signposts which indicate the general direction in which to look for the necessary measures, and the indications are mainly negative in character at that. Thus we know more or less what we must eliminate at the outset in order to free the road for a socialist economy. But when it comes to the nature of the thousand concrete, practical measures, large and small, necessary to introduce socialist principles into economy, law and all social relationships, there is no key in any socialist party programme or textbook. That is not a shortcoming but rather the very thing that makes scientific socialism superior to the utopian varieties. The socialist system of society should only be, and can only be, an historical product, born out of the school of its own experiences, born in the course of its realisation, as a result of the developments of living history, which – just like organic nature of which, in the last analysis, it forms a part – has the fine habit of always producing along with any real social need the means to its satisfaction, along with the task simultaneously the solution. However, if such is the case, then it is clear that socialism by its very nature cannot be decreed or introduced by *ukase*. It has as its prerequisite a number of measures of force – against property, etc. The negative, the tearing down, can be decreed; the building up, the positive, cannot. New territory. A thousand problems. Only experience is capable of correcting and opening new ways. Only unobstructed, effervescing life falls into a thousand new forms and improvisations, brings to light creative force, itself corrects all mistaken attempts. The public life of countries with limited freedom is so poverty-stricken, so miserable, so rigid, so unfruitful, precisely because, through the exclusion of democracy, it cuts off the living sources of all spiritual riches and progress. (Proof: the year 1905 and the months from February to October 1917.) There it was political in character; the same thing applies to economic and social life also. The whole mass of the people must take part in it. Otherwise, socialism will be decreed from behind a few official desks by a dozen intellectuals.

Public control is indispensably necessary. Otherwise the exchange of experiences remains only with the closed circle of the officials of the new regime. Corruption becomes inevitable. . . . Socialism in life demands a complete spiritual transformation in the masses degraded by centuries of bourgeois class rule. Social instincts in place of egotistical ones, mass initiative in place of inertia, idealism which conquers all suffering, etc., etc. No one knows this better, describes it more penetratingly; repeats it more stubbornly than Lenin. But he is completely mistaken in the means he employs. Decree, dictatorial force of the factory overseer, draconic penalties, rule by terror – all these things are but pallia-tives. The only way to a rebirth is the school of public life itself, the most unlimited, the broadest democracy and public opinion. It is rule by terror which demoralises.

When all this is eliminated, what really remains? In place of the representative bodies created by general, popular elections, Lenin and Trotsky have laid down the soviets as the only true representation of the labouring masses. But with the repression of political life in the land as a whole, life in the soviets must also become more and more crippled. Without general elections, without unrestricted freedom of press and assembly, without a free struggle of opinion, life dies out in every public institution, becomes a mere semblance of life, in which only the bureaucracy remains as the active element. Public life gradually falls asleep, a few dozen party leaders of inexhaustible energy and boundless experience direct and rule. Among them, in reality only a dozen outstanding heads do the leading and an élite of the working class is invited from time to time to meetings where they are to applaud the speeches of the leaders, and to approve proposed resolutions unanimously – at bottom, then, a clique affair – a dictatorship, to be sure, not the dictatorship of the proletariat, however, but only the dictatorship of a handful of politicans, that is a dictatorship in the bourgeois sense, in the sense of the rule of the Jacobins.

3 *Causes of Revolution*

3.1 ANOMIE AND THE SOCIAL NATURE OF DISCONTENT

From Emile Durkheim (1858–1917), Suicide: A Study in Sociology, translated by John A. Spaulding and George Simpson (London, 1952), pp. 249–53.

For this and the following extract, see 'Introduction', pp. 43–8. Durkheim's analysis of anomie *shows him arriving at the same position as de Tocqueville, on the essentially* relative *nature of our sense of deprivation.*

At every moment of history there is a dim perception, in the moral consciousness of societies, of the respective value of different social services, the relative reward due to each, and the consequent degree of comfort appropriate on the average to workers in each occupation. The different functions are graded in public opinion and a certain coefficient of well-being assigned to each, according to its place in the hierarchy. According to accepted ideas, for example, a certain way of living is considered the upper limit to which a workman may aspire in his efforts to improve his existence, and there is another limit below which he is not willingly permitted to fall unless he has seriously demeaned himself. Both differ for city and country workers, for the domestic servant and the day-labourer, for the business clerk and the official, etc. Likewise the man of wealth is reproved if he lives the life of a poor man, but also if he seeks the refinements of luxury overmuch. Economists may protest in vain; public feeling will always be scandalised if an individual spends too much wealth for wholly superfluous use, and it even seems that this severity relaxes only in times of moral disturbance. A genuine regimen exists, therefore, although not legally formulated, which fixes with relative precision the maximum degree of ease of living to which each social class may legitimately aspire. However, there is nothing immutable about such a scale. It changes with the increase or decrease of collective revenue and the changes occurring in the moral ideas of society. Thus what appears luxury to one period no longer does so to another; and the well-being which for long periods was granted to a class only by exception and supererogation, finally appears strictly necessary and equitable.

Under this pressure, each in his sphere vaguely realises the extreme limit set to his ambitions and aspires to nothing beyond. At least if he respects regulations and is docile to collective authority, that is, has a wholesome moral constitution, he feels that it is not well to ask more. Thus, an end and goal are set to the passions. Truly, there is nothing rigid nor absolute about such determination. The economic ideal assigned each class of citizens is itself confined to certain limits, within which the desires have free range. But it is not infinite. This relative limitation and the moderation it involves, make men contented with their lot while stimulating them moderately to improve it; and this average contentment causes the feeling of calm, active happiness, the pleasure in existing and living which characterises health for societies as well as for individuals. Each person is then at least, generally speaking, in harmony with his condition, and desires only what he may legitimately hope for as the normal reward of his activity. Besides, this does not condemn man to a sort of immobility. He may seek to give beauty to his life; but his attempts in this direction may fail without causing him to despair. For, loving what he has and not fixing his desire solely on what he lacks, his wishes and hopes may fail of what he has happened to aspire to, without his being wholly destitute. He has the essentials. The equilibrium of his happiness is secure because it is defined, and a few mishaps cannot disconcert him.

But it would be of little use for everyone to recognise the justice of the hierarchy of functions established by public opinion, if he did not also consider the distribution of these functions just. The workman is not in harmony with his social position if he is not convinced that he has his deserts. If he feels justified in occupying another, what he has would not satisfy him. So it is not enough for the average level of needs for each social condition to be regulated by public opinion, but another, more precise rule, must fix the way in which these conditions are open to individuals. There is no society in which such regulation does not exist. It varies with times and places. Once it regarded birth as the almost exclusive principle of social classification; today it recognises no other inherent inequality than hereditary fortune and merit. But in all these various forms its object is unchanged. It is also only possible, everywhere, as a restriction upon individuals imposed by superior authority, that is, by collective authority. For it can be established only by requiring of one or another group of men, usually of all, sacrifices and concessions in the name of the public interest. . . .

Man's characteristic privilege is that the bond he accepts is not physical but moral; that is, social. He is governed not by a material environment brutally imposed on him, but by a conscience superior to his own, the superiority of which he feels. Because the greater, better part of his existence transcends the body, he escapes the body's yoke, but is subject to that of society.

But when society is disturbed by some painful crisis or by beneficent but abrupt transitions, it is momentarily incapable of exercising this influence; thence come the sudden rises in the curve of suicides.

In the case of economic disasters, indeed, something like a declassification occurs which suddenly casts certain individuals into a lower state than their previous one. Then they must reduce their requirements, restrain their needs, learn greater self-control. All the advantages of social influence are lost so far as they are concerned; their moral education has to be recommenced. But society cannot adjust them instantaneously to this new life and teach them to practise the increased self-repression to which they are unaccustomed. So they are not adjusted to the condition forced on them, and its very prospect is intolerable; hence the suffering which detached them from a reduced existence even before they have made trial of it.

It is the same if the source of the crisis is an abrupt growth of power and wealth. Then, truly, as the conditions of life are changed, the standard according to which needs were regulated can no longer remain the same; for it varies with social resources, since it largely determines the share of each class of producers. The scale is upset; but a new scale cannot be immediately improvised. Time is required for the public conscience to reclassify men and things. So long as the social forces thus freed have not regained equilibrium, their respective values are unknown and so all regulation is lacking for a time. The limits are unknown between the possible and the impossible, what is just and what is unjust, legitimate claims and hopes and those which are immoderate. Consequently, there is no restraint upon aspirations. If the disturbance is profound, it affects even the principles controlling the distribution of men among various occupations. Since the relations between various parts of society are necessarily modified, the ideas expressing these relations must change. Some particular class especially favoured by the crisis is no longer resigned to its former lot, and, on the other hand, the example of its greater good fortune arouses all sorts of jealousy below and about it. Appetites, not being controlled by a public opinion, become disorientated, no longer recognise the limits proper to them. Besides, they are at the same time seized by a sort of natural erethism simply by the greater intensity of public life. With increased prosperity desires increase. At the very moment when traditional rules have lost their authority, the richer prize offered these appetites stimulates them and makes them more exigent and impatient of control. The state of deregulation or anomy is thus further heightened by passions being less disciplined, precisely when they need more disciplining.

3.2 SATISFACTION A RELATIVE CONCEPT

From Karl Marx, 'Wage Labour and Capital' (1847), in Marx and Engels, Selected Works in Two Volumes, vol. 1, pp. 93–4.

If capital grows, the mass of wage labour grows, the number of wage-workers grows; in a word, the domination of capital extends over a greater number of individuals. Let us assume the most favourable case: when productive capital grows, the demand for labour grows; consequently, the price of labour, wages, goes up.

A house may be large or small; as long as the surrounding houses are equally small it satisfies all social demands for a dwelling. But let a palace arise beside the little house, and it shrinks from a little house to a hut. The little house shows now that its owner has only very slight or no demands to make; and however high it may shoot up in the course of civilisation, if the neighbouring palace grows to an equal or even greater extent, the occupant of the relatively small house will feel more and more uncomfortable, dissatisfied and cramped within its four walls.

A noticeable increase in wages presupposes a rapid growth of productive capital. The rapid growth of productive capital brings about an equally rapid growth of wealth, luxury, social wants, social enjoyments. Thus, although the enjoyments of the worker have risen, the social satisfaction that they give has fallen in comparison with the increased enjoyments of the capitalist, which are inaccessible to the worker, in comparison with the state of development of society in general. Our desires and pleasures spring from society; we measure them, therefore, by society and not by the objects which serve for their satisfaction. Because they are of a social nature, they are of a relative nature.

3.3 TWO REQUISITES OF REVOLUTION

From V. I. Lenin, Selected Works in Three Volumes, *vol. III, pp. 430–1.*

For 3.3.–3.7, see 'Introduction', pp. 48–51.

The fundamental law of revolution, which has been confirmed by all revolutions, and particularly by all three Russian revolutions in the twentieth century, is as follows. It is not enough for revolution that the exploited and oppressed masses should understand the impossibility of living in the old way and demand changes; it is essential for revolution that the exploiters should not be able to live and rule in the old way. Only when the *'lower classes' do not want* the old way, and when the 'upper classes' *cannot carry on in the old way* – only then can revolution triumph. This truth may be expressed in other words: revolution is impossible without a nation-wide crisis (affecting both the exploited and the exploiters).

It follows that for revolution it is essential, first, that a majority of the workers (or at least a majority of the class-conscious, thinking, politically active workers) should fully understand that revolution is necessary and be ready to sacrifice their lives for it; secondly, that the ruling classes should be passing through a governmental crisis, which draws even the most backward masses into politics (a symptom of every real revolution is a rapid, tenfold and even hundredfold increase in the number of members of the working and oppressed masses – hitherto apathetic – who are capable of waging the political struggle), weakens the government and makes it possible for the revolutionaries to overthrow it rapidly.

3.4 GENERAL CAUSES OF THE DIVISION WITHIN THE RULING CLASS

From Leon Trotsky, The History of the Russian Revolution (1929–30), *3 vols., vol. 1, pp. 86–8.*

Robespierre once reminded the Legislative Assembly that the opposition of the nobility, by weakening the monarchy, had roused the bourgeoisie, and after them the popular masses. Robespierre gave warning at the same time that in the rest of Europe the revolution could not develop so swiftly as in France, for the privileged classes of other countries, taught by the experience of the French nobility, would not take the revolutionary initiative. In giving this admirable analysis, Robespierre was mistaken only in his assumption that with its oppositional recklessness the French nobility had given a lesson once for all to other countries. Russia proved again, both in 1905 and yet more in 1917, that a revolution directed against an autocratic and half-feudal regime, and consequently against a nobility, meets in its first step an unsystematic and inconsistent but nevertheless very real co-operation not only from the rank and file nobility, but also from its most privileged upper circles, including here even members of the dynasty. This remarkable historic phenomenon may seem to contradict the class theory of society, but in reality it contradicts only its vulgar interpretation.

A revolution breaks out when all the antagonisms of a society have reached their highest tension. But this makes the situation unbearable even for the classes of the old society – that is, those who are doomed to break up. Although I do not want to give a biological analogy more weight than it deserves, it is worth remarking that the natural act of birth becomes at a certain moment equally unavoidable both for the maternal organism and for the offspring. The opposition put up by the privileged classes expresses the incompatibility of their traditional social position with the demands of the further existence of society. Everything seems to slip out of the hands of the ruling bureaucracy. The aristocracy finding itself in the focus of a general hostility lays the blame upon the bureaucracy, the latter blames the aristocracy, and then together, or separately, they direct their discontent against the monarchical summit of their power.

Prince Sherbatov, summoned into the ministry for a time from his service in the hereditary institutions of the nobility, said:

Both Samarin and I are former heads of the nobility in our provinces. Up till now nobody has ever considered us as Left and we do not consider ourselves so. But we can neither of us understand a situation in a state where the monarch and his government find themselves in radical disagreement with all reasonable (we are not talking here of revolutionary intrigue) society – with the nobility, the merchants, the cities, the zemstovs, and even the army. If those above do not want to listen to our opinion, it is our duty to withdraw.

The nobility sees the cause of all its misfortunes in the fact that the monarchy is blind or has lost its reason. The privileged caste cannot believe that no policy whatever is possible which would reconcile the old society with the new. In other words, the nobility cannot accept its own doom and converts its death-weariness into opposition against the most sacred power of the old regime, that is the monarchy. The sharpness and irresponsibility of the aristocratic opposition is explained by history's having made spoiled children of the upper circles of the nobility, and by the unbearableness to them of their own fears in face of revolution. The unsystematic and inconsistent character of the noble discontent is explained by the fact that it is the opposition of a class which has no future. But as a lamp before it goes out, flares up with a bright although smoky light, so that nobility before disappearing gives out an oppositional flash, which performs a mighty service for its mortal enemy. Such is the dialectic of this process, which is not only consistent with the class theory of society, but can only by this theory be explained.

3.5 ROLE OF A REFORMING GOVERN-MENT IN THE CAUSATION OF THE FRENCH REVOLUTION

From Alexis de Tocqueville, On the State of Society in France Before the Revolution of 1789 (L'Ancien Régime et La Révolution), *translated by Henry Reeve, pp. 344–6.*

See 'Introduction', p. 56.

The government itself had long been at work to instil into and rivet in the minds of the common people many of the ideas which have since been called revolutionary – ideas hostile to individual liberty, opposed to private rights, and favourable to violence.

The King was the first to show with how much contempt it was possible to treat the most ancient, and apparently the best established, institutions. Louis xv shook the monarchy and hastened the Revolution quite as much by his innovations as by his vices, by his energy, as by his indolence. When the people beheld the fall and disappearance of a parliament almost contemporary with the monarchy itself, and which had until then seemed as immoveable as the throne, they vaguely perceived that they were drawing near a time of violence and of chance when everything may become possible, when nothing, however ancient, is respected, and nothing, however new, may not be tried.

During the whole course of his reign Louis xvi did nothing but talk of reforms to be accomplished. There are few institutions of which he did not foreshadow the approaching ruin, before the Revolution came to effect it. After removing from the statute-book some of the worst of these institutions he very soon replaced them; it seemed as if he wanted only to loosen their roots, leaving to others the task of striking them down. By some of the reforms which he effected himself, ancient and venerable customs were suddenly changed without sufficient preparation, and established rights were occasionally violated. These reforms prepared the way

163

for the Revolution, not so much by overthrowing the obstacles in its way, as by showing the people how to set about making it. The evil was increased by the very purity and disinterestedness of the intentions which actuated the King and his ministers; for no example is more dangerous than that of violence exerted for a good purpose by honest and well-meaning men.

At a much earlier period Louis xiv had publicly broached in his edicts the theory that all the land throughout the kingdom had originally been granted conditionally by the State, which was thus declared to be the only true owner, and that all others were possessors whose titles might be contested, and whose rights were imperfect. This doctrine has arisen out of the feudal system of legislation; but it was not proclaimed in France until feudalism was dying out, and was never adopted by the courts of justice. It is, in fact, the germ of modern socialism, and it is curious enough to see it first springing up under royal despotism.

3.6 A REMONSTRANCE OF THE PARLEMENT OF PARIS, 1788

From European Society in the Eighteenth Century, *Selected Documents edited by Robert and Elborg Forster (London, 1969), pp. 377–81.*

See 'Introduction', pp. 55–9. This remonstrance well illustrates the degree to which the parlements *had absorbed the language of the* philosophes, *which they employed freely in their struggle with the Crown.*

Sire,

It is the duty of your Parlement to keep a constant watch over the needs of the people and the rights of the sovereign: the people may be led astray by factions, and kings are only too exposed to rash advice. Your Parlement speaks of liberty to kings and of submission to the people. It gives dignity to this submission by its example, and it gives firmness to authority by its principles. In a word, Sire, it is your Parlement's function to attach royal authority to justice and public liberty to royalty. To do this has always been its aim and its reward in times of stress.

Still penetrated with these sentiments, still desiring to merit the benevolence of our kings and to ensure the liberty of our fellow citizens, we have come to the steps of the throne in order to bring before Your Majesty the most baneful error that can befall a sovereign; we have come, Sire, to invoke your justice, your wisdom, and your humanity against the use of the *lettres de cachet*.

These terrible words make every heart beat more slowly and throw all thinking into confusion. In terror, everyone hesitates, looks around him, and does not dare to explain himself; and the mute people hardly dares raise its thoughts to the inconceivable power which disposes of men without judging or even hearing them, which arbitrarily casts them into impenetrable darkness and keeps them there, in a place where the light of day often does not penetrate any more than the eye of the law, the cry of nature, or the voice of friendship. The people does not dare think of that power whose very essence is mystery and whose only justification is force; of that power which is exercised with impunity by ministers, underlings, and police spies; of that power, finally, which from the ministers down to the last tool of the police, forms a formidable chain of oppressors over our heads before which all the laws of nature and of state must remain silent.

No indeed, Sire, the laws of nature and the laws of the state shall not accuse your Parlement, the living law at the steps of the throne, of a guilty silence.

Man is born free, and his happiness depends on justice. Liberty is an inalienable right. It consists of being able to live according to the laws. Justice is a universal duty and precedes the very laws, which presuppose it and must direct it, but can never exempt kings or subjects from this duty.

Justice and liberty! These, Sire, are the principle and the aim of every society, these are the unshakeable foundations of all power and, happily for the human race, the admirable connection between these two goods is such that without them there is no reasonable authority and no solid obedience.

The use of the lettres de cachet reverses all these ideas. It reduces justice to a chimera, liberty to a word. It goes against reason, it is contrary to the statutes, and the motives by which one tries to justify it are only pretexts contradicted by the evidence.

It goes against reason; it is patently repugnant to human nature, to the nature of monarchy, and to the elementary notions of morality.

But such, precisely, is the essential character of the lettres de cachet.

It is not in human nature to be self-contained. For man, self-containment is a state of war, in which deviousness or force alternately command and in which justice, being without sanction, has no power. It is, therefore, in man's nature to unite with his fellow men and to live in society, submitting to general agreements, i.e. laws. But agreements which would subject him without protecting him would no longer be laws, they would be fetters. Force can impose these fetters, weakness or madness can bear them, but force does not create obligations, and weakness or madness cannot make commitments; all legitimate submission is voluntary by its very principle. A guilty citizen has consented in advance to the judgement that condemns him. Men who would say to other men: 'Do, by all means, pass an arbitrary judgement; we consent if, upon a word from your lips, a letter from your hand, we lose our fortune, our liberty, our wives, our children, and even the right to defend ourselves . . .', men, we contend who would speak thus would surely be insane. The consent of the people to the use of the lettres de cachet, therefore, would be incompatible with reason, but reason is the natural state of man as of society, so that the use of the lettres de cachet is repugnant to human nature, which is reasonable as well as sociable.

It is said that this usage is founded upon the nature of monarchical power? The answer to this is not very difficult to find.

Kings rule by conquest or by the law. If the victor misuses his conquest, if he violates the rights of man, if the conquest is not changed into a capitulation, if it is force which administers the fruits of victory, it will not give the conqueror subjects, but slaves. Kings who rule by law must come back to principles. Reason does not permit kings to order that which it would not permit peoples to consent to.

And how could reason tolerate such a reversal of morality?

Fortunately, Sire, the guardian principles of the human race are not in need of proofs, they are self-evident. It is evident that justice must protect weakness against power. It is evident that the scales must be balanced between the rich and the poor.

It is evident that dishonour and punishment must follow a crime after it has been judged, but then only.

If there were a power which could arbitrarily put a stop to legal procedures, which could make distinctions among offenders, protecting some and giving up others, it is evident that such a power, by compromising the justice of the sentences, would add the notion of partiality to that of the example.

And if this power were to constantly favour a certain class of citizens to the exclusion of all others, it is evident that the law, no longer having the function of punishing such and such crimes but such and such classes of society, would completely destroy the sense of justice and innocence in these proscribed classes, keeping them in a perpetual state of terror and degradation.

These incontestable truths can be applied directly to the use of the lettres de cachet. Two men meet, one of them is weak, the other powerful, one is poor, the other rich. The poor man can say to himself: If this man offends me, if he attacks my honour, my liberty, my life, the laws assure me of their support. But the laws deceive me: perhaps authority will feel differently about it, and in that case authority will have its way. But if I offend him, I shall be apprehended, imprisoned, dishonoured, abandoned, punished; that same authority will be mute, these same laws will be inexorable. Where, then, is justice? Is misery, then, a crime? Does simple humanity no longer mean anything? Is a simple man, a poor man, no longer a citizen? The statutes are as opposed to the lettres de cachet as the principles. At all times ambition, vindictiveness, flattery, and cupidity have besieged the throne, but at all times the laws have also warned the sovereigns and defended the people, if not with equal success, at least with equal energy; and this continuous struggle between arbitrary power and liberty has not extinguished the sense of liberty in the minds of people and of kings. The last Estates General held in Blois has beseeched the king to limit the lettres de cachet to his entourage, to use them not to remove these men from their business, their homes, and their families, but only to keep them away from his palace and to deprive them of his 'presence', without depriving them of justice. It is a maxim of our monarchy that no citizen can be imprisoned without a warrant from a judge. All the kings of the first two dynasties have recognised this maxim. Hugues Capet already found it when he came to the throne; all the statutes of the realm have confirmed it under the third dynasty. It has instituted the only distinction among prisoners our laws allow, that between prisoners for crime and prisoners for debts. The Ordinance of 1670, finally, conforming in this respect to all the previous ordinances, has given the official stamp to this maxim by stipulating that prisoners accused of crimes must be interrogated within twenty-four hours after their imprisonment; but this stipulation is a useless, derisory precaution as long as the lettres de cachet continue to be in use.

Thus the rights of the human race, the fundamental principles of society, the most enlightened reason, the most cherished interest of legitimate power, and the most elementary notions of morality and legality all unanimously condemn the use of the lettres de cachet.

3.7 GENERAL CAUSES OF REVOLUTION: THE CASE OF 1848

From Sir Lewis Namier, Vanished Supremacies *(London, 1962), pp. 34–6.*

A gale blows down whatever it encounters, and does not distinguish. Revolutions are anonymous, undenominational, and inarticulate. If there is an inherent programme, as in agrarian revolutions, it is of a most primitive character. The elemental forces of a mass movement can be made to do the work of men whose quest is alien to them. Most revolutions are filched or deflected: groups or parties with elaborate programmes – panaceas or nostrums – try to stamp them with their own ideology and, if successful, claim to be their spokesmen or even their makers. But revolutions are not made; they occur. Discontent with government there always is; still, even when grievous and well founded, it seldom engenders revolution till the moral bases of government have rotted away; the feeling of community between the masses and their rulers, and in the rulers a consciousness of their right and capacity to rule. Revolutions are usually preceded by periods of high intellectual achievement and travail, of critical analysis and doubt, of unrest among the educated classes, and of guilt-consciousness in the rulers; so it was in France in 1789, in Europe in 1848, and in Russia in 1917. If such corrosion of the moral and mental bases of government coincides with a period of social upheaval, and the conviction spreads, even to the rulers themselves, that the ramshackle building cannot last, government disintegrates and revolution ensues. Revolutions, as distinct from mere revolts, usually start at the centre of government, in the capital; but the nature of the actual outbreak and its purpose almost invariably escape analysis. What aim did the labouring poor of Paris pursue in the Great Revolution, and what did they attain? What was it that made them fight in July 1830, or in February 1848? And what would they have done had they been successful in the June Days or in the Paris Commune? Agrarian movements are far more articulate in form and aim, and therefore, if extensive and determined, are usually successful. The village is a living organism and its communal consciousness transcends other loyalties; and the peasants' demand to be relieved of dues, or to be given the land of the nobles and the church, can be met or enforced overnight. The weakness of agrarian movements usually is in that they break out sporadically, and therefore can be suppressed. But if linked with a rising in the urban centres and with self-doubt in the upper classes, if fanned by generalising factors, such as *la grande peur* in 1789 or the effect of war in 1917, they become overpowering; and then urban groups or parties graft on to them their own programmes.

The revolution of 1848 followed on a period of intellectual efflorescence such as Europe has never known before or since; it supervened at a time when the governments themselves came to feel unequal to the new circumstances and problems; in a period of financial crisis and economic distress, but of disjointed, or even contradictory, social movements. A numerous urban proletariat gathered in the rapidly growing capitals; the independent artisans were fighting a long-drawn losing battle against modern industry; the factory workers started their struggle for a human existence; while the incidence of the agrarian problem was uneven and varied. In France it had been solved by the Great Revolution; in Germany it was confined to several large areas; in the Habsburg Monarchy it was general and acute: there the peasants were determined to sweep away the surviving feudal burdens and jurisdictions. Before the first gusts of the revolutionary storm the governments

169

collapsed without offering serious resistance; there was a paralysis of will and a consciousness of defeat almost before the fight was joined. But there was no uniform or unified social-revolutionary force to continue the struggle; and the educated middle classes, the successors or new partners of the princes, from an exaggerated fear of the Reds quickly turned counter-revolutionary, though they still counted on preserving the conquests of the initial victory which they had appropriated. The peasants were bought off by timely and extensive concessions; the proletariat was defeated in Paris in the June Days, in Vienna in October, while in Berlin (as in 1933) it succumbed without fighting. In France, where 1789 had done most of the work which still awaited accomplishment elsewhere, 1848 followed a path apart; in the rest of Europe the conflict was between the principle of dynastic property in countries and that of national sovereignty: from which devolved the problems of self-government and self-determination, of constitutional rights and of national union and independence.

3.8 REVOLUTION PREDICTED ON THE EVE OF 1848

From Alexis de Tocqueville, The Recollections of Alexis de Tocqueville, *translated by Alexander Teixeira de Mattos (London, 1948), pp. 9–13.*

De Tocqueville was rightfully proud to recollect that his general knowledge of revolutions enabled him to foresee the coming revolution in France. In the next two extracts he also illustrates the negligible role of the professional revolutionaries in bringing about revolution.

The country was at that time divided into two unequal parts, or rather zones: in the upper, which alone was intended to contain the whole of the nation's political life, there reigned nothing but languor, impotence, stagnation, and boredom; in the lower, on the contrary, political life began to make itself manifest by means of feverish and irregular signs, of which the attentive observer was easily able to seize the meaning.

I was one of these observers; and although I was far from imagining that the catastrophe was so near at hand and fated to be so terrible, I felt a distrust springing up and insensibly growing in my mind, and the idea taking root more and more that we were making strides towards a fresh revolution. This denoted a great change in my thoughts; since the general appeasement and flatness that followed the Revolution of July had led me to believe for a long time that I was destined to spend my life amid an enervated and peaceful society. Indeed, anyone who had only examined the inside of the governmental fabric would have had the same conviction. Everything there seemed combined to produce with the machinery of liberty a preponderance of royal power which verged upon despotism; and, in fact, this result was produced almost without effort by the regular and tranquil movement of the machine. King Louis-Philippe was persuaded that, so long as he did not himself lay hand upon that fine instrument, and allowed it to work according to rule, he was safe from all peril. His only occupation was to keep it in order, and to make it work according to his own views, forgetful of society, upon which this ingenious piece of mechanism rested; he resembled the man who refused to believe that his house was on fire, because he had the key to it in his pocket. I could neither have the same interests nor the same cares, and this permitted me to see through the mechanism of institutions and the agglomeration of petty everyday facts, and to observe the state of morals and opinions in the country. There I clearly saw the appearance of several of the portents that usually denote the approach of revolutions, and I began to believe that in 1830 I had taken for the end of the play what was nothing more than the end of an act.

A short unpublished document which I composed at the time, and a speech which I delivered early in 1848, will bear witness to these pre-occupations of my mind. . . .

After commenting on the symptoms of languor in parliament, I continued:

. . . The time will come when the country will find itself once again divided between two great parties. The French Revolution which abolished all privileges and destroyed all exclusive rights, has allowed one to remain, that of property. Let not the proprietors deceive themselves as to the strength of their position, nor think that the rights of property form an insurmountable barrier because they have not as yet been surmounted; for our times are unlike any others. When the rights of property were merely the origin and commencement of a number of other rights, they were easily defended, or rather, they were never attacked; they then formed the surrounding wall of society, of which all other rights were the outposts; no blows reached them; no serious attempt was ever made to touch them. But today, when the rights of property are nothing more than the last remnants of an overthrown aristocratic world; when they alone are left intact, isolated privileges amid the universal levelling of society; when they are no longer protected behind a number of still more controvertible and odious rights, the case is altered, and they alone are left daily to resist the direct and unceasing shock of democratic opinion.

. . . Before long, the political struggle will be restricted to those who have and those who have not; property will form the great field of battle; and the principal political questions will turn upon the more or less important modifications to be introduced into the right of property. We shall then have once more among us great public agitations and great political parties.

How is it that these premonitory symptoms escape the general view? Can anyone believe that it is by accident, through some passing whim of the human mind, that we see appearing on every side these curious doctrines, bearing different titles, but all characterised in their essence by their denial of the rights of property, and all tending, at least, to diminish and weaken the exercise of these rights? Who can fail here to recognise the final symptom of the old democratic disease of the time, whose crisis would seem to be at hand?

. . . I am told that there is no danger because there are no riots; I am told that, because there is no visible disorder on the surface of society, there is no revolution at hand.

I was still more urgent and explicit in the speech which I delivered in the Chamber of Deputies on 29 January 1848, and which appeared in the *Moniteur* of the 30th.

The principal passages may be quoted here:

Gentlemen, permit me to say that I believe you are mistaken. True, there is no actual disorder; but it has entered deeply into men's minds. See what is preparing itself amongst the working classes, who, I grant, are at present quiet. No doubt they are not disturbed by political passions, properly so-called, to the same extent that they have been; but can you not see that their passions, instead of political, have become social? Do you not see that they are gradually forming opinions and ideas which are destined not only to upset this or that law, ministry, or even form of government, but society itself, until it totters upon the foundations on which it rests today? Do you not listen to what they say to themselves each day? Do you not hear them repeating unceasingly that all that is above them is incapable and unworthy of governing them; that the distribution of goods prevalent until now throughout the world is unjust; that property rests on a foundation which is not an equitable one? And do you not realise that when such opinions take root, when they spread in an almost universal manner, when they sink deeply into the masses, they are bound to bring with them sooner or later, I know not when or how, a most formidable revolution?

This, gentlemen, is my profound conviction: I believe that we are at this moment sleeping on a volcano. I am profoundly convinced of it. . . .

. . . I was saying just now that this evil would sooner or later, I know not how or whence it will come, bring with it a most serious revolution: be assured that that is so.

When I come to investigate what, at different times, in different periods, among different peoples, has been the effective cause that has brought about the downfall of the governing classes, I perceive this or that event, man, or accidental or superficial cause; but, believe me, the real reason, the effective reason which causes men to lose political power is that they have become unworthy to retain it.

Think, gentlemen, of the old Monarchy: it was stronger than you are, stronger in its origin; it was able to lean more than you do upon ancient customs, ancient habits, ancient beliefs; it was stronger than you are, and yet it has fallen to dust. And why did it fall? Do you think it was by particular mischance? Do you think it was by the act of some man, by the deficit, the oath in the Tennis Court, La Fayette, Mirabeau? No, gentlemen; there was another reason: the class that was then the governing class had become, through its indifference, its selfishness and its vices, incapable and unworthy of governing the country.

That was the true reason.

Well, gentlemen, if it is right to have this patriotic prejudice at all times, how much more is it not right to have it in our own? Do you not feel, by some intuitive instinct which is not capable of analysis, but which is undeniable, that the earth is quaking once again in Europe? Do you not feel – what shall I say? – as it were a gale of revolution in the air? This gale, no one knows whence it springs, whence it blows, nor, believe me, whom it will carry with it.

3.9 GENERAL CAUSES OF THE FEBRUARY REVOLUTION OF 1848

From Alexis de Tocqueville, Recollections, *pp. 68–70.*

The Revolution of February, in common with all other great events of this class, sprang from general causes, impregnated, if I am permitted the expression, by accidents; and it would be as superficial a judgement to ascribe it necessarily to the former or exclusively to the latter.

The industrial revolution which, during the past thirty years, had turned Paris into the principal manufacturing city of France and attracted within its walls an entire new population of workmen (to whom the works of the fortifications had added another population of labourers at present deprived of work), together with the excess in material pleasures fostered by the government itself, tended more and more to inflame this multitude. Add to this the democratic disease of envy, which was silently permeating it; the economical and political theories which were beginning to make their way and which strove to prove that human misery was the work of laws and not of Providence, and that poverty could be changing the conditions of society; the contempt into which the governing class, and especially the men who led it, had fallen, a contempt so general and so profound that it paralysed the resistance even of those who were most interested in maintaining the power that was being overthrown; the centralisation which reduced the whole revolutionary movement to the overmastering of Paris and the seizing of the machinery of government; and lastly, the mobility of all this, institutions, ideas, men and customs, in a fluctuating state of society which had, in less than sixty years, undergone the shock of seven great revolutions, without numbering a multitude of smaller, secondary upheavals. These were the general causes without which the Revolution of February would have been impossible. The principal accidents which led to it were the passions of the dynastic Opposition, which brought about a riot in proposing a reform; the suppression of this riot, first over-violent and then abandoned; the sudden disappearance of the old Ministry, unexpectedly snapping the threads of power, which the new ministers, in their confusion, were unable either to seize upon or to reunite; the mistakes and disorder of mind of these ministers, so powerless to re-establish that which they had been strong enough to overthrow; the vacillation of the generals; the absence of the only princes who possessed either personal energy or popularity; and above all, the senile imbecility of King Louis-Philippe, his weakness, which no one could have foreseen, and which still remains almost incredible, after the event has proved it.

3.10 REVOLUTION NOT CAUSED BY REVOLUTIONARIES

From Alexis de Tocqueville, Recollections, pp. 35-6.

Portalis, who became Attorney-General of Paris a few days later, was among us. . . . His coarse, violent, perverse mind had quite naturally entered into all the false ideas and extreme opinions of our times. Although he was in relation with most of those who are regarded as the authors and leaders of the Revolution of 1848, I can conscientiously declare that he did not that night expect the revolution any more than we did. I am convinced that, even at that supreme moment, the same might have been said of the greater number of his friends. It would be a waste of time to try to discover what secret conspiracies brought about events of this kind. Revolutions accomplished by means of popular risings are generally longed for beforehand rather than premeditated. Those who boast of having contrived them have done no more than turn them to account. They spring spontaneously into being from a general malady of men's minds, brought suddenly to the critical stage by some fortuitous and unforeseen circumstance. As to the so-called originators or leaders of these revolutions, they originate and lead nothing; their only merit is identical with that of the adventurers who have discovered most of the unknown countries. They simply have the courage to go straight before them as long as the wind impels them.

3.11 A REVOLUTIONARY SITUATION: RUSSIA

From Friedrich Engels, 'On Social Relations in Russia' (1875), in Marx and Engels, *Selected Works in Two Volumes, vol. ii, pp. 60–1.*

Russia undoubtedly is on the eve of a revolution. Her financial affairs are in extreme disorder. Taxes cannot be screwed any higher, the interest on old state loans is paid by means of new loans, and every new loan meets with greater difficulties; money can now only be raised under the pretext of building railways! The administration, as of old, corrupt from top to bottom, the officials living more from theft, bribery and extortion than on their salaries. The entire agricultural production – by far the most essential for Russia – completely dislocated by the redemption settlement of 1861; the big landowners without sufficient labour power, the peasants without sufficient land, oppressed by taxation and sucked dry by usurers, agricultural production declining from year to year. The whole held together with great difficulty and only outwardly by an Oriental despotism whose arbitrariness we in the West simply cannot imagine; a despotism which not only from day to day comes into more glaring contradiction with the views of the enlightened classes and in particular with those of the rapidly developing bourgeoisie of the capital, but which, in the person of its present bearer, has lost its head, one day making concessions to liberalism and the next, frightened, cancelling them again and thus bringing itself more and more into disrepute. With all that a growing recognition among the enlightened strata of the nation concentrated in the capital that this position is untenable, that a revolution is impending, and the illusion that it will be possible to guide this revolution into a smooth, constitutional channel. Here all the conditions of a revolution are combined, of a revolution which, started by the upper classes of the capital, perhaps even by the government itself, must be rapidly carried further, beyond the first constitutional phase, by the peasants; of a revolution which will be of the greatest importance for the whole of Europe if only because it will destroy at one blow the last, so far intact, reserve of the entire European reaction.

3.12 ROLE OF THE ZEMSTVOS IN THE RUSSIAN REVOLUTION

From P. Milyoukov, Russia and its Crisis *(Chicage, 1905), pp. 528–33.*

See 'Introduction', pp. 65–6. In this summary of the events immediately preceding the Revolution of 1905, Milyoukov, as a Liberal participant, illustrates the importance of the zemstvos *in mobilising educated opinion against the autocracy.*

The members of the Zemstvos, taken as a whole, are not at all identical with the 'Emancipation Party'. Yet so powerful is the present current of liberal public opinion that their programme, recently formulated in the petition presented to the Tsar, is that of the 'Emancipation'. We have seen that as early as 1902 voices were heard in the local committees advocating the introduction of a constitution. But these voices were indistinct, and such as had a more positive ring were stifled, and their possessors sent into exile. The cry was, however, raised again – this time not by three or four isolated individuals, but by fully a hundred; and it was not in the local assemblies legally summoned in the districts, but in a semi-official meeting of the members of all the Zemstvos, first invited by the minister Svyatopolk-Mirskee, then forbidden, and finally tolerated to meet at St Petersburg.

This was the first meeting in Russian history which represented the opinion of the Zemstvos, not about local and economic, but about general and political questions. This meeting formulated a demand which was much more positive than that of the few exiled members of 1902. In its petition it enumerated all the fundamental rights of the individual and the citizen: the inviolability of the person and of the private home; no sentence without trial, and no diminution of rights except by judgement of an independent court; liberty of conscience and of belief; liberty of the press and of speech; equal rights – civil and political – for all social orders, and as a consequence, enfranchisement of the peasants; a large measure of local and municipal self-government; and last, as a general condition and a guarantee for all the preceding rights, 'a regular representation in a separate elective body, which must participate

177

in legislation, in working out the budget, and in controlling the administration'. Of the ninety-eight members present, seventy-one voted for this last clause as a whole, while the minority of twenty-seven was satisfied with its first half; i.e. the most conservative asked for a 'regular representation in a separate elective body, which must participate in legislation'; and they found this reform 'absolutely necessary for the normal development of the state and of society'. In the last paragraph of their petition the members of the Zemstvos requested that the anticipated reform be carried out with the assistance of the 'freely elected representatives of the people'; i.e. demanded the convocation of the 'constitutional assembly'.

This degree of unanimity in the St Petersburg assembly has surpassed the boldest expectations even of those observers who have closely followed the latest events in the political life of Russia. 'The Petition of Rights' of 19–21 November 1904, will remain a beautiful page in our annals; and whatever be its immediate practical consequences, its political importance cannot be over-estimated. It was the first political programme of the Russian Liberal party, openly proclaimed in an assembly which had full moral right to represent liberalism throughout the empire. More-over, this petition of the Zemstvo men from all Russia was officially handed to the Tsar, and a deputation of the assembly was received by him. The pacification of Russia depended at that moment on the satisfactory answer of the Tsar to the petition. This answer seemed to have been more or less determined upon in advance; otherwise there would have been no political sense in permitting the assembly to gather in St Petersburg, and in receiving the petitioners in a formal audience. All Russia was in a state of feverish expectation; and meanwhile all social groups – writers and journalists, professors and men of science, lawyers, engineers, individual Zemstvos, provincial circles of intellectuals, working men, students, learned societies, the general public in the street, each in his own way in demonstrations, banquets, resolutions covered with thousands of signatures, etc., etc. – hastened to endorse the petition of the Zemstvo. No more united and 'co-ordinated' political action has ever been witnessed in the history of the country. To be sure, socialistic publications drew a sharp line between their own demands and those of the liberals, proposing to include in their resolutions a more positive demand for a 'direct, equal, and secret' general vote, freedom of strikes and a constitutional convention, as well as for the immediate cessation of the war. In many cases these demands were agreed to, as practically they did not contradict – and often were even implied in – the demands of the liberals themselves. The freedom of discussion and the boldness of speech in these assemblies surpassed everything that Russia had ever seen before; and the same spirit pervaded the press. Conservative newspapers – as *Novoya Vraimya* – became liberal; liberal newspapers became radical; and two new daily papers were started in St Petersburg to advocate the claims of the more advanced public opinion. Though severely censored, they used a bold, open language, which, with perhaps two exceptions – at the beginning of the era of the 'Great Reforms' (1859–61), and in 1881 – was unprecedented in the history of our press. Public manifestations in the streets, though peaceful, were treated with relentless cruelty. Policemen and 'janitors' in groups of four or five fell upon single unarmed students and girls, beat them with their fists, and struck them with drawn swords, until the poor disabled victims lost consciousness. Some of them died; others were maimed for life. Evidently this was a deliberate and systematised attempt, intended to inspire horror. Instead, it only inspired hatred and a feeling of revenge.

At the same time the question of reform was under discussion in the Tsar's palace, Tsarskoya Selo; and in a cabinet session on 15 December, under the presidency of the Tsar, it received a fatal solution which, instead of ending the conflict, hopelessly enlarged the gulf between the Tsar and his people. Mr Mooravyov, the minister of justice, who was the first to speak, tried to prove that the Tsar had no right to change the existing political order. Mr Pobedonostsev attempted to prove the same proposition by arguments from religion. He thought – in his own peculiar language – that Russia 'would fall into sin and return to a state of barbarism', if the Tsar should renounce his power; religion and morality would suffer, and the law of God would be violated. It was such arguments as these which for a time decided the fate of Russia. Mr Svyatopolk-Mirksee tried in vain to prove that the minister of justice talked nonsense; and Mr Witte grimly concluded: 'If it should become known that the emperor is forbidden by law and religion to introduce fundamental reforms of his own will – well, then a part of the population will come to the conclusion that these reforms must be achieved by way of violence. It would be equivalent to an actual appeal to revolution!' Mr Witte played the prophet.

3.13 THE PLACE OF THE RUSSIAN REVOLUTION IN THE EUROPEAN REVOLUTIONARY TRADITION

From E. H. Carr, A History of Soviet Russia, *vol. 1 (London, 1960), pp. 38–44.*

See 'Introduction', pp. 87–9.

The dispute between Bolsheviks and Mensheviks, though it appeared to turn on esoteric points of Marxist doctrine, raised issues fundamental to the history of the Russian revolution. The Mensheviks, clinging to the original Marxist sequence of bourgeois-democratic and proletarian-socialist revolutions, never really accepted Lenin's hypothesis, thrown out as early as 1898, of an indissoluble link between them. The bourgeois revolution had to come first; for it was only through the bourgeois revolution that capitalism could receive its full development in Russia, and, until that development occurred, the Russian proletariat could not become strong enough to initiate and carry out the socialist revolution. This formal separation between the two revolutions, however satisfying to the theorist, had consequences which would have proved embarrassing to more practical revolutionaries than the Mensheviks. Narrowing their horizon to the bourgeois revolution, the Mensheviks found difficulties in imparting to their political programme any socialist or proletarian appeal. The bourgeois revolution was the necessary and predestined precursor of the proletarian revolution, and was therefore, at long range, a vital interest of the proletariat. But the immediate effect would be to put in power those who were the oppressors of the proletariat and, once more at long range, its most formidable enemies. From this dilemma the Mensheviks could escape only by concentrating on a short-term policy of support for the bourgeoisie in destroying the autocracy and completing the bourgeois revolution, and of pressure on the eventual bourgeois revolutionary government to accord to the proletariat such material alleviations of their lot as formed the staple of social policy in advanced capitalist countries (recognition of trade unions, the eight-hour day, social insurance and so forth).

In essence, therefore, as Lenin frequently pointed out, the Bolshevik argument against the Mensheviks repeated the controversies with the legal Marxists and the Economists against whom the whole party had formerly stood united; and it echoed the controversy with the 'revisionists' in the German Social-Democratic party. Wedded to the cut-and-dried thesis that Russia was on the eve of a bourgeois, but not of a socialist, revolution, the Mensheviks followed the legal Marxists in their emphasis on revolutionary theory and in their postponement of revolutionary action to some still remote future; they followed the Economists in preferring the economic concept of class to the political concept of party and believing that the only concrete aim that could be offered to the workers at the present stage was the improvement of their economic lot; they followed the German revisionists in advocating parliamentary pressure on a bourgeois government to secure reforms favourable to the workers rather than revolutionary action to overthrow it. Menshevism was not an isolated or accidental phenomenon. The Mensheviks came to stand for a series of ideas familiar in the practice of western European socialism – a legal opposition, progress through reform rather than revolution, compromise and co-operation with other parliamentary parties, economic agitation through trade unions. Menshevism was firmly rooted in western thought and western tradition (and, after all, Marx was a westerner). The Russian *narodniks*, like the Slavophils, had asserted the uniqueness of Russia's development; unlike the west, Russia was destined to avoid the capitalist stage. Plekhanov, refuting the *narodniks*, based his whole teaching on the axiom that Russia must follow precisely the same development as the west. In this sense, he too was a whole-hearted westerner; and the Mensheviks were Plekhanov's disciples. They always found it easier than the Bolsheviks to win sympathy and understanding among the social-democratic leaders of the west. It was a quip of Radek many years later that 'western Europe begins with the Mensheviks'.

It was symptomatic of this contrast that, when the Bolshevik and

Menshevik wings of the party came to be clearly differentiated in Russia itself (which happened later and much less sharply than among the *émigrés*), the Mensheviks found their adherents among the most highly skilled and organised workers, the printers, the railwaymen and steel-workers in the modern industrial centres of the south, whereas the Bolsheviks drew their main support from the relatively unskilled labour of the mass industries – the old-fashioned heavy industry of the Petersburg region and the textile factories of Petersburg and Moscow. Most of the trade unions were predominantly Menshevik. The Economists had argued that, while the instructed workers of the west were capable of political indoctrination, only economic agitation could appeal to the mass of the Russian 'factory proletariat'; and Lenin himself appeared to accept the view that the appeal of the Economists was to the 'lowest and least developed strata of the proletariat'. This diagnosis was, however, contradicted both by the experience of the west (where, from the days of the First International onwards, it was the most advanced section of the workers, the English trade unionists, who exalted the economic at the expense of the political struggle) and by contemporary Russian realities. The most highly skilled, educated, organised and privileged Russian workers, who approximated most nearly to the organised workers of the west, were least susceptible to revolutionary appeals and most easily induced to believe in the possibility of improving their economic lot within a bourgeois political framework. The unskilled mass of Russian factory workers who, standing in all respects at a lower level than the lowest grades of western industrial labour, had 'nothing to lose but their chains', were most readily accessible to the Bolshevik plea for political revolution as the sole avenue to economic improvement.

The failure of Menshevism, a failure marked both by tragedy and by futility, was a result of its alienation from Russian conditions. The Russian social and political order provided none of the soil in which a bourgeois-democratic regime could flourish. History rarely repeats itself; and an interpretation of Marxism which supposed that the successive stages of revolution elsewhere in the world would precisely conform to a pattern established in western Europe was deterministic and therefore false. In Germany it proved impossible throughout the latter half of the nineteenth century to complete the bourgeois-democratic revolution in its classical form; German social and political development was twisted and stultified by the abortion of 1848. In Russia, if the Mensheviks could have had their way, the bankruptcy of the German revolution in 1848 would have been matched by the bankruptcy of 1905. Nor was this merely because the German bourgeoisie of 1848 and the Russian bourgeoisie of 1905 were too weak and undeveloped to achieve their own revolutionary ambitions. That they were weak was undeniable. But a more significant cause of their hesitancy was that they were already conscious of the growing menace to themselves of an eventual proletarian revolution. One reason why history so rarely repeats itself is that the dramatis personae at the second performance have prior knowledge of the *dénouement*. The Marxist scheme of revolution required the bourgeoisie to overthrow the feudal order as a prelude to its own overthrow by the proletariat. The weakness of the scheme was that, once it had penetrated the bourgeois consciousness, it could no longer be carried out. Once bourgeois democracy was recognised as a stepping-stone to socialism, it could be brought into being only by those who believed also in socialism. This was the profound truth which Lenin expressed when he argued that only the proletariat could take the lead in carrying out the bourgeois revolution. The trouble was not that conditions in Russia were not yet ripe for the western revolutionary drama; it was that the drama had been played out in the west, and could no longer be re-acted elsewhere. The Mensheviks, who waited for conditions in Russia to ripen, were doomed to sterility and frustration.

The Bolshevik standpoint, though it took far more account of specifically Russian conditions and was thus spared the humiliation of failure, was also not free from inner contradictions. According to this standpoint the bourgeois-democratic revolution, though carried out by the proletariat with the support of the peasantry, was none the less essentially bourgeois in character: it was a stage which could not be skipped, and must not be confused with the subsequent proletarian-socialist revolution. That a revolution carried out in these conditions could and should adopt many measures which were in fact not socialist and were perfectly compatible with bourgeois capitalism – such as the distribution of land to the

183

peasants, the eight-hour day or the separation of church and state –
was, of course, undeniable: these measures and many like them
were inscribed in the minimum programme of the party. But that
such a revolution, boycotted or actively opposed by the bourgeoisie, could achieve that 'bourgeois freedom and bourgeois
progress' which Lenin himself had described as the only 'path to
real freedom for the proletariat and the peasantry', was a conception whose difficulties Lenin never appears seriously to have faced.
In later speeches and writings he frequently denounced 'bourgeois
freedom' as a hollow sham. This involved him in no inconsistency,
since he was speaking of two different epochs. So long as the bourgeoisie was a revolutionary force taking the offensive against the
remnants of medievalism and feudalism, bourgeois freedom was
real and progressive; so soon as the bourgeoisie, having consolidated
its power, was on the defensive against the rising forces of socialism
and the proletariat, 'bourgeois freedom' became reactionary and
false. But the verbal contradiction helped to unmask the real
problem. The Bolshevik argument required the establishment in
Russia of a bourgeois freedom and bourgeois democracy which
had and could have no social roots in Russia (since it would have to
be established without the support of the bourgeoisie), and declared
that failing this there could be no path to the higher freedom of
socialism. The Menshevik scheme which waited for the Russian
bourgeoisie to establish bourgeois freedom was scarcely more
unreal than the Bolshevik scheme which required it to be established by a revolutionary dictatorship of the proletariat and the
peasantry.

The tragic dilemma of the Russian revolution, which neither
Mensheviks nor Bolsheviks could wholly solve, rested on an error
or prognostication in the original Marxist scheme. Marx believed
that bourgeois capitalism, once established, would everywhere run
its full course, and that, when it began to decay through its own
inherent contradictions, then and only then would it be overthrown by a socialist revolution. What in fact happened was that
capitalism, in the countries where it was most fully and powerfully
developed, built around itself a vast network of vested interests
embracing a large sector of the industrial working class, so that,
even after the process of decay had manifestly set in, it continued
for a long period to resist without much difficulty the forces of

revolution, whereas it was a nascent and immature capitalism which succumbed easily to the first revolutionary onslaught. The economic consequences of this departure from the preconceived plan were apparent: the young revolutionary government, instead of being able to take over the efficient industrial organisation and trained man-power of a fully developed capitalism, was compelled to rely, for the building of the socialist order, on the inadequate resources of a backward country, so that the new socialism had to bear the handicap and the reproach of being a regime of scarcity and not, as Marxists had always expected, a regime of abundance. The political consequences were not less embarrassing: the new repositories of political power were a proletariat innocent of the political training and experience which are acquired under a bourgeois constitution from the exercise of universal suffrage and from association in trade unions and workers' organisations, and a peasantry mainly illiterate and almost wholly devoid of political consciousness. The difficulties of this situation, and the disappointments resulting from it, were attributed by the Mensheviks to the wilful abandonment by the Bolsheviks of the Marxist scheme of revolution. But that scheme was bound to break down when the proletarian revolution occurred in the most backward of capitalist countries.

4 *Formation of Revolutionary Movements*

4.1 CONDITIONS FOR THE DEVELOP-MENT OF A REVOLUTIONARY PROLETARIAT

From Karl Marx and Friedrich Engels, 'Manifesto of the Communist Party' (1848), in Marx and Engels, Selected Works in Two Volumes, vol. I, pp. 41–3.

The lower strata of the middle class – the small tradespeople, shopkeepers, and retired tradesmen generally, the handicraftsmen and peasants – all these sink gradually into the proletariat, partly because their diminutive capital does not suffice for the scale on which Modern Industry is carried on, and is swamped in the competition with the large capitalists, partly because their special-ised skill is rendered worthless by new methods of production. Thus the proletariat is recruited from all classes of the population.

The proletariat goes through various stages of development. With its birth begins its struggle with the bourgeoisie. At first the contest is carried on by individual labourers, then by the workpeople of a factory, then by the operatives of one trade, in one locality, against the individual bourgeois who directly exploits them. They direct their attacks not against the bourgeois condi-tions of production, but against the instruments of production themselves; they destroy imported wares that compete with their labour, they smash to pieces machinery, they set factories ablaze, they seek to restore by force the vanished status of the workman of the Middle Ages.

At this stage the labourers still form an incoherent mass scattered over the whole country, and broken up by their mutual competition. If anywhere they unite to form more compact bodies, this is not yet the consequence of their own active union, but of the union of the bourgeoisie, which class, in order to attain its own political ends, is compelled to set the whole proletariat in motion, and is moreover yet, for a time, able to do so. At this stage, therefore, the proletarians do not fight their enemies, but the enemies of their enemies, the remnants of absolute monarchy, the landowners, the non-industrial bourgeois, the petty bourgeoisie. Thus the whole historical movement is concentrated in the hands of the bourgeoisie; every victory so obtained is a victory for the bourgeoisie.

But with the development of industry the proletariat not only increases in number; it becomes concentrated in greater masses, its strength grows, and it feels that strength more. The various interests and conditions of life within the ranks of the proletariat are more and more equalised, in proportion as machinery obliterates all distinctions of labour, and nearly everywhere reduces wages to the same low level. The growing competition among the bourgeois, and the resulting commercial crises, make the wages of the workers ever more fluctuating. The unceasing improvement of machinery, ever more rapidly developing, makes their livelihood more and more precarious; the collisions between individual workmen and individual bourgeois take more and more the character of collisions between two classes. Thereupon the workers begin to form combinations (Trades' Unions) against the bourgeois; they club together in order to keep up the rate of wages; they found permanent associations in order to make provision beforehand for these occasional revolts. Here and there the contest breaks out into riots.

Now and then the workers are victorious, but only for a time. The real fruit of their battles lies, not in the immediate result, but in the ever-expanding union of the workers. This union is helped on by the improved means of communication that are created by modern industry and that place the workers of different localities in contact with one another. It was just this contact that was needed to centralise the numerous local struggles, all of the same character, into one national struggle between classes. But every class struggle

187

is a political struggle. And that union, to attain which the burghers of the Middle Ages, with their miserable highways, required centuries, the modern proletarians, thanks to railways, achieve in a few years.

This organisation of the proletarians into a class, and consequently into a political party, is continually being upset again by the competition between the workers themselves. But it ever rises up again, stronger, firmer, mightier. It compels legislative recognition of particular interests of the workers, by taking advantage of the divisions among the bourgeoisie itself. Thus the ten-hours' bill in England was carried.

Altogether collisions between the classes of the old society further, in many ways, the course of development of the proletariat. The bourgeoisie finds itself involved in a constant battle. At first with the aristocracy; later on, with those portions of the bourgeoisie itself, whose interests have become antagonistic to the progress of industry; at all times, with the bourgeoisie of foreign countries. In all these battles it sees itself compelled to appeal to the proletariat, to ask for its help, and thus, to drag it into the political arena. The bourgeoisie itself, therefore, supplies the proletariat with its own elements of political and general education, in other words, it furnishes the proletariat with weapons for fighting the bourgeoisie.

Further, as we have already seen, entire sections of the ruling classes are, by the advance of industry, precipitated into the proletariat, or are at least threatened in their conditions of existence. These also supply the proletariat with fresh elements of enlightenment and progress.

Finally, in times when the class struggle nears the decisive hour, the process of dissolution going on within the ruling class, in fact within the whole range of old society, assumes such a violent, glaring character, that a small section of the ruling class cuts itself adrift, and joins the revolutionary class, the class that holds the future in its hands. Just as, therefore, at an earlier period, a section of the nobility went over to the bourgeoisie, so now a portion of the bourgeoisie goes over to the proletariat, and in particular, a portion of the bourgeois ideologists, who have raised themselves to the level of comprehending theoretically the historical movement as a whole.

4.2 'RIPENESS IS ALL...'

From Karl Marx, Selected Writings in Sociology and Social Philosophy, edited by T. B. Bottomore and Maximilien Rubel (London, Pelican edn., 1963), pp. 244–5. This was written in 1847. See 'Introduction', pp. 34–6.

If the proletariat destroys the political rule of the bourgeoisie, that will only be a temporary victory, only an element in the service of the *bourgeois revolution* itself, as in 1794, so long as in the course of history, in its 'movement', the material conditions are not yet created which make necessary the abolition of the bourgeois mode of production and thus the definitive overthrow of bourgeois political rule. The reign of terror in France could only serve, therefore, to clear away from the soil of France, through its powerful blows, the remnants of feudalism. The anxious and considerate bourgeoisie would never have completed this task in decades. The bloody action of the people thus only prepared the way for it. Similarly, the collapse of the absolute monarchy would have been temporary, had not the economic conditions for the rule of the bourgeois class already ripened. Men do not build themselves a new world out of the fruits of the earth, as *vulgar* superstition believes, but out of the historical accomplishments of their declining civilisation. They must, in the course of their development, begin by themselves *producing* the *material* conditions of a new society, and no effort of mind or will can free them from this destiny.

4.3 THE NECESSITY OF A MYTH: EXAMPLE OF THE GENERAL STRIKE

From Georges Sorel, Reflections on Violence (1908) translated by T. E. Hulme and J. Roth (1961 edn.), pp. 49–50, 122–8.

On the whole, in this century it is the radical Right, not Left, which has most successfully exploited the device of the revolutionary 'myth'. But Sorel first elaborated it with reference to the Syndicalist strategy of the General Strike.

As long as there are no myths accepted by the masses, one may go on talking of revolts indefinitely, without ever provoking any revolutionary movement; this is what gives such importance to the general strike and renders it so odious to socialists who are afraid of a revolution; they do all they can to shake the confidence felt by the workers in the preparations they are making for the revolution; and in order to succeed in this they cast ridicule on the idea of the general strike – the only idea that could have any value as a motive force. One of the chief means employed by them is to represent it as a Utopia; this is easy enough, because there are very few myths which are perfectly free from any Utopian element.

The revolutionary myths which exist at the present time are almost free from any such mixture; by means of them it is possible to understand the activity, the feelings and the ideas of the masses preparing themselves to enter on a decisive struggle; the myths are not descriptions of things, but expressions of a determination to act. A Utopia is, on the contrary, an intellectual product; it is the work of theorists who, after observing and discussing the known facts, seek to establish a model to which they can compare existing society in order to estimate the amount of good and evil it contains. It is a combination of imaginary institutions having sufficient analogies to real institutions for the jurist to be able to reason about them; it is a construction which can be taken to pieces, and certain parts of it have been shaped in such a way that they can (with a few alterations by way of adjustment) be fitted into approaching legislation. Whilst contemporary myths lead men to prepare themselves for a combat which will destroy the existing state of things, the effect of Utopias has always been to direct men's minds towards reforms which can be brought about by patching up the existing system; it is not surprising, then, that so many makers of Utopias were able to develop into able statesmen when they had acquired a greater experience of political life. A myth cannot be refuted, since it is, at bottom, identical with the convictions of a group, being the expression of these convictions in the language of movement; and it is, in consequence, unanalysable into parts which could be placed on the plane of historical descriptions. A Utopia, on the contrary, can be discussed like any other social constitution; the spontaneous movements it presupposes can be compared with the movements actually observed in the course of history, and we can in this way evaluate its verisimilitude; it is possible to refute Utopias by showing that the economic system on which they have been made to rest is incompatible with the necessary conditions of modern production. . . .

Syndicalism endeavours to employ methods of expression which throw a full light on things, which put them exactly in the place assigned to them by their nature, and which bring out the whole value of the forces in play. Oppositions, instead of being glozed over, must be thrown into sharp relief if we desire to obtain a clear idea of the Syndicalist movement; the groups which are struggling one against the other must be shown as separate and as compact as possible; in short, the movements of the revolted masses must be represented in such a way that the soul of the revolutionaries may receive a deep and lasting impression.

These results could not be produced in any very certain manner by the use of ordinary language; use must be made of a body of images which, *by intuition alone*, and before any considered analyses are made, is capable of evoking as an undivided whole the mass of sentiments which corresponds to the different manifestations of the war undertaken by Socialism against modern society. The Syndicalists solve this problem perfectly, by concentrating the whole of Socialism in the drama of the general strike; there is thus no longer any place for the reconciliation of contraries in the equivocations of the professors; everything is clearly mapped out, so that only one interpretation of Socialism is possible. This method has all the advantages which 'integral' knowledge has over analysis, according to the doctrine of Bergson; and perhaps it would not be possible to cite another example which would so perfectly demonstrate the value of the famous professor's doctrines.

The possibility of the actual realisation of the general strike has been much discussed; it has been stated that the Socialist war could not be decided in one single battle. To the people who think themselves cautious, practical, and scientific the difficulty of setting great masses of the proletariat in motion at the same moment seems prodigious; they have analysed the difficulties of detail which such an enormous struggle would present. It is the opinion of the Socialist-sociologists, as also of the politicians, that the general strike is a popular dream, characteristic of the beginnings of a working-class movement; we have had quoted against us the authority of Sidney Webb, who has decreed that the general strike is an illusion of youth, of which the English workers – whom the monopolists of sociology have so often presented to us as the depositaries of the true conception of the working-class movement – soon rid themselves.

That the general strike is not popular in contemporary England is a poor argument to bring against the historical significance of the idea, for the English are distinguished by an extraordinary lack of understanding of the class war; their ideas have remained very much dominated by medieval influences: the guild, privileged, or at least protected by laws, still seems to them the ideal of working-class organisation; it is for England that the term *working-class aristocracy*, as a name for the trades unionists, was invented, and, as a matter of fact, trades unionism does pursue the acquisition of legal privileges. We might therefore say that the aversion felt by England for the general strike should be looked upon as strong presumptive evidence in favour of the latter by all those who look upon the class war as the essence of Socialism. . . .

Neither do I attach any importance to the objections made to the general strike based on considerations of a practical order. The attempt to construct hypotheses about the nature of the struggles of the future and the means of suppressing capitalism, on the mode furnished by history, is a return to the old methods of the Utopists. There is no process by which the future can be predicted scientifically, nor even one which enables us to discuss whether one hypothesis about it is better than another; it has been proved by too many memorable examples that the greatest men have committed prodigious errors in thus desiring to make predictions about even the least distant future.

And yet without leaving the present, without reasoning about this future, which seems for ever condemned to escape our reason, we should be unable to act at all. Experience shows that the *framing of a future, in some indeterminate time*, may, when it is done in a certain way, be very effective, and have very few inconveniences; this happens when the anticipations of the future take the form of those myths, which enclose with them, all the strongest inclinations of a people, of a party or of a class, inclinations which recur to the mind with the insistence of instincts in all the circumstances of life; and which give an aspect of complete reality to the hopes of immediate action by which, more easily than by any other method, men can reform their desires, passions, and mental activity. We know, moreover, that these social myths in no way prevent a man profiting by the observations which he makes in the course of his life, and form no obstacle to the pursuit of his normal occupations.

The truth of this may be shown by numerous examples.

The first Christians expected the return of Christ and the total ruin of the pagan world, with the inauguration of the kingdom of the saints, at the end of the first generation. The catastrophe did not come to pass, but Christian thought profited so greatly from the apocalyptic myth that certain contemporary scholars maintain that the whole preaching of Christ referred solely to this one point. The hopes which Luther and Calvin had formed of the religious exaltation of Europe were by no means realised; these fathers of the Reformation very soon seemed men of a past era; for present-day Protestants, they belong rather to the Middle Ages than to modern times, and the problems which troubled them most occupy very little place in contemporary Protestantism. Must we for that reason deny the immense result which came from their dreams of Christian renovation? It must be admitted that the real developments of the Revolution did not in any way resemble the enchanting pictures which created the enthusiasm of its first adepts; but without those pictures would the Revolution have been victorious? Many Utopias were mixed up with the Revolutionary myth, because it had been formed by a society passionately fond of imaginative literature, full of confidence in the 'science', and very little acquainted with the economic history of the past. These Utopias came to nothing; but it may be asked whether the Revolution was not a much more profound transformation than those dreamed of by the people who in the eighteenth century had invented social Utopias. In our own times Mazzini pursued what the wiseacres of his time called a mad chimera; but it can no longer be denied that, without Mazzini, Italy would never have become a great power, and that he did more for Italian unity than Cavour and all the politicians of his school.

A knowledge of what the myths contain in the way of details which will actually form part of the history of the future is then of small importance; they are not astrological almanacs; it is even

possible that nothing which they contain will ever come to pass –
as was the case with the catastrophe expected by the first Christians.
In our own daily life, are we not familiar with the fact that what
actually happens is very different from our pre-conceived notion
of it? And that does not prevent us from continuing to make
resolutions. Psychologists say that there is heterogeneity between
the ends in view and the ends actually realised: the slightest
experience of life reveals this law to us, which Spencer transferred
into nature, to extract therefrom his theory of the multiplication
of effects.

The myth must be judged as a means of acting on the present;
any attempt to discuss how far it can be taken literally as future
history is devoid of sense. *It is the myth in its entirety which is alone
important*: its parts are only of interest in so far as they bring out
the main idea. No useful purpose is served, therefore, in arguing
about the incidents which may occur in the course of a social war,
and about the decisive conflicts which may give victory to the
proletariat; even supposing the revolutionaries to have been wholly
and entirely deluded in setting up this imaginary picture of the
general strike, this picture may yet have been, in the course of the
preparation for the Revolution, a great element of strength, if it
has embraced all the aspirations of Socialism, and if it has given to
the whole body of Revolutionary thought a precision and a rigidity
which no other method of thought could have given. . . .

. . . We know that the general strike is indeed what I have said:
the *myth* in which Socialism is wholly comprised, i.e. a body of
images capable of evoking instinctively all the sentiments which
correspond to the different manifestations of the war undertaken
by Socialism against modern society. Strikes have engendered in
the proletariat the noblest, deepest, and most moving sentiments
that they possess; the general strike groups them all in a co-ordinated picture, and, by bringing them together, gives to each one of
them its maximum intensity, appealing to their painful memories
of particular conflicts, it colours with an intense life all the details
of the composition presented to consciousness. We thus obtain
that intuition of Socialism which language cannot give us with
perfect clearness – and we obtain it as a whole, perceived instantaneously.

4.4 THE INDISPENSABILITY OF THE INTELLECTUALS

From V. I. Lenin, Selected Works in Three Volumes *(Moscow, n.d.), vol. I, pp. 148–9. Written in 1902.*

In this and the following two extracts, it is argued that the lower classes of society cannot develop a revolutionary consciousness on their own, but only through the educative and organising influence of intellectuals and a tightly-knit party. Lenin, in particular, is arguing against the view that the working class will 'spontaneously' revolt, in the form of a general strike, etc.

[W]e pointed out how *universally* absorbed the educated youth of Russia was in the theories of Marxism in the middle of the ninetics. In the same period the strikes that followed the famous St Petersburg industrial war of 1896 assumed a similar general character. Their spread over the whole of Russia clearly showed the depth of the newly awakening popular movement, and if we are to speak of the 'spontaneous element' then, of course, it is this strike movement which, first and foremost, must be regarded as spontaneous. But there is spontaneity and spontaneity. Strikes occurred in Russia in the seventies and sixties (and even in the first half of the nineteenth century), and they were accompanied by the 'spontaneous' destruction of machinery, etc. Compared with these 'revolts', the strikes of the nineties might even be described as 'conscious', to such an extent do they mark the progress which the working-class movement made in that period. This shows that the 'spontaneous element', in essence, represents nothing more nor less than consciousness in an *embryonic form*. Even the primitive revolts expressed the awakening of consciousness to a certain extent. The workers were losing their age-long faith in the permanence of the system which oppressed them and began ... I shall not say to understand, but to sense the necessity for collective resistance, definitely abandoning their slavish submission to the authorities. But this was, nevertheless, more in the nature of outbursts of desperation and vengeance than of *struggle*. The strikes of the nineties revealed far greater flashes of consciousness; definite demands were advanced, the strike was carefully timed, known cases and instances in other places were discussed, etc. The revolts were simply the resistance of the oppressed, whereas the systematic strikes represented the class struggle in embryo, but only in embryo. Taken by themselves, these strikes were simply trade union struggles, not yet Social-Democratic struggles. They marked the awakening antagonisms between workers and employers; but the workers were not, and could not be, conscious of the irreconcilable antagonism of their interests to the whole of the modern political and social system, i.e. theirs was not yet Social-Democratic consciousness. In this sense, the strikes of the nineties, despite the enormous progress they represented as compared with the 'revolts', remained a purely spontaneous movement.

We have said that *there could not have been* Social-Democratic consciousness among the workers. It would have to be brought to them from without. The history of all countries shows that the working class, exclusively by its own effort, is able to develop only trade union consciousness, i.e. the conviction that it is necessary to combine in unions, fight the employers, and strive to compel the government to pass necessary labour legislation, etc. The theory of socialism, however, grew out of the philosophic, historical, and economic theories elaborated by educated representatives of the propertied classes, by intellectuals. By their social status, the founders of modern scientific socialism, Marx and Engels, themselves belonged to the bourgeois intelligentsia. In the very same way, in Russia, the theoretical doctrine of Social-Democracy arose altogether independently of the spontaneous growth of the working-class movement; it arose as a natural and inevitable outcome of the development of thought among the revolutionary socialist intelligentsia.

4.5 THE MASSES AND THE REVOLUTIONARY INTELLECTUALS

From Robert Michels, Political Parties (1915), *translated by Eden and Cedar Paul (New York, 1962 edn.), pp. 227–31)*

The masses are not easily stirred. Great events pass before their eyes and revolutions are accomplished in economic life without their minds undergoing profound modifications. Very slowly do they react to the influence of new conditions.

For decades, and even for centuries, the masses continue to endure passively outworn political conditions which greatly impede legal and moral progress. Countries which from the economic point of view are fairly well advanced, often continue to endure for lengthy periods a political and constitutional regime which derives from an earlier economic phase. This is especially noteworthy in Germany, where an aristocratic and feudal form of government, the outcome of economic conditions which the country has outlived, has not yet been able to adapt itself to an economic development of the most advanced capitalist character.

These historical phenomena, which at first sight appear paradoxical, arise from causes of two different orders. In the first place it may happen that classes or sub-classes representing an extinct economic form may survive from a time in which they were the authentic exponents of the then dominant economic relationships; they have been able to save from the wreck a sufficiency of moral prestige and effective political force to maintain their dominion in the new phase of economic and civil development, and to do this even in opposition to the expressed will of the majority of the people. These classes succeed in maintaining themselves in power by the strength of their own political energy and with the assistance of numerous elements essentially foreign to themselves, but which they can turn to their own advantage by suggestive influences. Most commonly, however, we find that the classes representing a past economic order continue to maintain their social predominance only because the classes representing the present or future economy have as yet failed to become aware of their strength, of their political and economic importance, and of the wrongs which they suffer at the hands of society. Moreover, a sense of fatalism and a sad conviction of impotence exercise a paralysing influence in social life. As long as an oppressed class is influenced by this fatalistic spirit, as long as it has failed to develop an adequate sense of social injustice, it is incapable of aspiring towards emancipation. It is not the simple *existence* of oppressive conditions, but it is the *recognition of these conditions by the oppressed*, which in the course of history has constituted the prime factor of class struggles.

The mere existence of the modern proletariat does not

suffice *per se* to produce a 'social problem'. The class struggle, if it is not to remain a nebulous theory, in which the energy is for ever latent, requires to be animated by class consciousness.

It is the involuntary work of the bourgeoisie to arouse in the proletariat that class consciousness which is necessarily directed against the bourgeoisie itself. History is full of such ironies. It is the tragical destiny of the bourgeoisie to be instructor of the class which from the economic and social point of view is its own deadly enemy. As Karl Marx showed in his *Communist Manifesto*, the principal reason for this is found in the unceasing struggle which the bourgeoisie is forced to carry on 'at once with the aristocracy, with those sections of its own class whose interests are opposed to industrial progress, and with the bourgeoisie of all foreign countries.' Unable to carry on this struggle effectively by its own unaided powers, the bourgeoisie is continually forced 'to appeal to the proletariat, to demand its aid, and thus to launch the proletariat into the political mêlée, thus putting into the hands of the proletariat a weapon which the latter will turn against the bourgeoisie itself'. Under yet another aspect the bourgeoisie appears as the instructor, as the fencing-master of the working class. Through its daily contact with the proletariat there results the detachment from its own body of a small number of persons who devote their energies to the service of the working classes, in order to inflame these for the struggle against the existing order, to make them feel and understand the deficiencies of the prevailing economic and social regime. It is true that the number of those who are detached from the bourgeoisie to adhere to the cause of the proletariat is never great. But those who thus devote themselves are among the best of the bourgeoisie; they may, in a sense, be regarded as supermen, raised above the average of their class, it may be by love of their neighbours, it may be by compassion, it may be by moral indignation against social injustice or by a profound theoretical understanding of the forces at work in society, or, finally, by a greater energy and logical coherence in the translation of their principles into practice. In any case, they are exceptional individualities, these bourgeois who, deserting the class in which they were born, give a deliberate direction to the instincts still slumbering in the proletariat, and thus hasten the emancipation of the proletarian class as a whole.

The proletarian mass is at first aware by instinct alone of the oppression by which it is burdened, for it entirely lacks the instruction which might give a clue to the understanding of that historical process which is in appearance so confused and labyrinthine. It would seem to be a psychological-historical law that any class which has been enervated and led to despair in itself through prolonged lack of education and through deprivation of political rights, cannot attain to the possibility of energetic action until it has received instruction concerning its ethical rights and politico-economical powers, not alone from members of its own class, but also from those who belong to, what in vulgar parlance are termed a 'higher' class. Great class movements have hitherto been initiated in history solely by the simple reflection: it is not we alone, belonging to the masses without education and without legal rights, who believe ourselves to be oppressed, but that belief as to our condition is shared by those who have a better knowledge of the social mechanism and who are therefore better able to judge; since the cultured people of the upper classes have also conceived the ideal of our emancipation, that ideal is not a mere chimera.

The socialist theory has arisen out of the reflections of philosophers, economists, sociologists, and historians. In the socialist programmes of the different countries, every word represents a synthesis of the work of numerous learned men. The fathers of modern socialism were with few exceptions men of science primarily, and in the second place only were they politicians in the strict sense of the term. It is true that before the days of such men there were spontaneous proletarian movements initiated by an instructive aspiration towards a higher intellectual and economic standard of life. But these movements manifest themselves rather as the mechanical outcome of an unreflecting though legitimate discontent, than as the consequence of a genuine sentiment of revolt inspired by a clear consciousness of oppression. It was only when science placed itself at the service of the working class that the *proletarian* movement became transformed into a *socialist* movement, and that instinctive, unconscious, and aimless rebellion was replaced by conscious aspiration, comparatively clear, and strictly directed towards a well-defined end.

Similar phenomena are apparent in all earlier class struggles. Every great class movement in history has arisen upon the instigation, with the co-operation, and under the leadership of men sprung from the very class against which the movement was directed. Spartacus, who urged the slaves to revolt on behalf of their freedom, was, it is true, of servile origin, but he was a freed-man, a Thracian property owner. Thomas Münzer, to whose agitation the Thuringian Peasants' War was largely due, was not a peasant but a man of learning. Florian Geier was a knight. The most distinguished leaders of the movement for the emancipation of the *tiers état* at the outset of the French Revolution, Lafayette, Mirabeau, Roland, and Sieyès, belonged to the privileged classes, and Philippe-Égalité, the regicide, was even a member of the royal house. The history of the modern labour movement furnishes no exception to this rule. ... The great precursors of political socialism and leading representatives of philosophical socialism, St Simon, Fourier, and Owen; the founders of political socialism, Louis Blanc, Blanqui, and Lassalle; the fathers of economic and scientific socialism, Marx, Engels, and Rodbertus, were all bourgeois intellectuals. Of comparatively trifling importance in the international field, alike in respect of theory and of practice, were Wilhelm Weitling, the tailor's apprentice, and Pierre Leroux, the self-taught philosopher. It is only Proudhon, the working printer, a solitary figure, who attains to a position of superb grandeur in this field. Even among the great orators who during recent years have been devoted to the cause of labour, ex-bourgeois constitute the great majority, while men of working-class origin are altogether exceptional. Pages could be filled with the names of leading socialist politicians sprung from the bourgeoisie, whereas in a single breath we could complete the list of political leaders of truly working-class origin whose names will be immortalised in the history of their class. We have Benoît Malon, August Bebel, and Eduard Anseele; but not one of these, although they are great practical leaders of the working class, and potent organisers, is numbered among the creative theorists of socialism.

4.6 THE PLACE OF CONSPIRACY IN REVOLUTION

From Leon Trotsky, The History of the Russian Revolution (1929–30), 3 vols., translated by Max Eastman (Sphere Books edn., 1967), vol. III, *pp. 159–65.*

Conspiracy is ordinarily contrasted to insurrection as the deliberate undertaking of a minority to a spontaneous movement of the majority. And it is true that a victorious insurrection, which can only be the act of a class called to stand at the head of the nation, is widely separated both in method and historic significance from a governmental overturn accomplished by conspirators acting in concealment from the masses. . . .

This does not mean, however, that popular insurrection and conspiracy are in all circumstances mutually exclusive. An element of conspiracy almost always enters to some degree into any insurrection. Being historically conditioned by a certain stage in the growth of a revolution, a mass insurrection is never purely spontaneous. Even when it flashes out unexpectedly to a majority of its own participants, it has been fertilised by those ideas in which the insurrectionaries see a way out of the difficulties of existence. But a mass insurrection can be foreseen and prepared. It can be organised in advance. In this case the conspiracy is subordinate to the insurrection, serves it, smoothes its path, hastens its victory. The higher the political level of a revolutionary movement and the more serious its leadership, the greater will be the place occupied by conspiracy in a popular insurrection. . . .

To overthrow the old power is one thing; to take the power in one's own hands is another. The bourgeoisie may win the power in a revolution not because it is revolutionary, but because it is bourgeois. It has in its possession property, education, the press, a network of strategic positions, a hierarchy of institutions. Quite otherwise with the proletariat. Deprived in the nature of things of all social advantages, an insurrectionary proletariat can count only on its numbers, its solidarity, its cadres, its official staff.

Just as a blacksmith cannot seize the red hot iron in his naked hand, so the proletariat cannot directly seize the power; it has to have an organisation accommodated to this task. The co-ordination of the mass insurrection with the conspiracy, the subordination of the conspiracy to the insurrection, the organisation of the insurrection through the conspiracy, constitutes that complex and responsible department of revolutionary politics which Marx and Engels called 'the art of insurrection'. It presupposes a correct general leadership of the masses, a flexible orientation in changing conditions, a thought-out plan of attack, cautiousness in technical preparation, and a daring blow. . . .

From his observations and reflections upon the failure of the many insurrections he witnessed or took part in, Auguste Blanqui derived a number of tactical rules which if violated will make the victory of any insurrection extremely difficult, if not impossible. Blanqui demanded these things: a timely creation of correct revolutionary detachments, their centralised command and adequate equipment, a well calculated placement of barricades, their definite construction, and a systematic, not a mere episodic, defence of them. All these rules, deriving from the military problems of the insurrection, must of course change with social conditions and military technique, but in themselves they are not by any means 'Blanquism' in the sense that this word approaches the German 'putschism', or revolutionary adventurism.

Insurrection is an art, and like all arts it has its laws. The rules of Blanqui were the demands of a military revolutionary realism. Blanqui's mistake lay not in his direct but his inverse theorem. From the fact that tactical weakness condemns an insurrection to defeat, Blanqui inferred that an observance of the rules of insurrectionary tactics would itself guarantee the victory. Only from this point on is it legitimate to contrast Blanquism with Marxism. Conspiracy does not take the place of insurrection. An active minority of the proletariat, no matter how well organised, cannot seize power regardless of the general conditions of the country. In this point history has condemned Blanquism. But only in this. His affirmative theorem retains all its force. In order to conquer the power, the proletariat needs more than a spontaneous insurrection. It needs a suitable organisation, it needs a plan; it needs a conspiracy. Such is the Leninist view of this question.

Engel's criticism of the fetishism of the barricade was based upon the evolution of military technique and of technique in general. The insurrectionary tactic of Blanquism corresponded to the character of the old Paris, the semi-handicraft proletariat, the narrow streets and the military system of Louis-Philippe. Blanqui's mistake in principle was to identify revolution with insurrection. His technical mistake was to identify insurrection with the barricade. The Marxian criticism has been directed against both mistakes. Although at one with Blanquism in regarding insurrection as an art, Engels discovered not only the subordinate place occupied by insurrection in a revolution, but also the declining role of the barricade in an insurrection. Engels' criticism had nothing in common with a renunciation of the revolutionary methods in favour of pure parliamentarism, as the philistines of the German Social Democracy, in co-operation with the Hohenzollern censorship, attempted in their day to pretend. For Engels the question about barricades remained a question about one of the technical elements of an uprising. The reformists have attempted to infer from his rejection of the decisive importance of the barricade, a rejection of revolutionary violence in general. That is about the same as to infer the destruction of militarism from considerations of the probable decline in importance of trenches in future warfare.

The organisation by means of which the proletariat can both overthrow the old power and replace it, is the soviets. This afterwards became a matter of historic experience, but was up to the October revolution a theoretical prognosis – resting, to be sure, upon the preliminary experience of 1905. The soviets are organs of preparation of the masses for insurrection, organs of insurrection, and after the victory, organs of government.

However, the soviets by themselves do not settle the question. They may serve different goals according to the programme and leadership. The soviets receive their programme from the party. Whereas the soviets in revolutionary conditions – and apart from revolution they are impossible – comprise the whole class with the exception of its altogether backward, inert or demoralised strata, the revolutionary party represents the brain of the class. The problem of conquering the power can be solved only by a definite combination of party with soviets – or with other mass organisations more or less equivalent to soviets.

When headed by a revolutionary party the soviet consciously and in good season strives towards a conquest of power. Accommodating itself to changes in the political situation and the mood of the masses, it gets ready the military bases of the insurrection, unites the shock-troops upon a single scheme of action, works out a plan for the offensive and for the final assault. And this means bringing organised conspiracy into mass insurrection. . . .

But if it is true that an insurrection cannot be evoked at will, and that nevertheless in order to win it must be organised in advance, then the revolutionary leaders are presented with a task of correct diagnosis. They must feel out the growing insurrection in good season and supplement it with a conspiracy. The interference of the midwife in labour pains – however this image may have been abused – remains the clearest illustration of this conscious intrusion into an elemental process. Herzen once accused his friend Bakunin of invariably in all his revolutionary enterprises taking the second month of pregnancy for the ninth. Herzen himself was rather inclined to deny even in the ninth that pregnancy existed. In February the question of determining the date of birth hardly arose at all, since the insurrection flared up unexpectedly without centralised leadership. But exactly for this reason the power did not go to those who had accomplished the insurrection, but to those who had applied the brakes. It was quite otherwise with the second insurrection. This was consciously prepared by the Bolshevik Party. The problem of correctly seizing the moment to give the signal for the attack was thus laid upon the Bolshevik staff.

Moment here is not to be taken too literally as meaning a definite day and hour. Physical births also present a considerable period of uncertainty – their limits interesting not only to the art of the midwife, but also the casuistics of the Surrogate's Court. Between the moment when an attempt to summon an insurrection must inevitably prove premature and lead to a revolutionary miscarriage, and the moment when a favourable situation must be considered hopelessly missed, there exists a certain period – it may be measured in weeks, and sometimes in a few months – in the course of which an insurrection may be carried out with more or less chance of success. To discriminate this comparatively short period and then choose the definite moment – now in the more accurate sense of the very day and hour – for the last blow, constitutes the most responsible task of the revolutionary leaders. It can with full justice be called the key problem, for it unites the policy of revolution with the technique of insurrection – and it is needless to add that insurrection, like war, is a continuation of politics with other instruments.

4.7 THE ROLE OF THE *PHILOSOPHES* IN THE FRENCH REVOLUTION

The following two extracts illustrate the revolutionary influence of the most significant group of political intellectuals of modern times: the French philosophes of the eighteenth century.

4.7.1 *From Alexis de Tocqueville,* On the State of Society in France before the Revolution of 1789, *translated by Henry Reeve (1856), pp. 253–71.*

France had long been the most literary of all the nations of Europe; although her literary men had never exhibited such intellectual powers as they displayed about the middle of the eighteenth century, or occupied such a position as that which they then assumed. Nothing of the kind had ever been seen in France, or perhaps in any other country. They were not constantly mixed up with public affairs as in England: at no period, on the contrary, had they lived more apart from them. They were invested with no authority whatever, and filled no public offices in a society crowded with public officers; yet they did not, like the greater part of their brethren in Germany, keep entirely aloof from the arena of politics and retire into the regions of pure philosophy and polite literature. They busied themselves incessantly with matters appertaining to government, and this was, in truth, their special occupation. Thus they were continually holding forth on the origin and primitive forms of society, the primary rights of the citizen and of government, the natural and artificial relations of men, the wrong or right or customary laws, and the principles of legislation. While they thus penetrated to the fundamental basis of the constitution of their time, they examined its structure with minute care and criticised its general plan. All, it is true, did not make a profound and special study of these great problems: the greater part only touched upon them cursorily, and as it were in sport: but they all dealt with them

205

more or less. This species of abstract and literary politics was scattered in unequal doses through all the works of the period: from the ponderous treatise to the popular song, not one of these but contained some grains of it. . . .

All those who felt themselves aggrieved by the daily application of existing laws were soon enamoured of these literary politics. The same taste soon reached even those who by nature or by their condition of life seemed the farthest removed from abstract speculations. Every taxpayer wronged by the unequal distribution of the *taille* was fired by the idea that all men ought to be equal; every little landowner devoured by the rabbits of his noble neighbour was delighted to be told that all privileges were without distinction contrary to reason. Every public passion thus assumed the disguise of philosophy; all political action was violently driven back into the domain of literature; and the writers of the day, undertaking the guidance of public opinion, found themselves at one time in that position which the heads of parties commonly hold in free countries. No one in fact was any longer in a condition to contend with them for the part they had assumed.

An aristocracy in all its vigour not only carries on the affairs of a country, but directs public opinion, gives a tone to literature, and the stamp of authority to ideas; but the French nobility of the eighteenth century had entirely lost this portion of its supremacy: its influence had followed the fortunes of its power; and the position it had occupied in the direction of the public mind had been left entirely vacant to the writers of the day, to stretch themselves out in at their ease. Nay more, this very aristocracy whose place they thus assumed, favoured their undertaking. So completely had it forgotten the fact that general theories once admitted, inevitably transform themselves in time into political passions and deeds, that doctrines the most adverse to the peculiar rights, and even to the existence of the nobility, were looked upon as ingenious exercises of the mind; the nobles even shared as a pleasant pastime in these discussions, and quietly enjoyed their immunities and privileges whilst they serenely discussed the absurdity of all established customs.

In England those who wrote on the subject of government were connected with those who governed; the latter applied new ideas to practice – the former corrected or controlled their theories by practical observation. But in France the political world remained divided into two separate provinces, with no mutual intercourse. One portion governed; the other established abstract principles on which all government ought to be founded. Here measures were taken in obedience to routine; there general laws were propounded, without even a thought as to the means of their application. These kept the direction of affairs; those guided the intelligence of the nation.

Above the actual state of society – the constitution of which was still traditional, confused, and irregular, and in which the laws remained conflicting and contradictory, ranks sharply sundered, the conditions of the different classes fixed whilst their burdens were unequal – an imaginary state of society was thus springing up, in which everything appeared simple and co-ordinate, uniform, equitable, and agreeable to reason. The imagination of the people gradually deserted the former state of things in order to seek refuge in the latter. Interest was lost in what was, to foster dreams of what might be; and men thus dwelt in fancy in this ideal city, which was the work of literary invention.

The French Revolution has been frequently attributed to that of America. The American Revolution had certainly considerable influence upon the French; but the latter owed less to what was actually done in the United States than to what was thought at the same time in France. Whilst to the rest of Europe the Revolution of America still only appeared a novel and strange occurrence, in France it only rendered more palpable and more striking that which was already supposed to be known. Other countries it astonished; to France it brought more complete conviction. The Americans seemed to have done no more than execute what the literary genius of France had already conceived; they gave the substance of reality to that which the French had excogitated. It was as if Fénélon had suddenly found himself in Salentum.

This circumstance, so novel in history, of the whole political education of a great people being formed by its literary men, contributed more than anything perhaps to bestow upon the French Revolution its peculiar stamp, and to cause those results which are still perceptible.

The writers of the time not only imparted their ideas to the people who effected the Revolution, but they gave them also their peculiar temperament and disposition. The whole nation ended, after being so long schooled by them, in the absence of all other leaders and in profound ignorance of practical affairs, by catching up the instincts, the turn of mind, the tastes, and even the humours of those who wrote; so that, when the time for action came, it transported into the arena of politics all the habits of literature.

A study of the history of the French Revolution will show that it was carried on precisely in that same spirit which has caused so many abstract books to be written on government. There was the same attraction towards general theories, complete systems of legislation, and exact symmetry in the laws – the same contempt of existing facts – the same reliance upon theory – the same love of the original, the ingenious, and the novel in institutions – the same desire to reconstruct, all at once, the entire constitution by the rules of logic, and upon a single plan, rather than to seek to amend it in its parts. The spectacle was an alarming one; for that which is a merit in a writer is often a fault in a statesman: and the same things which have often caused great books to be written, may lead to great revolutions.

4.7.2 *From Gustave Le Bon (1841–1931),* The Psychology of Revolution, *translated by Bernard Miall (London, 1913), pp. 149–51.*

The actual influence of the philosophers in the genesis of the Revolution was not that which was attributed to them. They revealed nothing new, but they developed the critical spirit which no dogma can resist once the way is prepared for its downfall.

Under the influence of this developing critical spirit things which were no longer very greatly respected came to be respected less and less. When tradition and prestige had disappeared the social edifice suddenly fell.

This progressive disaggregation finally descended to the people, but was not commenced by the people. The people follows examples, but never sets them.

The philosophers, who could not have exerted any influence over the people, did exert a great influence over the enlightened portion of the nation. The unemployed nobility, who had long been ousted from their old functions, and who were consequently inclined to be censorious, followed their leadership. Incapable of foresight, the nobles were the first to break with the traditions that were their only raison d'être. As steeped in humanitarianism and rationalism as the *bourgeoisie* of today, they continually sapped their own privileges by their criticism. As today, the most ardent reformers were found among the favourites of fortune. The aristocracy encouraged dissertations on the social contract, the rights of man, and the equality of citizens. At the theatre it applauded plays which criticised privileges, the arbitrariness and the incapacity of men in high places, and abuses of all kinds.

As soon as men lose confidence in the foundations of the mental framework which guides their conduct they feel at first uneasy and then discontented. All classes felt their old motives of action gradually disappearing. Things that had seemed sacred for centuries were now sacred no longer.

The censorious spirit of the nobility and of the writers of the day would not have sufficed to move the heavy load of tradition, but that its action was added to that of other powerful influences. . . . Under the *ancien régime* the religious and civil governments, widely separated in our days, were intimately connected. To injure one was inevitably to injure the other. Now, even before the monarchical idea was shaken the force of religious tradition was greatly diminished among cultivated men. The constant progress of knowledge had sent an increasing number of minds from theology to science by opposing the truth observed to the truth revealed.

This mental evolution, although as yet very vague, was sufficient to show that the traditions which for so many centuries had guided men had not the value which had been attributed to them, and that it would soon be necessary to replace them.

But where discover the new elements which might take the place of tradition? Where seek the magic ring which would raise a new social edifice on the remains of that which no longer contented men?

Men were agreed in attributing to reason the power that tradition and the gods seemed to have lost. How could its force be doubted? Its discoveries having been innumerable, was it not legitimate to suppose that by applying it to the construction of societies it would entirely transform them? Its possible function increased very rapidly in the thoughts of the more enlightened, in proportion as tradition seemed more and more to be distrusted.

The sovereign power attributed to reason must be regarded as the culminating idea which not only engendered the Revolution but governed it throughout. During the whole Revolution men gave themselves up to the most persevering efforts to break with the past, and to erect society upon a new plan dictated by logic.

Slowly filtering downward, the rationalistic theories of the philosophers meant to the people simply that all the things which had been regarded as worthy of respect were now no longer worthy. Men being declared equal, the old masters need no longer be obeyed.

The multitude easily succeeded in ceasing to respect what the upper classes themselves no longer respected. When the barrier of respect was down the Revolution was accomplished.

4.8 THE CHARACTER OF THE REVOLUTIONARY INTELLIGENTSIA: THE CASE OF RUSSIA

From F. F. Seeley, 'The Heyday of the "Superfluous Man" in Russia', Slavonic and East European Review, vol XXXI (1952), pp. 92–6.

See 'Introduction', pp. 59–64.

Although the term 'intelligentsia' has gained international currency, and despite the extreme shortness of its history even in Russian, there is no uniformity in its use and meaning. Russian uses might perhaps be plotted along a scale running from that of the uncultured or, in a broad sense, semi-literate, for whom anyone with a smattering of culture or higher education is an *intelligent*, through the elastic and somewhat nebulous definition of the intelligentsia as the whole of cultured society in so far as it contributes to the development of spiritual values (Ovsyaniko-Kulikovsky), to the rigid conceptualism of Ivanov-Razumnik equating the intelligentsia with the body of critical thinkers in his society. In other words an *intelligent* may be anyone from 'a man of some education' to 'an intellectual', but the first of these meanings is too broad for our purposes and the last too narrow, quite apart from the dubiousness of some of the *differentiae* adduced by Ivanov-Razumnik. Of course the intellectuals will be the core of the intelligentsia, but the intelligentsia may fairly be understood to include many less specialised workers in the fields of thought.

At this point two questions arise. First, is the intelligentsia simply the intellectual *élite* of Russia, i.e. are the differences between the intelligentsia and the intellectual élite of any West European country of the same kind – however different in degree – as the differences between the intellectual élites of any two such countries? If not, secondly, is the intelligentsia a phenomenon peculiar to Russia (as Berdyayev, for instance, contends), or may it not arise – has it not already arisen – elsewhere? Professor A. J. Toynbee has suggested that an essential characteristic of an intelligentsia is that it acts as a channel for the introduction and acclimatisation in its own country of an alien culture; to which I would add: when the intrusive culture is recognised as in some sense superior to the native culture and yet the native culture is not just submerged, but persists as a living force seeking to come to terms with the intrusive culture. No doubt the relative superiority and inferiority of cultures must be a more or less arbitrary notion, but as a rough working criterion I would propose to call one culture superior to another in a given period in so far as it influences that other either without being influenced by it or at any rate to a much greater degree than it is itself influenced.

If these conceptions be accepted, our second question answers itself. For in the last three or four hundred years West European culture has been spreading itself over the globe and impinging on very unequal terms on all the cultures it has met. So one would expect to find intelligentsia arising in India, China, the Islamic countries and elsewhere, and indeed there have arisen groups to which it would seem possible to give that name. But how much of common character and common development is implied in a common name and the common factor of Western influence must be left to future research. (Of course one night expect to find not only important psychological similarities, but differences reflecting the differences in the duration and form of West European domination.)

The soul of the intelligentsia is thus necessarily a house divided against itself. Such a state has some sort of parallel among the intellectuals of a society in course of transition from one form of politico-economic organisation to another (e.g. from feudalism to mercantilism, from mercantilism to industrialism). Then too the intellectuals are torn between the two sets of values – those of the old order and those of the new. But there are two differences which should tend to make the conflict less acute. First, the two sets of values are both national values, and in modern times the cult of country has tended to take precedence over even that of class, so the humiliation should be less; and secondly, the values of a rising class are neither as organically integrated in themselves nor are they recognised to be as absolutely superior by the superseded class as the values of an intrusive culture are and seem to an intelligentsia, and so, instead of an entirely or largely one-way traffic, there is apt to be an interchange, a fusion, a compromise, which partly compensates the defeated for their defeat.

The Russian intelligentsia, however, was in the unhappy position of experiencing both sets of stresses simultaneously, since the impact of European culture became effective in Russia at the very time when the feudal order was beginning to break up. Moreover, the intellectuals, even in a stage of social transition, may often enjoy the indulgence and admiration of large sections both of the declining and of the rising class and even of the authorities. But an intelligentsia is in the nature of things spiritually isolated, since its own people see in it the representatives and embodiment of a foreign culture, while to the bearers of that culture the intelligentsia appears as so many poor relations or spiritual hangers-on – at best amusing and quaint, but often merely pitiful or absurd.

Thus the drama of an intelligentsia lies in its struggles to break out of its isolation, which means to achieve organic reunion with its own people and, by bridging the outer gulf which divides it from them, to heal also the inner rift which festers and aches in its soul. The history of the Russian intelligentsia suggests a division of that drama into three acts – *sc.* where the drama runs its full course and the intelligentsia accomplishes its mission,

The first act is a period of happy growth, extending in Russia over the greater part of the eighteenth century. The intelligentsia accepts unquestioningly the superiority of the alien culture and is largely absorbed in the tasks of assimilating it as fully as possible and of passing it on to as many of its compatriots as are capable of profiting by it. Though sundered from his people in dress and outlook and only tenuously linked to them by the formalities of religious observance and – more important – by the memories of his nursery years presided over by serf *dyad'ki* and *nyan'ki*: at this stage the *intelligent* is less conscious of what he is leaving behind than of the prospects opening before him, of what he has lost than of what he stands to gain, of his isolation than of his mission. This is all the more natural, because his divorce from the people is partly compensated by his collaboration with the authorities, who use him, as an instrument indeed, and with little consideration or respect for his person or his function, but yet on the whole freely enough and confidently enough to afford him scope and satisfaction, a sense of purpose and a sense of achievement.

The second act opens when the *intelligent*'s estrangement from the people is capped by his estrangement from the authorities, so that the circle of his isolation is complete, and he is thrown back on himself (or small groups of his fellows). A breach between the intelligentsia and the government is inevitable, because their association is based on cross-purposes: the government regards the intelligentsia as an instrument for running the state and maintaining the powers and privileges of the rulers, while the intelligentsia sees its vocation as the transplanting and acclimatising of values and as soon as these values cut across the vested interests of the authorities, a rupture is in sight.

But this break faces the intelligentsia with two problems. It must find fresh allies, for to remain in utter isolation is to condemn itself to futility and destruction, and it must re-think its mission. We should, therefore, expect this second act to fall into various phases such as we actually find in the history of the Russian intelligentsia in the nineteenth century: first, the break itself, which is not a sudden catastrophe but a protracted process; then a period, more or less prolonged, of questing uncertainty, of protest and revolt, when the *intelligent* inveighs against the society which has rejected him without actually seeking any fresh alliance and jangles the chains of his frustration without being able to shake them off, and this phase in turn is followed by a series of experiments: in seeking allies, in adopting objectives and in choosing ways towards them.

Finally, the third act of the drama comprises the effective re-integration of the intelligentsia (or, at all events a part of it) within its people: the evolution of the intelligentsia (in our sense) into a vanguard of intellectuals and leaders of the national life.

The struggle of the Russian intelligentsia was particularly painful and bitter for a number of reasons. There was the might and malevolent obscuration of the central government and its machinery. There was the incubus of serfdom which meant that the nobility, from which in our period the intelligentsia was largely drawn, had to contend not only with the estrangement but often enough with the hostility of their people: this or their own principles naturally bred in the more sensitive members of the intelligentsia guilt-feelings – conscious or subconscious – making for emotional disequilibrium. Another handicap was the widespread disintegration of family life. A high proportion of the homes from which the leading *intelligenty* came offered neither the love nor the stability needed for the normal development of happy human beings. Again and again as we glance through the biographies of the intelligentsia we find that the child was illegitimate (Pnin, Zhukovsky, Polezhayev, Herzen), or early lost one or both parents and was brought up by remoter relations or servants (Chaadayev, Lermontov, Tolstoy, Kropotkin), or grew up in a home shadowed by the indifference or unhappy temperament of one or both parents (Pushkin, Belinsky, Turgenev, Dostoyevsky).

There were thus all the factors to produce a fine crop of neuroses: the schism in the soul; the conflict with authority; deep-seated feelings of guilt; insecure and loveless childhoods.

4.9 ARMIES AND REVOLUTION

From C. K. Chorley, Armies and the Art of Revolution *(London, 1943), pp. 241-7.*

The position of the armed forces in a modern state runs parallel to that of the civil service. The armed forces are responsible for the maintenance of law and order and for the defence of the realm. The civil service is responsible for the administration of communal life. Both are at the orders of the duly chosen government of the day and are constitutionally bound to carry out the policy of that government. This position is, however, rather a constitutional conception than a constitutional fact. So far as the armed forces are concerned the theory has been evolved with the evolution of standing armies in order to guard against the perils of irresponsible military force. But in practical political life it is found that the theory is apt to break down in application at times of crisis; it puts too great a strain on political human nature. Armies are not in fact set apart from politics. In smooth political periods, where there are no particular clashes of interest between governors and governed, or between various sections of a community, the army is to all appearance merely a part of the machinery of government and politically innocuous. But in communities where deep fissures of angry opinion develop to separate classes and political parties the soldiers appear in their true colours and take their political stand on whatever side their sentiments may lie.

Broadly speaking, an army reproduces in its own character the structure of society in which it has grown up. Where this is a class structure it means in practice that the main features of army character will square with those of the traditionally strongest classes in the community. The corps of officers will be chosen from those classes and the rank and file will be subjected to a system of discipline and influence designed to make them so much docile material in the hands of their officers. Experience proves that the process of politically sterilising the rank and file can be carried through, given favourable conditions of service, to an astonishing degree of success. The importance attached by a politician like Pitt to keeping the army from civil contacts is significant. As a result, an enormous reservoir of power is in effect placed at the disposal of the officers and can be used by them without let or hindrance to further their own political aims. Experience also proves that the officers have seldom hesitated to use this power when their interests have been seriously threatened. Hence, when they are drawn mainly from one particular class of the community, or from the ranks of one particular political party, their power will effectually be at the beck and call of that class or party.

In a static society this condition of affairs offers no particular danger, but where a society is gradually but steadily changing in character it is a different story. In such a case it may easily happen that the army does not keep pace with the rest of society and that its structure still reflects the social forces of an earlier time. Here the danger from the army is obvious. It may at any time clash with the progressive drive of the community. . . .

In modern times, these dangers are enormously increased owing to the complexity and power of modern weapons of war which put a regular army in an invincible position as against amateur levies. The exclusive or preponderating weight of guns, tanks, and aeroplanes, besides munitions, on one side of the balance is decisive. Hence the more modern and efficient the technical equipment of an army, the more it is to be feared by a government with whose policy it seriously disagrees. It follows then that the position of the army in almost any society is the pivot on which that society swings; and in practice this usually means the position of the corps of officers.

Owing to the immense technical superiority of trained and fully equipped troops, it can be laid down that no revolution will be won against a modern army when that army is putting out its full strength against the insurrection. Practical experience proves this to be the case. No revolution has in fact been won under those conditions. And apparent exceptions to this rule show on investigation special features which mean that the striking power of the army has been in effect seriously curtailed and weakened. In a revolutionary situation the attitude of the army is therefore of supreme importance. It is the decisive factor on which will depend success or failure. The army's attitude will be determined in part by the corps of officers and in part by the rank and file. The evidence suggests that widespread disaffection among officers is generally sufficient in practice to paralyse the striking power of the army. We have the testimony of 1688 and of 1913–14 in this country, and in Spain the witness of 1936, where the disaffected officer corps not only paralysed the army by depriving it of leadership but dragged it over almost intact to its own side. Since most armies, and this has been particularly true of the British, are officered by men drawn from the propertied classes of the community, it is scarcely reasonable to suppose that the officers will in any circumstances be drawn over to support a proletarian revolution. In modern times, disaffection in an officers' corps is likely to have other aims. It may be used to further a Fascist revolt against a democratic government as it has been in Spain; or it may be used to hamstring some particular policy of an advanced government bent on reform of the social system, and which has not had the foresight or perhaps the power to reform its army before attacking the system on whose character that army has been modelled.

Revolutionary leaders of the Left depend upon disaffection in the rank and file if they are to gain the support of the army or paralyse its opposition during a revolution. In practice, the rank and file, whatever may be their apparent class interests and sympathies, are far more politically sluggish than their officers and far less easily moved to mutinous action on their own account. This is due to the care with which a ring fence is built round them in order to cut them off from civilian interests and provide an empty field in which they may be conditioned to accept unquestioningly their officers' influence. Again and again . . . the rank and file have accepted their officers' lead to the extent of breaking an insurrection on whose success their own class interests depended. . . .

History suggests that the only solvent likely to disintegrate the rank and file against the will of their officers is an unsuccessful large-scale war. The army will be ripe for disintegration either immediately after the war or towards its end when it is disillusioned by suffering and defeat. The way is cleared for disintegration by two fundamental changes in the character of the army brought about by wartime conditions. One change regards the rank and file. The enormous wastage of modern war added to the necessary expansion of the armed forces means that the ranks must be filled on a vast scale from the civilian population. And the civilians must be taught soldiering in the shortest possible space of time. Hence there is no opportunity to wean them from their civilian interests and cut them off from their civilian background. The rank and file approximates to the type of a citizen army and the soldiers of citizen armies . . . are not politically emasculated. The terms of their service prevent this; they carry with them into their military life all the political and class affiliations and sympathies of their civilian life.

The second change regards the corps of officers. Here again the wastage and expansion are both enormous. Thus, as the war drags on, it will be found that the officers' corps is manned more and more by men who have little or nothing in common with those sections of the community from which the old officers' corps was drawn and do not share the old professional and social ideals. It will be manned by promotion from the ranks and by a wide recruitment from all classes of the civil population. In practice this means that the old influence of the officers' corps over the rank and file is completely undermined. It is undermined partly because the rank and file are now politically alive on their own account and partly because the officers' corps has lost every characteristic of a military caste. The army, both officers and men, is in fact the nation in arms. It is an army of individuals subject like other individual citizens to every storm of political passion which may sweep over the country. . . .

The object of a revolution is to win it. It follows therefore that the first business of revolutionary leaders will be to assess, before launching the revolution, the probable strength and attitude of the armed forces which will be opposed to them. This assessment will be made, not only in regard to the objective strength and the subjective character of those forces, but also in regard to the special conditions in which the revolution will be fought out. It may happen that the political strength of the opposing forces is in practice sufficiently weakened owing to the circumstances, sometimes geographical, sometimes political, and sometimes both, in which they have to operate. This is particularly true of the American Revolution, where the distance from the base in England and the extreme difficulty of the transport of men and supplies, coupled with the fact that the British Army was on the whole fighting to penetrate a hostile area, contributed in no small measure to the ultimate success of the Colonists. It is also to a large extent true of the Sinn Fein Revolution, where the opposition of a large section of public opinion in England and the fear of awkward repercussions abroad added to the advantages which the Irish derived from conducting guerrilla warfare against the background of a friendly population and in a rural territory, crippled the effective striking power of the British Army and police. These favourable conditions will be more likely to occur in nationalist than in social revolts. In social revolts it is unlikely that the revolutionaries will have the benefit of a homogeneous population behind them. Nor is it likely that they will have the benefit of any compact geographical region to use as an undisturbed base for training their levies and assembling their supplies.

The social revolt presents, therefore, on the whole a more difficult problem than the nationalist revolt. Under certain rather rare conditions, as in France in 1830 and 1848, and in Spain in 1931, social revolt has succeeded without active disintegration of the army. The explanation of this is simple. The government of the *status quo* feels weak and uncertain and prefers to abdicate without provoking a serious armed clash. Charles x, Louis Philippe, and Alphonso xiii never tried out the issue between troops and people. Thus the question of army disintegration did not seriously arise. It was never put to the test whether the common soldier would follow his general or swing back to his natural social place among the revolting populace. But under a strong and courageous government, which is prepared and able to fight out the issue to the bitter end, the disintegration of the armed forces is essential for success. Where armies of the old non-democratic type are in question this disintegration will almost certainly only take place towards the end of or after an unsuccessful war, since it is probable that only unsuccessful war produces a set of conditions sufficiently strong to act as solvents of army unity. Hence, where severe opposition is to be expected, the chances for revolutionary action are most favourable at this period. The apparent exception to this rule, presented by the swing-over of the French Army to the Revolution in 1789, can be explained in terms of special conditions. Outstanding among them was the fact that the officers at first encouraged discontent by their attitude and at no period presented a united active front against the revolution except as émigrés.

In planned insurrections the leaders are in a position to work before the outbreak to increase all conditions favouring disintegration of the army. Practical grievances of the soldiers can be exploited, political propaganda can be carried on, the insurrection can be timed for an advantageous date. Finally, at the moment of outbreak, fraternisation can be attempted.

In spontaneous mass uprisings, which catch revolutionary leaders unawares, or before their plans are matured, less will be effected beforehand. It will then be their business to gain control as rapidly as possible of the instinctive revolutionary movement and direct it to the best advantage. Fraternisation will be the only means open to them of influencing the morale of the troops.

In those armies which have the character described for citizen armies, the influence of the officers' corps over the rank and file is weak. Hence, at the impact of social revolution, the armed forces may be expected to split according to their class and political interests. This conclusion, however, is based on general reasoning from the behaviour of citizen armies. It has never been put to a large-scale practical test, since no serious social revolution has taken place in those countries which maintain exclusively armies of the militia type.

The long-service army with a professional officers' corps is not amenable to influence from the Left in any serious degree, but it does appear markedly amenable to fascist influences coming through Right channels. The reasons for this lie in the character of the officers' corps which makes it in effect the custodian of conservatism and the privileges of property, in the tendency of the officers' corps to support party politics with the sanction of force when their political interests are gravely threatened or their political emotions aroused, and in the ascendancy which the officers' corps gains over the rank and file.

A progressive government which is driving its way along the road of social reconstruction by constitutional means may find itself hamstrung if it maintains an army of this type.

A democracy, struggling against some storm of political disillusion and economic depression which finds a fascist focus, may discover too late that its armed forces are no defence.

5 *Course of Revolution*

5.1 THE GENERAL STAGES OF HISTORICAL 'CRISES'

From Jakob Burckhardt (1818–97), Reflections on History, *translated by M. D. Hottinger (London, 1943), pp. 142–57.*

See 'Introduction', pp. 74–5.

In that extraordinarily complex condition of life in which the State, religion and culture, in extremely derivative forms are intimately associated, and in which most things, as they exist, have forfeited the link with their origin which justified their existence, one of the three will long since have attained an undue expansion of power, and, after the fashion of all earthly things, will abuse it, while the other powers must suffer undue restriction.

According to its nature, however, the suppressed power can either lose or enhance its resilience in the process. Indeed, the national spirit in the finest sense of the word may become aware of itself by having suffered oppression. In the latter case, something breaks out, subverting the public order. Either it is suppressed, whereupon the ruling power, if it is a wise one, will find some remedy, or, unexpectedly to most people, a crisis in the whole state of things is produced, involving whole epochs and all or many peoples of the same civilisation, since invasions, undertaken and suffered, ensue of themselves. The historical process is suddenly accelerated in terrifying fashion. Developments which otherwise take centuries seem to flit by like phantoms in months or weeks, and are fulfilled. . . .

It is not the most wretched, but the energetic spirits which make the real start. It is they who cast an ideal light on the nascent crisis, whether by their oratory or by other personal gifts.

And now the curtain rises on the brilliant farce of hope, this time for vast classes of people on a gigantic scale. Even in the masses, the protest against the past is blended with a radiant vision of the future which frustrates any cool consideration. Sometimes that vision may reveal the imprint of the people which conceived it. Promises of rejuvenation may illuminate it, to deaden the rheumatic twinges of age. . . .

In the Civil War in England, quite particularly, we find nothing of the kind. It has no place in the present discussion because it did not for one moment attack the principles of civic life, never stirred up the supreme powers of the nation, spent its early years as a slow legal process, and by 1644 had passed into the hands of the Parliamentary army and its Napoleon, thus sparing the nation the years 1792–94. Moreover, all true Calvinism and Puritanism is of its very nature too pessimistic to indulge in brilliant visions. Hence the wild preachings of the Independents were powerless to convulse life.

The power of the original vision, on the other hand, is beautifully demonstrated in the *Cahiers* of 1789; its guiding principle was Rousseau's doctrine of the goodness of human nature and the value of feeling as a warrant of virtue. It was the time of flags and festivals, which saw its last brilliant moment in 1790 on the Champ de Mars. It is as though human nature, at such moments, had to give full rein to its power of hope.

We are too prone to take the vision for the specific spirit of a crisis. The vision is merely its wedding finery, which must be laid aside for the bitter workaday life which follows. . . .

The official arenas of crises are the great national assemblies. But they often fall very rapidly into obsolescence, and are incompatible with the presence of a really strong man (as Napoleon emphasised in 1815). The real barometer of power is rather to be sought in clubs and *hetairia*, which can be reconstituted at any moment and are mainly characterised by their frivolity.

In the first stage of the crisis, when old oppressions have to be swept away and their representatives persecuted, we already find the phenomenon which causes so much foolish amazement, namely that the initiators of the movement are ousted and replaced.

Either they had been the agents of very diverse forces, while from now on *one* force stands revealed as the real leader, annihilating the others or carrying them with it; this, for instance, was the case in the Civil War in England, which was set in motion by the Cavaliers but carried through by the Roundheads alone, a proof that the essential impulse was not the defence of the constitution but the Independent movement.

Or else those initiators were carried away by imagination (their own or others'), with their minds in a state of confusion, and thus found themselves at the head of affairs without any right to be there, perhaps by the mere effect of their oratory.

The bright and bellying sail conceives itself to be the cause of the ship's motion, but it only catches the wind, which may change or drop at any moment.

Any man who flags for an instant, or can no longer keep pace with the increasing momentum of the movement, is replaced with astonishing rapidity. In the shortest space of time, a second generation of leaders has found time to mature, and is already representative of the crisis alone, and of its essential, specific spirit. They feel their bond with the former state of things far less strongly than the men who came first. It is at such times that power can least suffer suspension. Whenever a man – or a party – wearies, another is waiting to take his place, and though he may, in his turn, be extremely inadequate to his moment, the whole movement may crystallise round him just for that moment. Men take for granted that every power must ultimately behave rationally, i.e. in the long run recognise and restore to honour the general conditions of existence. Even so-called anarchy is, as quickly as possible, shaped into separate fragments of power, i.e. into representatives of a whole, however crude they may be. Both in the north of France and later in Italy, the Normans began as pirates but soon founded firmly established states. . . .

In its further progress, a great crisis brings into play that 'social' phenomenon which makes the hair of its idealistic originators stand on end, namely distress and greed, due partly to the stoppage of ordinary traffic, partly to the spoils which have become available and partly to impunity.

According to the circumstances, Religion will soon take sides for or against it, or else the principle of the crisis will be a rift through religion, a religious split, so that all its battles also partake of the character of a war of religion.

Indeed, all the rest of the world's life is involved in the ferment, is implicated in the crisis in a thousand ways, friendly or hostile. It would even seem as if the crisis absorbed into itself the whole mobility of an epoch, just as other diseases decline in an epidemic, the movement hastening, slowing down, relapsing and re-starting according to the main impulses operative at the moment. . . .

And now the opposing forces. These include all antecedent institutions which have long since become vested rights, or even law, to whose existence morals and culture have become linked up in all kinds of ways; further, the individuals who incorporate those institutions at the time of the crisis and are chained to them by duty or interest. (For this there are phrases but no remedy.)

Hence the fierceness of these struggles, the unleashing of passion on both sides. Each side defends 'what it holds most sacred' – on the one hand, an abstract loyalty and a religion; on the other, a new 'world order'.

And hence also the indifference as to methods, which may go as far as an exchange of weapons, so that the secret reactionary may play the democrat and the 'man of liberty' turn his hand to every kind of arbitrary violence. . . .

At such times the necessity of reaping success at all costs soon leads to an utter unscrupulousness in methods and a complete oblivion of the principles originally appealed to; thus men bring upon themselves a terrorism which frustrates any really fruitful, forward-looking activity and compromises the whole crisis. In its initial stage, that terrorism is wont to put forward the time-worn plea of threats from outside, while it is actually born of a fury keyed up to the highest pitch against elusive enemies at home, and further, of the necessity of finding an easy method of government and the growing awareness of being in the minority. In its progress, this terrorism comes to be taken for granted, for should it flag, retribution for what has already been committed would immediately descend. . . .

Now and then, however, the aftermath of terrorism falls upon the crisis itself. *La révolution dévore ses enfants.* Every stage of the crisis, moreover, devours the representatives of the preceding stage as 'moderates'.

Now, while the crisis is affecting a number of countries belonging to the same civilization (it is particularly prone to carry small countries along with it), combining there with repressed forces and passion, and producing its own peculiar reflection in the minds of their inhabitants, it may, in the country of its origin, be already weakening and waning. In this process its original tendency may be reversed, i.e. what is called a reaction sets in. The causes of that reaction are the following:

1. The very excesses committed must, by any normal human reckoning, lead to fatigue.

2. The masses, whose irritability is great only at the beginning, either fall away or are overcome by apathy. They may already have conveyed their spoils to safety, or perhaps have never had their hearts in the matter at all. It has merely been blindly assumed that they had. Indeed, the vast majority of the rural population has never been really consulted.

3. Violence having been once unchained, a host of latent forces have been aroused and now take up their stand, suddenly demand their spoils from the chaos and devour the movement without a thought for its quondam ideals. The majority of both the Guelfs and the Ghibellines were so minded.

4. Since the scaffold has already despatched those who were the most obvious representatives of the successive climaxes of the crisis, the most powerful men have already disappeared. The so-called second generation already have a look of epigoni about them.

5. The surviving representatives of the movement have passed through an inward change. Some want to enjoy, some to save their lives if nothing else. . . .

And now wars and militarism have their part to play. Infallibly, wars and armies come into existence. They may be necessary to quell recalcitrant provinces; for instance, Cromwell had to fight the Irish, and the French generals the Fédéralistes and the Vendée. Or they may be used for purposes of offence or defence against other countries, threatened or threatening, as in the case of the resistance of the House of Orange to the Spaniards, and of the French to the Coalitions after 1792. Moreover, the movement itself requires some manifest power if all the currents which have been released are to be conducted into one channel. As a rule, however, what it fears is their effect on its principle. The first symptom of that fear is terrorism directed against its own military leaders. In a certain way we can see this as early as the impeachments of the generals after the battle of Arginusae, and very distinctly in the behaviour of the French in 1793 and 1794.

But the one man who is never caught is the right man, because he is still unknown.

And then, as soon as the crisis has gathered too much momentum and fatigue sets in, the former instruments of power of the antecedent dispensation, namely the police and the army, reorganise themselves spontaneously in their old discipline. Some element, however, a prey to mortal weariness, inevitably falls into the hands of the strongest element that happens to be in the field – and this does not consist of newly elected, moderate assemblies, but of soldiers.

Now come the *coups d'état*. One form is the abolition by military force of political representation regarded as constitutional, and surviving the crisis, while the nation applauds or looks on indifferent. This was ventured by Caesar in 49 BC, by Cromwell in 1653 and by the two Napoleons. At such moments the constitutional aspect of public life is *pro forma* retained and re-constituted, or even expanded; Caesar enlarged the Senate, and Napoleon introduced universal suffrage, which had been restricted by the decree of May 31, 1850.

The spirit of the military, however, will, after some transitional stages, tend towards a monarchy, and a despotic one. It re-forms the State in its own image.

Not every army vanishes as quietly as Cromwell's, which, of course, was only called into being during the Civil War and therefore had no monarchist or militarist institutions to fall back on. It had *not* given the crown even to Cromwell, but had been and remained the army of a republican despotism. And since Monk deceived it, it was not responsible for the Restoration. In the end, in 1661, it melted into private life, not unlike the American Army after the last war. In both cases, of course, the respective nations were by temperament utterly non-militaristic.

When the crisis has affected other nations in such a way that the converse movement (provoked, perhaps, by attempts at imitation) has been established, while in the country of its origin it has also gone into reverse, it comes to an end in purely national wars waged by despot against despot.

Despotism following crises is primarily a restoration of purposeful command and willing obedience, in which the loosened bonds of State are reknotted, and more firmly. It is born not so much of the openly confessed realisation that the people is incapable of government as of the horror men feel of what they have just experienced, namely the rule of anyone ruthless and terrible enough to take the reins into his hands. The abdication men desire is less their own than that of a gang of ruffians. . . .

Then come the restorations. These must be distinguished from those [where] it was a question of the re-establishment of a people or a State, but here it is a question of the re-establishment of a defeated party within the same nation, i.e. of those partial political restorations which are carried out by émigrés returning home after crises.

In themselves, they may be a restoration of justice, or even a closing of the breach in the nation. In practice, they are dangerous in exact proportion to the severity of the crisis.

Thus even in Greece we can see a large number of exiled bodies of citizens returning to their cities. But, since for the most part, they had to share those cities with their new owners, their return was not always a blessing for the cities and themselves.

For while the homecomers are striving to restore some of the relics and principles of the past, they are confronted with the new generation which has grown up since the crisis and has on its side the privilege of youth. And this absolutely new form of life is founded on the destruction of what has gone before, is largely guiltless of that destruction, and hence regards the restitution demanded of it as an infringement of an acquired right. And at the same time it has a transfigured and alluring awareness of how easy revolution was, and in that feeling the memory of suffering fades.

It would be better for émigrés never to return, or at any rate not to return with claims for compensation. It would be better for them to accept their sufferings as their share of the common lot, recognising a law of superannuation which would pronounce judgement not merely according to the lapse of time but also according to the greatness of the breach.

The new generation, who are expected, for their part, to retire within themselves, do nothing of the sort, but scheme for new revolutions to blot out the shame that has been put upon them. And so the spirit of change rises again, and the more often, the more inexorably an institution has triumphed over it, the more inevitable becomes that institution's ultimate overthrow by the secondary and tertiary creations of the crisis. 'Institutions are destroyed by their triumphs' (Renan).

5.2 THE 'IRRESISTIBILITY' OF THE REVOLUTIONARY PROCESS: THE FRENCH REVOLUTION

From The Works of Joseph de Maistre, *selected, translated and introduced by Jack Lively (London, 1965), Pp. 48–50.*

De Maistre (1753–1821), an émigré of the French Revolution, saw the Revolution as a divine punishment for the irreligious and subversive doctrines of the Enlightenment. This allows him to see the course of the Revolution as having a necessary, God-inspired, logic; a view which in different forms commended itself to many social thinkers of the nineteenth century, and which affected the revolutionaries themselves.

For this and the following extract, see 'Introduction, pp. 72–3.

Doubtless, because its primary condition lays it down, there are no means of preventing a revolution, and no success can attend those who wish to impede it. But never is purpose more apparent, never is Providence more palpable, than when divine replaces human action and works alone. That is what we see at this moment.

The most striking aspect of the French Revolution is this overwhelming force which turns aside all obstacles. Its current carries away like a straw everything human power has opposed to it. No one has run counter to it unpunished. Purity of motive has been able to make resistance honourable, but that is all; and this jealous force, moving inexorably to its objective, rejects equally Charette, Dumouriez, and Drouet.

It has been said with good reason that the French Revolution leads men more than men lead it. This observation is completely justified; and, although it can be applied more or less to all great revolutions, yet it has never been more strikingly illustrated than at the present time, The very villians who appear to guide the Revolution take part in it only as simple instruments; and as soon as they aspire to dominate it, they fall ingloriously. Those who established the Republic did so without wishing it and without realising what they were creating; they have been led by events: no plan has achieved its intended end.

Never did Robespierre, Collot, or Barère think of establishing the revolutionary government or the Reign of Terror; they were led imperceptibly by circumstances, and such a sight will never be seen again. Extremely mediocre men are exercising over a culpable nation the most heavy despotism history has seen, and, of everyone in the kingdom, they are certainly the most astonished at their power.

But at the very moment when these tyrants have committed every crime necessary to this phase of the Revolution, a breath of wind topples them. This gigantic power, before which France and Europe trembled, could not stand before the first gust; and because there could be no possible trace of greatness or dignity in such an entirely criminal revolution, Providence decreed that the first blow should be struck by the Septembrists, so that justice itself might be degraded.

It is often astonishing that the most mediocre men have judged the French Revolution better than the most talented, that they have believed in it strongly while skilled men of affairs were still unbelievers. This conviction was one of the foremost elements of the Revolution, which could succeed only because of the extent and vigour of the revolutionary spirit or, if one can so express it, because of the revolutionary *faith*. So untalented and ignorant men have ably driven what they call *the revolutionary chariot*; they have all ventured without fear of counter-revolution; they have always driven on without looking behind them; and everything has fallen into their lap because they were only the instruments of a force more far-sighted than themselves. They have taken no false steps in their revolutionary career, for the same reason that the flutist of Vaucanson never played a false note.

The revolutionary current has taken successively different courses; and the most prominent revolutionary leaders have acquired the kind of power and renown appropriate to them only by following the demands of the moment. Once they attempted to oppose it or even to turn it from its predestined course, by isolating themselves and following their own bent, they disappeared from the scene. . . .

In short, the more one examines the apparently more active personalities of the Revolution, the more one finds something passive and mechanical about them. It cannot be too often repeated that men do not at all guide the Revolution; it is the Revolution that uses men. It is well said that it has its own impetus. This phrase shows that never has the Divinity revealed itself so clearly in any human event. If it employs the most vile instruments, it is to regenerate by punishment.

5.3 THE CONSEQUENCES OF A REVOLUTION BASED ON REASON

From Matthew Arnold (1822–88), 'The Function of Criticism at the Present Time' (1864), in Matthew Arnold's Essays, Literary and Critical (London, 1906), pp. 6–8.

Arnold's comment on the French Revolution is a lucid paraphrase of Hegel's influential analysis.

At first sight it seems strange that out of the immense stir of the French Revolution and its age should not have come a crop of works of genius equal to that which came out of the stir of the great productive time of Greece, or out of that of the Renaissance, with its powerful episode the Reformation. But the truth is that the stir of the French Revolution took a character which essentially distinguished it from such movements as these. These were, in the main, disinterestedly intellectual and spiritual movements; movements in which the human spirit looked for its satisfaction in itself and in the increased play of its own activity: the French Revolution took a political, practical character. This Revolution – the object of so much blind love and so much blind hatred – found indeed its motive-power in the intelligence of men, and not in their practical sense; – this is what distinguishes it from the English Revolution of Charles the First's time; this is what makes it a more spiritual event than our Revolution, an event of much more powerful and world-wide interest, though practically less successful – it appeals to an order of ideas which are universal, certain, permanent. 1789 asked of a thing, Is it rational? 1642 asked of a thing, Is it legal? or, when it went furthest, Is it according to conscience? This is the English fashion, a fashion to be treated, within its own sphere, with the highest respect; for its success, within its own sphere, has been prodigious. But what is law in one place is not law in another; what is law here today is not law even here tomorrow; and as for conscience, what is binding on one man's conscience is not binding on another's, the old woman who threw her stool at the head of the surpliced minister in the Tron Church at Edinburgh obeyed an impulse to which millions of the human race may be permitted to remain strangers. But the prescriptions of reason are absolute, unchanging, of universal validity; *to count by tens is the easiest way of counting*, – that is a proposition of which everyone, from here to the Antipodes, feels the force; at least I should say so if we did not live in a country where it is not impossible that any morning we may find a letter in the *Times* declaring that a decimal coinage is an absurdity. That a whole nation should have been penetrated with an enthusiasm for pure reason, and with an ardent zeal for making its prescriptions triumph, is a very remarkable thing, when we consider how little of mind, or anything so worthy and quickening as mind, comes into the motives which alone, in general *impel* great masses of men. In spite of the extravagant direction given to this enthusiasm, in spite of the crimes and follies in which it lost itself, the French Revolution derives from the force, truth, and universality of the ideas which it took for its law, and from the passion with which it could inspire a multitude for these ideas, a unique and still living power; it is – it will probably long remain – the greatest, the most animating event in history. And as no sincere passion for the things of the mind, even though it turn out in many respects an unfortunate passion, is ever quite thrown away and quite barren of good, France has reaped from hers one fruit, the natural and legitimate fruit, though not precisely the grand fruit she expected; she is the country in Europe where *the people* is most alive.

But the mania for giving an immediate political and practical application to all these fine ideas of the reason was fatal. Here an Englishman is in his element: on this theme we can all go for hours. And all we are in the habit of saying on it has undoubtedly a great deal of truth. Ideas cannot be too much prized in and for themselves, cannot be too much lived with; but to transport them abruptly into the world of politics and practice, violently to revolutionise this world to their bidding – that is quite another thing. There is the world of ideas and there is the world of practice; the French are often for suppressing the one and the English the other; but neither is to be suppressed. A member of the House of Commons said to me the other day: 'That a thing is an anomaly, I consider to be no objection to it whatever.' I venture to think he was wrong; that a thing is an anomaly *is* an objection to it, but absolutely and in the sphere of ideas: it is not necessarily, under such and such circumstances, or at such and such a moment, an objection to it in the sphere of politics and practice. Joubert has said beautifully: *'C'est la force et le droit qui règlent toutes choses dans le monde ; la force en attendant le droit.'* Force and right are the governors of this world; force till right is ready. *Force till right is ready*; and till right is ready, force, the existing order of things, is justified, is the legitimate ruler. But right is something moral, and implies inward recognition, free assent of the will; we are not ready for right – *right*, so far as we are concerned, *is not ready* – until we have attained this sense of seeing it and willing it. The way in which for us it may change and transform force, the existing order of things, and become, in its turn, the legitimate ruler of the world, will depend on the way in which, when our time comes, we see it and will it. Therefore for other people enamoured of their own newly discerned right, to attempt to impose it upon us as ours, and violently to substitute their right for our force, is an act of tyranny, and to be resisted. It sets at nought the second great half of our maxim, *force till right is ready*. This was the grand error of the French Revolution; and its movement of ideas, by quitting the intellectual sphere, and rushing furiously into the political sphere, ran, indeed, a prodigious and memorable course, but produced no such intellectual fruit as the movement of ideas of the Renaissance. . . .

5.4 THE INEVITABLE MARCH TO MILITARY DICTATORSHIP

From Edmund Burke (1728–97), 'Reflections on the Revolution in France, 1790', in The Works of the Right Honourable Edmund Burke, *vol.* IV *(London, 1907), pp. 243, 245–6.*

See 'Introduction', pp. 77–8.

It is known that armies have hitherto yielded a very precarious and uncertain obedience to any senate, or popular authority; and they will least of all yield it to an assembly which is only to have a continuance of two years. The officers must totally lose the characteristic disposition of military men, if they see with perfect submission and due admiration, the dominion of pleaders; especially when they find that they have a new court to pay to an endless succession of those pleaders; whose military policy, and the genius of whose command (if they should have any), must be as uncertain as their duration is transient. In the weakness of one kind of authority, and in the fluctuation of all, the officers of an army will remain for some time mutinous and full of faction, until some popular general, who understands the art of conciliating the soldiery, and who possesses the true spirit of command, shall draw the eyes of all men upon himself. Armies will obey him on his personal account. There is no other way of securing military obedience in this state of things. But the moment in which that event shall happen, the person who really commands the army is your master; the master (that is little) of your king, the master of your assembly, the master of your whole republic. . . .

Everything depends upon the army in such a government as yours; for you have industriously destroyed all the opinions and prejudices, and as far as in you lay, all the instincts which support government. Therefore the moment any difference arises between your National Assembly and any part of the nation, you must have recourse to force. Nothing else is left to you; or rather you have left nothing else to yourselves. You see, by the report of your war minister, that the distribution of the army is in a great measure made with a view of internal coercion. You must rule by an army; and you have infused into that army by which you rule, as well as

233

into the whole body of the nation, principles which after a time must disable you in the use you resolve to make of it. The king is to call out troops to act against his people, when the world has been told, and the assertion is still ringing in our ears, that troops ought not to fire on citizens. The colonies assert to themselves an independent constitution and a free trade. They must be constrained by troops. In what chapter of your code of the rights of men are they able to read that it is a part of the rights of men to have their commerce monopolised and restrained for the benefit of others? As the colonists rise on you, the negroes rise on them. Troops again – massacre, torture, hanging! These are your rights of men! These are the fruits of metaphysic declarations wantonly made, and shamefully retracted! It was but the other day that the farmers of land in one of your provinces refused to pay some sorts of rents to the lord of the soil. In consequence of this, you decree, that the country people shall pay all rents and dues except those which as grievances you have abolished; and if they refuse, then you order the king to march troops against them. You lay down metaphysic propositions which infer universal consequences, and then you attempt to limit logic by despotism. The leaders of the present system tell them of their rights, as men, to take fortresses, to murder guards, to seize on kings, without the least appearance of authority even from the assembly, whilst, as the sovereign legislative body, that assembly was sitting in the name of the nation – and yet these leaders presume to order out the troops which have acted in these very disorders, to coerce those who shall judge on the principles, and follow the examples, which have been guaranteed by their own approbation.

5.5 THE FORCE OF REVOLUTIONARY TRADITION: 1789 AND 1848

From Alexis de Tocqueville, Recollections, *pp. 56–7.*

For this and the following extract, see 'Introduction', pp. 3–4.

In the course of the Revolution of February, I was present at two or three scenes which possessed the elements of grandeur; but this scene lacked them entirely, for the reason that there was nothing genuine in it. We French, especially in Paris, are prone to introduce our literary or theatrical reminiscences into our most serious demonstrations; this often gives rise to the belief that the sentiments we express are not genuine, whereas they are only clumsily adorned. In this case the imitation was so evident that the terrible originality of the facts remained concealed beneath it. It was a time when every imagination was besmeared with the crude colours with which Lamartine had been daubing his *Girondins*. The men of the first Revolution were living in every mind, their deeds and words present to every memory. All that I saw that day bore the visible impress of those recollections; it seemed to me throughout as though they were engaged in acting the French Revolution, rather than continuing it.

Despite the presence of drawn swords, bayonets and muskets, I was unable to persuade myself for a single instant not only that I was in danger of death, but that anybody was, and I honestly believe that no one really was. Bloodthirsty hatreds only showed themselves later: they had not yet had the time to spring up; the special spirit which was to characterise the Revolution of February did not yet manifest itself. Meantime, men were fruitlessly endeavouring to warm themselves at the fire of our fathers' passions, imitating their gestures and attitudes as they had seen them represented on the stage, but unable to imitate their enthusiasm or to be inflamed with their fury. It was the tradition of violent deeds that was being imitated by cold hearts, which understood not the spirit of it. Although I clearly saw that the catastrophe of the piece would be a terrible one, I was never able to take the actors very seriously, and the whole seemed to me like a bad tragedy performed by provincial actors.

5.6 1848: HISTORY REPEATS ITSELF AS FARCE

From Karl Marx, 'The Eighteenth Brumaire of Louis Napoleon'
(1852), in Marx and Engels, Selected Works in Two Volumes,
vol. 1, pp. 247–50.

Hegel remarks somewhere that all facts and personages of great importance in world history occur, as it were, twice. He forgot to add: the first time as tragedy, the second as farce. Causidiere for Danton, Louis Blanc for Robespierre, the *Montagne* of 1848 to 1851 for the *Montagne* of 1793 to 1795, the Nephew for the Uncle. And the same caricature occurs in the circumstances attending the second edition of the eighteenth Brumaire!

Men make their own history, but they do not make it just as they please; they do not make it under circumstances chosen by themselves, but under circumstances directly encountered, given and transmitted from the past. The tradition of all the dead generations weighs like a nightmare on the brain of the living. And just when they seem engaged in revolutionising themselves and things, in creating something that has never yet existed, precisely in such periods of revolutionary crisis they anxiously conjure up the spirits of the past to their service and borrow from them names, battle cries and costumes in order to present the new scene of world history in this time-honoured disguise and this borrowed language. Thus Luther donned the mask of the Apostle Paul, the Revolution of 1789 to 1814 draped itself alternately as the Roman republic and the Roman empire, and the Revolution of 1848 knew nothing better to do than to parody, now 1789, now the revolutionary tradition of 1793 to 1795. In like manner a beginner who has learnt a new language always translates it back into his mother tongue, but he has assimilated the spirit of the new language and can freely express himself in it only when he finds his way in it without recalling the old and forgets his native tongue in the use of the new.

Consideration of this conjuring up of the dead of world history reveals at once a salient difference. Camille Desmoulins, Danton, Robespierre, Saint-Just, Napoleon, the heroes as well as the parties and the masses of the old French Revolution, performed the task of their time in Roman costume and with Roman phrases, the task of unchaining and setting up modern *bourgeois* society. The first ones knocked the feudal basis to pieces and mowed off the feudal heads which had grown on it. The other created inside France the conditions under which alone free competition could be developed, parcelled landed property, exploited and employed the unchained industrial productive power of the nation; and beyond the French borders he everywhere swept the feudal institutions away, so far as was necessary to furnish bourgeois society in France with a suitable up-to-date environment on the European Continent. The new social formation once established, the antediluvian Colossi disappeared and with them resurrected Romanity – the Brutuses, Gracchi, Publicolas, the tribunes, the senators, and Caesar himself. Bourgeois society in its sober reality had begotten its true interpreters and mouthpieces in the Says, Cousins, Royer-Collards, Benjamin Constants and Guizots; its real military leaders sat behind the office desks, and the hogheaded Louis XVIII was its political chief. Wholly absorbed in the production of wealth and in peaceful competitive struggle, it no longer comprehended that ghosts from the days of Rome had watched over its cradle. But unheroic as bourgeois society is, it nevertheless took heroism, sacrifice, terror, civil war and battles of peoples to bring it into being. And in the classically austere traditions of the Roman republic its gladiators found the ideals and the art forms, the self-deceptions that they needed in order to conceal from themselves the bourgeois limitations of the content of their struggles and to keep their enthusiasm on the high plane of the great historical tragedy. Similarly, at another stage of development, a century earlier, Cromwell and the English people had borrowed speech, passions and illusions fron the Old Testament for their bourgeois revolution. When the real aim had been achieved, when the bourgeois transformation of English society had been accomplished, Locke supplanted Habakkuk.

Thus the awakening of the dead in those revolutions served the purpose of glorifying the new struggles, not of parodying the old: of magnifying the given task in imagination, not of fleeing from its solution in reality; of finding once more the spirit of revolution, not of making its ghost walk about again.

From 1848 to 1851 only the ghost of the old revolution walked about, from Marrast, the *républicain en gants jaunes*, who disguised himself as the old Bailly, down to the adventurer, who hides his commonplace repulsive features under the iron death mask of Napoleon. An entire people, which had imagined that by means of a revolution it had imparted to itself an accelerated power of motion, suddenly finds itself set back into a defunct epoch and, in order that no doubt as to the relapse may be possible, the old dates arise again, the old chronology, the old names, the old edicts, which had long become a subject of antiquarian erudition, and the old minions of the law, who had seemed long decayed. .... The French, so long as they were engaged in revolution, could not get rid of the memory of Napoleon, as the election of December 10 proved. They hankered to return from the perils of revolution to the flesh-pots of Egypt, and December 2, 1851 was the answer. They have not only a caricature of the old Napoleon, they have the old Napoleon himself, caricatured as he must appear in the middle of the nineteenth century.

The social revolution of the nineteenth century cannot draw its poetry from the past, but only from the future. It cannot begin with itself before it has stripped off all superstition in regard to the past. Earlier revolutions required recollections of past world history in order to drug themselves concerning their own content. In order to arrive at its own content, the revolution of the nineteenth century must let the dead bury their dead. There the phrase went beyond the content; here the content goes beyond the phrase.

5.7 A NEW REVOLUTIONARY FORCE REVEALED: THE COURSE OF THE FEBRUARY REVOLUTION OF 1848

From Karl Marx, 'The Eighteenth Brumaire of Louis Napoleon', Selected Works, vol. 1, pp. 252–5, 268–9.

See 'Introduction', pp. 73–4. This and the following two extracts show various responses to the bloody events of the 'June Days' in the February Revolution. The most serious thinkers were impressed by the fact that a new revolutionary force, the working class, had been summoned up as a natural consequence of the working out of the principles of the French Revolution of 1789.

Let us recapitulate in general outline the phases that the French Revolution went through from February 24, 1848, to December 1851.

Three main periods are unmistakable: *the February period*; May 4, 1848, to May 28, 1849: *the period of the constitution of the the republic*, or *of the Constituent National Assembly*; May 28, 1849, to December 2, 1851: *the period of the constitutional republic* or *of the Legislative National Assembly*.

The *first period*, from February 24, or the overthrow of Louis Philippe, to May 4, 1848, the meeting of the Constituent Assembly, the *February period* proper, may be described as the *prologue* to the revolution. Its character was officially expressed in the fact that the government improvised by it itself declared that it was *provisional* and, like the government, everything that was mooted, attempted or enunciated during this period proclaimed itself to be only *provisional*. Nothing and nobody ventured to lay claim to the right of existence and of real action. All the elements that had prepared or determined the revolution, the dynastic opposition, the republican bourgeoisie, the democratic-republican petty bourgeoisie and the social-democratic workers, provisionally found their place in the February *government*.

It could not be otherwise. The February days originally intended an electoral reform, by which the circle of the politically privileged among the possessing class itself was to be widened and the exclusive domination of the aristocracy of finance overthrown. When it came to the actual conflict, however, when the people mounted the barricades, the National Guard maintained a passive attitude, the army offered no serious resistance and the monarchy ran away, the republic appeared to be a matter of course. Every party construed it in its own way. Having secured it arms in hand, the proletariat impressed its stamp upon it and proclaimed it to be a *social republic*. There was thus indicated the general content of the modern revolution, a content which was in most singular contradiction to everything that, with the material available, with the degree of education attained by the masses, under the given circumstances and relations, could be immediately realised in practice. On the other hand, the claims of all the remaining elements that had collaborated in the February Revolution were recognised by the lion's share that they obtained in the government. In no period do we, therefore, find a more confused mixture of high-flown phrases and actual uncertainty and clumsiness, of more enthusiastic striving for innovation and more deeply-rooted domination of the old routine, of more apparent harmony of the whole of society and more profound estrangement of its elements. While the Paris proletariat still revelled in the vision of the wide prospects that had opened before it and indulged in seriously-meant discussions on social problems, the old powers of society had grouped themselves, assembled, reflected and found unexpected support in the mass of the nation, the peasants and petty bourgeois, who all at once stormed on to the political stage, after the barriers of the July monarchy had fallen.

The *second period*, from May 4, 1848, to the end of May 1849, is the period of the *constitution*, the *foundation, of the bourgeois republic*. Directly after the February days not only had the dynastic opposition been surprised by the republicans and the republicans by the Socialists, but all France by Paris. The National Assembly, which met on May 4, 1848, had emerged from the national elections and represented the nation. It was a living protest against the pretensions of the February days and was to reduce the results of the revolution to the bourgeois scale. In vain the Paris proletariat, which immediately grasped the character of this National Assembly, attempted on May 15, a few days after it met, forcibly to negate its existence, to dissolve it, to disintegrate again into its constituent parts the organic form in which the proletariat was threatened by the reacting spirit of the nation. As is known, May 15 had no other result save that of removing Blanqui and his comrades, that is, the real leaders of the proletarian party, from the public stage for the entire duration of the cycle we are considering.

The *bourgeois monarchy* of Louis Philippe can be followed only by a *bourgeois republic*; that is to say, whereas a limited section of the bourgeoisie ruled in the name of the king, the whole of the bourgeoisie will now rule on behalf of the people. The demands of the Paris proletariat are utopian nonsense, to which an end must be put. To this declaration of the Constituent National Assembly the Paris proletariat replied with the *June Insurrection*, the most colossal event in the history of European civil wars. The bourgeois republic triumphed. On its side stood the aristocracy of finance, the industrial bourgeoisie, the middle class, the petty bourgeois, the army, the *lumpenproletariat* organised as the Mobile Guard, the intellectual lights, the clergy and the rural population. On the side of the Paris proletariat stood none but itself. More than three thousands insurgents were butchered after the victory, and fifteen thousand were transported without trial. With this defeat the proletariat passes into the *background* of the revolutionary stage. It attempts to press forward again on every occasion, as soon as the movement appears to make a fresh start, but with ever decreased expenditure of strength and always slighter results. As soon as one of the social strata situated above it gets into revolutionary ferment, the proletariat enters into an alliance with it and so shares all the defeats that the different parties suffer, one after another. But these subsequent blows become the weaker, the greater the surface of society over which they are distributed. The more important leaders of the proletariat in the Assembly and in the press successively fall victims to the courts, and ever more equivocal figures come to head it. In part it throws itself into doctrinaire experiments, exchange banks and workers associations, hence into a movement in which it renounces the revolutionising of the old world by means of the latter's own great, combined resources, and seeks, rather, to achieve its salvation behind society's back, in private fashion, within its limited conditions of existence, and hence necessarily suffers shipwreck. It seems to be unable either to rediscover revolutionary greatness in itself or to win new energy from the connections newly entered into, until *all classes* with which it contended in June themselves lie prostrate beside it. But at least it succumbs with the honours of the great, world-historic struggle; not only in France, but all Europe trembles at the June earthquake, while the ensuing defeats of the upper classes are so cheaply bought that they require bare-faced exaggeration by the victorious party to be able to pass for events at all, and become the more ignominious the further the defeated party is removed from the proletarian party.

The defeat of the June insurgents, to be sure, had now prepared, had levelled the ground on which the bourgeois republic could be founded and built up, but it had shown at the same time that in Europe the questions at issue are other than that of 'republic or monarchy'. It had revealed that here *bourgeois republic* signifies the unlimited despotism of one class over other classes. It had proved that in countries with an old civilisation, with a developed formation of classes, with modern conditions of production and with an intellectual consciousness in which all traditional ideas have been dissolved by the work of centuries, *the republic* signifies *in general only the political form of revolution of bourgeois society*. . . .

On May 28, 1849, the Legislative National Assembly met. On December 2, 1851, it was dispersed. This period covers the span of life of the *constitutional*, or *parliamentary*, *republic*.

In the first French Revolution the rule of the *Constitutionalists* is followed by the rule of the *Girondins* and the rule of the *Girondins* by the rule of the *Jacobins*. Each of these parties relies on the more progressive party for support. As soon as it has brought the revolution far enough to be unable to follow it further, still less to go ahead of it, it is thrust aside by the bolder ally that stands behind it and sent to the guillotine. The revolution thus moves along an ascending line.

It is the reverse with the Revolution of 1848. The proletarian party appears as an appendage of the petty-bourgeois-democratic party. It is betrayed and dropped by the latter on April 16, May 15, and in the June days. The democratic party, in its turn, leans on the shoulders of the bourgeois-republican party. The bourgeois-republicans no sooner believe themselves well established than they shake off the troublesome comrade and support themselves on the shoulders of the party of Order. The party of Order hunches its shoulders, lets the bourgeois-republicans tumble and throws itself on the shoulders of armed force. It fancies it is still sitting on its shoulders when, one fine morning, it perceives that the shoulders have transformed themselves into bayonets. Each party kicks back at the one behind, which presses upon it, and leans against the one in front, which pushes backwards. No wonder that in this ridiculous posture it loses its balance and, having made the inevitable grimaces, collapses with curious capers. The revolution thus moves in a descending line. It finds itself in this state of retrogressive motion before the last February barricade has been cleared away and the first revolutionary authority constituted.

5.8 THE SECRET OF 1848: SOCIALISM

From Alexis de Tocqueville, Recollections, *pp. 78–9, 81–5.*

Although the working classes had often played the leading part in the events of the First Revolution, they had never been the sole leaders and masters of the State, either *de facto* or *de jure*; it is doubtful whether the Convention contained a single man of the people; it was composed of *bourgeois* and men of letters. The war between the Mountain and the Girondists was conducted on both sides by members of the middle class, and the triumph of the former never brought power down into the hands of the people alone. The Revolution of July was effected by the people, but the middle class had stirred it up and led it, and secured the principal fruits of it. The Revolution of February, on the contrary, seemed to be made entirely outside the *bourgeoisie* and against it.

In this great concussion, the two parties of which the social body in France is mainly composed had, in a way, been thrown more completely asunder, and the mass of the people, which had stood alone, remained in sole possession of power. Nothing more novel had been known in our annals. Similar revolutions had taken place, it is true, in other countries and other days; for the history of our own times, however new and unexpected it may seem, always belongs at bottom to the old history of humanity, and what we call new facts are oftenest nothing more than facts forgotten. Florence, in particular, towards the close of the Middle Ages, had presented on a small scale a spectacle analogous to ours; the noble classes had first been succeeded by the burgher classes, and then one day the latter were, in their turn, expelled from the government, and a *gonfalonier* was seen marching barefoot at the head of the people, and thus leading the Republic. But in Florence this popular revolution was the result of transient and special causes, while with us it was brought about by causes very permanent and of a kind so general that, after stirring up France, it was to be expected that it would excite all the rest of Europe. This time it was not only a question of the triumph of a party; the aim was to establish a social science, a philosophy, I might almost say a religion, fit to be

I

243

learned and followed by all mankind. This was the really new portion of the old picture. . . .

For the first time in sixty years, the priests, the old aristocracy and the people met in a common sentiment – a feeling of revenge, it is true, and not of affection; but even that is a great thing in politics, where a community of hatred is almost always the foundation of friendships. The real, the only vanquished were the middle class; but even this had little to fear. Its reign had been exclusive rather than oppressive: corrupt, but not violent; it was despised rather than hated. Moreover, the middle class never forms a compact body in the heart of the nation, a part very distinct from the whole; it always participates a little with all the others, and in some places merges into them. This absence of homogeneity and of exact limits makes the government of the middle class weak and uncertain, but it also makes it intangible, and, as it were, invisible to those who desire to strike it when it is no longer governing.

From all these united causes proceeded that languor of the people which had struck me as much as its omnipotence, a languor which was the more discernible, in that it contrasted strangely with the turgid energy of the language used and the terrible recollections which it evoked. The truth is that never was a greater change in the government, and even in the very condition of a nation, brought about by citizens who were themselves so little moved. The *History of the Revolution* by M. Thiers, *The Girondins* by M. Lamartine, as well as other works, particularly plays, which are less well known, had rehabilitated the period of the Terror and brought it to some extent into fashion. The luke-warm passions of the time were made to speak in the bombastic periods of '93, and one heard cited at every moment the name and example of the illustrious ruffians whom no one possessed either the energy or even a sincere desire to resemble.

It was the Socialistic theories which I have already described as the philosophy of the Revolution of February that later kindled genuine passion, embittered jealousy, and ended by stirring up war between the classes. If the actions at the commencement were less disorderly than might have been feared, on the very morrow of the Revolution there was displayed an extraordinary agitation, an unequalled disorder, in the ideas of the people.

From the 25th of February onwards, a thousand strange systems came issuing pell-mell from the minds of innovators, and spread among the troubled minds of the crowd. Everything still remained standing except Royalty and Parliament; yet it seemed as though the shock of the Revolution had reduced society itself to dust, and as though a competition had been opened for the form that was to be given to the edifice about to be erected in its place. Everyone came forward with a plan of his own: this one printed it in the papers, that other on the placards with which the walls were soon covered, a third proclaimed his loud-mouthed in the open air. One aimed at destroying inequality of fortune, another inequality of education, a third undertook to do away with the oldest of all inequalities, that between man and woman. Specifics were offered against poverty, and remedies for the disease of work which has tortured humanity since the first days of its existence.

These theories were of very varied natures, often opposed and sometimes hostile to one another; but all of them, aiming lower than the government and striving to reach society itself, on which government rests, adopted the common name of Socialism.

Socialism will always remain the essential characteristic and most redoubtable remembrance of the Revolution of February. The Republic will only appear to the onlooker to have come upon the scene as a means, not as an end.

It does not come within the scope of these Recollections that I should seek for the causes which gave a socialistic character to the Revolution of February, and I will content myself with saying that the discovery of this new facet of the French Revolution was not of a nature to cause so great surprise as it did. Had it not long been perceived that the people had continually been improving and raising its condition, that its importance, its education, its desires, its power had been constantly increasing? Its prosperity had also grown greater, but less rapidly, and was approaching the limit which it hardly ever passes in old societies, where there are many men and but few places. How should the poor and humbler and yet powerful classes not have dreamt of issuing from their poverty and inferiority by means of their power, especially in an epoch when our view into another world has become dimmer, and the miseries of this world become more visible and seem more intolerable? They had been working to this end for the last sixty years. The people had first endeavoured to help itself by changing every

245

political institution, but after each change it found that its lot was in no way improved, or was only improving with a slowness quite incompatible with the eagerness of its desire. Inevitably, it must sooner or later discover that that which held it fixed in its position was not the constitution of the government but the unalterable laws that constitute society itself; and it was natural that it should be brought to ask itself if it had not both the power and the right to alter those laws, as it had altered all the rest. And to speak more specially of property, which is, as it were, the foundation of our social order – all the privileges which covered it and which, so to speak, concealed the privilege of property having been destroyed, and the latter remaining the principal obstacle to equality among men, and appearing to be the only sign of inequality – was it not necessary, I will not say that it should be abolished in its turn, but at least that the thought of abolishing it should occur to the minds of those who did not enjoy it?

This natural restlessness in the minds of the people, this inevitable perturbation of its thoughts and its desires, these needs, these instincts of the crowd formed in a certain sense the fabric upon which the political innovators embroidered so many monstrous and grotesque figures. Their work may be regarded as ludicrous, but the material on which they worked is the most serious that it is possible for philosophers and statesmen to contemplate.

5.9 THE 'JUNE DAYS' AND THE END OF LIBERALISM

From Alexander Herzen, From the Other Shore *(1855), translated from the Russian by Moura Budberg (London, 1956), pp. 59–61.*

For a long time the liberals played happily with the idea of revolution, and the end of their play was February 24th. The popular hurricane swept them up to the top of a high steeple from which they could see where they were going and where they were leading others. Glancing down at the abyss that opened before their eyes, they grew pale. They saw that what was crumbling was not only what they had considered prejudice, but also everything else – what they had considered true and eternal. They were so terrified that some clutched at the falling walls, while others stopped half-way, repentant, and began to swear to all passers-by that this was not at all what they had wanted. This is why the men who proclaimed the republic became the assassins of freedom; this is why the liberal names that had resounded in our ears for a score of years or so, are today those of reactionary deputies, traitors, inquisitors. They want freedom and even a republic provided that it is confined to their own cultivated circle. Beyond the limits of their moderate circle they become conservatives. In the same way, rationalists were fond of explaining the mysteries of religion, they liked to reveal the meaning and essence of myths, they gave not a thought to where this would lead, nor did they suppose that their investigations, beginning with the fear of God, would end in atheism, that their criticism of church ritual would end in the denial of religion.

Since the Restoration liberals in all countries have called the people to the destruction of the monarchic and feudal order, in the name of equality, of the tears of the unfortunate, of the suffering of the oppressed, of the hunger of the poor. They have enjoyed hounding down various ministers with a series of impossible demands; they rejoiced when one feudal prop collapsed after another, and in the end became so excited that they outstripped their own desires. They came to their senses when, from behind the half-demolished walls, there emerged the proletarian, the worker with his axe and his blackened hands, hungry and half-naked in rags – not as he appears in books or in parliamentary chatter or in philanthropic verbiage, but in reality. This 'unfortunate brother' about whom so much has been said, on whom so much pity has been lavished, finally asked what was to be his share in all these blessings, where were *his* freedom, *his* equality, *his* fraternity? The liberals were aghast at the impudence and ingratitude of the worker. They took the streets of Paris by assault, they littered them with corpses, and then they hid from their *brother* behind the bayonets of martial law in their effort to save *civilisation and order*!

They are right, but they are inconsistent. For in that case, why did they ever try to undermine the monarchy? How did they not see that in abolishing the monarchic principle the revolution could not stop at merely flinging out some dynasty or other? They were as happy as children because Louis-Philippe hadn't had time to reach St Cloud before there was a new government installed in the Hôtel de Ville and everything appeared to be taking its normal course – although the very smoothness of the upheaval should have opened their eyes to its unreality. The liberals were satisfied. But the people were not; and now they raised their voices, they echoed the words and promises of the liberals; but the liberals, like Peter, thrice denied their words and their promises, once they saw that things had taken a serious turn, and began the killing. In the same way Luther and Calvin drowned the anabaptists, the protestants repudiated Hegel, and the Hegelians Feuerbach. This is the position of *reformers* in general: all they do is to lay down the pontoons across which the peoples whom they have roused cross from one shore to the other. They like nothing better than the dreary, constitutional atmosphere of neither one being nor another. And it is in this world of logomachy, discord, irreconcilable contradictions, that these futile men wished, without changing it, to achieve their *pia desideria* of liberty, equality and fraternity.

5.10 PROFESSIONAL REVOLUTIONARIES AND REVOLUTIONARY EXILES

From Alexander Herzen (1812–70), My Past and Thoughts, 4 vols., translated by Constance Garnett (revised edn., London 1968), vol. II, pp. 673–4, vol. III, pp. 1045–6.

Herzen was a Russian nobleman who exiled himself from his native land. He witnessed the European Revolutions of 1848 at first hand, before settling in London, where he became acquainted with many of the continental exiles. In the following two passages he sketches the class of professional revolutionaries thrown up by the European revolutions, whom he sees as the heirs of a now bankrupt tradition.

(i)

In the café various *habitués* of the revolution were sitting with dignity at a dozen little tables, looking darkly and consequentially about them from under wide-brimmed felt hats and caps with tiny peaks. These were the perpetual suitors of the revolutionary Penelope, those inescapable actors who take part in every popular demonstration and form its *tableau*, its background, and who are as menacing from afar as the paper dragons with which the Chinese wished to intimidate the English.

In the troubled times of social storms and reconstructions in which states forsake their usual grooves for a long time, a new generation of people grows up who may be called the choristers of the revolution; grown on shifting, volcanic soil, nurtured in an atmosphere of alarm when work of every kind is suspended, they become inured from their earliest years to an environment of political ferment, and like the theatrical side of it, its brilliant, pompous *mise en scène*. Just as to Nicholas marching drill was the most important part of the soldier's business, to them all those banquets, demonstrations, protests, gatherings, toasts, banners, are the most important part of the revolution.

Among them there are good, valiant people, sincerely devoted and ready to face a bullet; but for the most part they are very limited and extraordinarily pedantic. Immobile conservatives in everything revolutionary, they stop short at some programme and do not advance.

Dealing all their lives with a small number of political ideas, they only know their rhetorical side, so to speak, their sacerdotal vestments, that is the commonplaces which successively cut the same figure, *à tour de rôle*, like the ducks in the well-known children's toy – in newspaper articles, in speeches at banquets and in parliamentary devices.

In addition to naïve people and revolutionary doctrinaires, the unappreciated artists, unsuccessful literary men, students who did not complete their studies, brief-less lawyers, actors without talent, persons of great vanity but small capability, with huge pretensions but no perseverance or power of work, all naturally drift into this *milieu*. The external authority which guides and pastures the human herd in a lump in ordinary times is weakened in times of revolution; left to themselves people do not know what to do. The younger generation is struck by the ease, the apparent ease, with which celebrities float to the top in times of revolution, and rushes into futile agitation; this inures the young people to violent excitements and destroys the habit of work. Life in the clubs and cafés is attractive, full of movement, flattering to vanity and free from restraint. One must not be left behind, there is no need to work:

what is not done today may be done tomorrow, or may even not be done at all.

(ii)

If one had conceived the idea of writing from the outside the inner history of the political *émigrés* and exiles from the year 1848 in London, what a melancholy page he would have added to the records of contemporary man. What sufferings, what privations, what tears . . . and what triviality, what narrowness, what poverty of intellectual powers, of resources, of understanding, what obstinacy in wrangling, what pettiness of wounded vanity! . . .

On one hand those simple-hearted men, who by heart and instinct have understood the business of revolution and have made for its sake the greatest sacrifice a man can make, that of voluntary beggary, form the small group of the blessed. On the other hand there are men, actuated by secret, ill-concealed ambition, for whom the revolution meant office, *position sociale*, and who scuttled into exile when they failed to attain a position. Then there were all kinds of fanatics, monomaniacs with every sort of monomania, madmen with every variety of madness. It was due to this nervous, strained irritable condition that table-turning numbered so many victims among the exiles. Almost every one was turning tables, from Victor Hugo and Ledru-Rollin to Quirico Filopanti who went farther still and found out everything that a man was doing a thousand years ago.

And with all that not a step forward. They are like the court clock at Versailles, which pointed to one hour, the hour at which the King died . . . And, like the clock, it has been forgotten to move them on from the time of the death of Louis xv. They point to one event, the extinction of some event. They talk about it, they think about it, they go back to it. Meeting the same men, the same groups, in five or six months, in two or three years, one becomes frightened: the same arguments are still going on, the same personalities and recriminations: only the furrows drawn by poverty and privation are deeper; jackets and overcoats are shabbier; there are more grey hairs, and they are all older together and bonier and more gloomy . . . and still the same things are being said over and over again.

The revolution with them has remained the philosophy of social order, as it was in the 'nineties, but they have not and cannot have the naïve passion for the struggle which in those days gave vivid colouring to the most meagre generalisations and body to the dry outlines of their political framework; generalisations and abstract concepts were a joyful novelty, a revelation in those days. At the end of the eighteenth century men for the first time – not in books but in actual fact – began to free themselves from the fatal, mysteriously oppressive world of theological tradition, and were trying to base on conscious understanding the whole political system which had grown apart from will or consciousness. In the attempt at a rational state, as in the attempt to found a religion of reason, there was in 1793 a mighty titanic poetry, which bore its fruits, but for all that, has withered and weakened in the last sixty years. Our heirs of the Titans do not notice this. They are like the monks of Mount Athos, who busy themselves about their own affairs, deliver the same speeches which were delivered in the time of Chrysostom and keep up a manner of life blocked long ago by the Turkish sovereignty, which now is drawing towards an end itself ... and they go on meeting together on certain days to commemorate certain events with the same ritual, the same prayers.

5.11 COURSE OF THE RUSSIAN REVOLUTION, 1917

From Rosa Luxemburg, The Russian Revolution *(Ann Arbor paperback edn., 1961), pp. 30–3, 35–8. Written in 1918.*

The first period of the Russian Revolution, from its beginning in March to the October Revolution, corresponds exactly in its general outlines to the course of development of both the Great English Revolution and the Great French Revolution. It is the typical course of every first general reckoning of the revolutionary forces begotten within the womb of bourgeois society.

Its development moves naturally in an ascending line: from moderate beginnings to an ever-greater radicalisation of aims and, parallel with that, from a coalition of classes and parties to the sole rule of the radical party.

At the outset in March 1917, the 'Cadets', that is the liberal bourgeoisie, stood at the head of the revolution. The first general rising of the revolutionary tide swept everyone and everything along with it. The Fourth Duma, ultra-reactionary product of the ultra-reactionary four-class right of suffrage and arising out of the *coup d'état*, was suddenly converted into an organ of the revolution. All bourgeois parties, even those of the nationalistic right, suddenly formed a phalanx against absolutism. The latter fell at the first attack almost without a struggle, like an organ that had died and needed only to be touched to drop off. The brief effort, too, of the liberal bourgeoisie to save at least the throne and the dynasty collapsed within a few hours. The sweeping march of events leaped in days and hours over distances that formerly, in France, took decades to traverse. In this, it became clear that Russia was realising the result of a century of European development, and above all, that the revolution of 1917 was a direct continuation of that of 1905–07, and not a gift of the German 'liberator'. The movement of March 1917 linked itself directly on to the point where, ten years earlier, its work had broken off. The democratic republic was the complete, internally ripened product of the very first onset of the revolution.

Now, however, began the second and more difficult task. From the very first moment, the driving force of the revolution was the mass of the urban proletariat. However, its demands did not limit themselves to the realisation of political democracy but were concerned with the burning question of international policy – immediate peace. At the same time, the revolution embraced the mass of the army, which raised the same demand for immediate peace, and the mass of the peasants, who pushed the agrarian question into the foreground, that agrarian question which since 1905 had been the very axis of the revolution. Immediate peace and land – from these two aims the internal split in the revolutionary phalanx followed inevitably. The demand for immediate peace was in most irreconcilable opposition to the imperialist tendencies of the liberal bourgeoisie for whom Milyukov was the spokesman. On the other hand, the land question was a terrifying spectre for the other wing of the bourgeoisie, the rural landowners. And, in addition, it represented an attack on the sacred principle of private property in general, a touchy point for the entire propertied class.

Thus, on the very day after the first victories of the revolution, there began an inner struggle within it over the two burning questions – peace and land. The liberal bourgeoisie entered upon the tactics of dragging out things and evading them. The labouring masses, the army, the peasantry, pressed forward ever more impetuously. There can be no doubt that with the questions of peace and land, the fate of the political democracy of the republic was linked up. The bourgeois classes, carried away by the first stormy wave of the revolution, had permitted themselves to be dragged along to the point of republican government. Now they began to seek a base of support in the rear and silently to organise a counter-revolution. The Kaledin Cossack campaign against Petersburg was a clear expression of this tendency. Had the attack been successful, then not only the fate of the peace and land questions would have been sealed, but the fate of the republic as well. Military dictatorship, a reign of terror against the proletariat, and then return to monarchy, would have been the inevitable results. . . .

The party of Lenin was the only one in Russia which grasped the true interest of the revolution in that first period. It was the element that drove the revolution forward, and, thus it was the only party which really carried on a socialist policy.

It is this which makes clear, too, why it was that the Bolsheviks, though they were at the beginning of the revolution a persecuted, slandered and hunted minority attacked on all sides, arrived within the shortest time to the head of the revolution and were able to bring under their banner all the genuine masses of the people: the urban proletariat, the army, the peasants, as well as the revolutionary elements of democracy, the left wing of the Socialist-Revolutionaries.

The real situation in which the Russian Revolution found itself, narrowed down in a few months to the alternative: victory of the counter-revolution or dictatorship of the proletariat – Kaledin or Lenin. Such was the objective situation, just as it quickly presents itself in every revolution after the first intoxication is over, and as it presented itself in Russia as a result of the concrete, burning questions of peace and land, for which there was no solution within the framework of bourgeois revolution.

In this, the Russian Revolution has but confirmed the basic lesson of every great revolution, the law of its being, which decrees: either the revolution must advance at a rapid, stormy and resolute tempo, break down all barriers with an iron hand and place its goals ever farther ahead, or it is quite soon thrown backward behind its feeble point of departure and suppressed by counter-revolution. To stand still, to mark time on one spot, to be contented with the first goal it happens to reach, is never possible in revolution. And he who tries to apply the home-made wisdom derived from parliamentary battles between frogs and mice to the field of revolutionary tactics only shows thereby that the very psychology and laws of existence of revolution are alien to him and that all historical experience is to him a book sealed with seven seals.

Take the course of the English Revolution from its onset in 1642. There the logic of things made it necessary that the first feeble vacillations of the Presbyterians, whose leaders deliberately evaded a decisive battle with Charles I and victory over him, should inevitably be replaced by the Independents, who drove them out of Parliament and seized the power for themselves. And in the same way, within the army of the Independents, the lower petty-bourgeois mass of the soldiers, the Lilburnian 'Levellers' constituted the driving force of the entire Independent movement; just as, finally, the proletarian elements within the mass of the soldiers, the elements that went farthest in their aspirations for social revolution and who found their expression in the Digger movement, constituted in their turn the leaven of the democratic party of the 'Levellers'.

Without the moral influence of the revolutionary proletarian elements on the general mass of the soldiers, without the pressure of the democratic mass of the soldiers upon the bourgeois upper layers of the party of the Independents, there would have been no 'purge' of the Long Parliament of its Presbyterians, nor any victorious ending to the war with the army of the Cavaliers and Scots, nor any trial and execution of Charles I, nor any abolition of the House of Lords and proclamation of a republic.

And what happened in the Great French Revolution? Here, after four years of struggle, the seizure of power by the Jacobins proved to be the only means of saving the conquests of the revolution, of achieving a republic, of smashing feudalism, of organising a revolutionary defence against inner as well as outer foes, of suppressing the conspiracies of counter-revolution and spreading the revolutionary wave from France to all Europe.

254

Kautsky and his Russian co-religionists who wanted to see the Russian Revolution keep the 'bourgeois character' of its first phase, are an exact counterpart of those German and English liberals of the preceding century who distinguished between the two well-known periods of the Great French Revolution: the 'good' revolution of the first Girondin phase and the 'bad' one after the Jacobin uprising. The Liberal shallowness of this conception of history, to be sure, doesn't care to understand that, without the uprising of the 'immoderate' Jacobins, even the first, timid and half-hearted achievements of the Girondin phase would soon have been buried under the ruins of the revolution, and that the real alternative to Jacobin dictatorship – as the iron course of historical development posed the question in 1793 – was not 'moderate' democracy, but . . . restoration of the Bourbons! The 'golden mean' cannot be maintained in any revolution. The law of its nature demands a quick decision: either the locomotive drives forward full steam ahead to the most extreme point of the historical ascent, or it rolls back of its own weight again to the starting point at the bottom; and those who would keep it with their weak powers half-way up the hill, it but drags down with it irredeemably into the abyss.

Thus it is clear that in every revolution only that party is capable of seizing the leadership and power which has the courage to issue the appropriate watchwords for driving the revolution ahead, and the courage to draw all the necessary conclusions from the situation. This makes clear, too, the miserable role of the Russian Mensheviks, the Dans, Zeretellis, etc., who had enormous influence on the masses at the beginning, but, after their prolonged wavering and after they had fought with both hands and feet against taking over power and responsibility were driven ignobly off the stage.

The party of Lenin was the only one which grasped the mandate and duty of a truly revolutionary party and which, by the slogan – 'All power in the hands of the proletariat and peasantry' – insured the continued development of the revolution.

5.12 LAW OF COMBINED AND UNEVEN DEVELOPMENT

From Leon Trotsky, The History of the Russian Revolution *(1929-30), 3 vols., translated by Max Eastman (Sphere Books edn., 1967), vol. 1, pp. 22-31.*

For this and the following extract, see 'Introduction', pp. 87-8.

A backward country assimilates the material and intellectual conquests of the advanced countries. But this deos not mean that it follows them slavishly, reproduces all the stages of their past. The theory of the repetition of historic cycles – Vico and his more recent followers – rests upon an observation of the orbits of old pre-capitalistic cultures, and in part upon the first experiments of capitalistic development. A certain repetition of cultural stages in ever new settlements was in fact bound up with the provincial and episodic character of that whole process. Capitalism means, however, an overcoming of those conditions. It prepares and in a certain sense realises the universality and permanence of man's development. By this a repetition of the forms of development by different nations is ruled out. Although compelled to follow after the advanced countries, a backward country does not take things in the same order. The privilege of historic backwardness – and such a privilege exists – permits, or rather compels, the adoption of whatever is ready in advance of any specified date, skipping a whole series of intermediate stages. Savages throw away their bows and arrows for rifles all at once, without travelling the road which lay between those two weapons in the past. The European colonists in America did not begin history all over again from the beginning. The fact that Germany and the United States have now economically outstripped England was made possible by the very backwardness of their capitalist development. On the other hand, the conservative anarchy in the British coal industry – as also in the heads of Mac-Donald and his friends – is a paying-up for the past when England played too long the role of capitalist pathfinder. The development of historically backward nations leads necessarily to a peculiar combination of different stages in the historic process. Their development as a whole acquires a planless, complex combined character.

The possibility of skipping over intermediate steps is of course by no means absolute. Its degree is determined in the long run by the economic and cultural capacities of the country. The backward nation, moreover, not infrequently debases the achievements borrowed from outside in the process of adapting them to its own more primitive culture. In this the very process of assimilation acquires a self-contradictory character. Thus the introduction of certain elements of Western technique and training, above all military and industrial, under Peter I, led to a strengthening of serfdom as the fundamental form of labour organisation. European armament and European loans – both indubitable products of a higher culture – led to a strengthening of czarism, which delayed in its turn the development of the country.

The laws of history have nothing in common with a pedantic schematism. Unevenness, the most general law of the historic process, reveals itself most sharply and complexly in the destiny of the backward countries. Under the whip of external necessity their backward culture is compelled to make leaps. From the universal law of unevenness thus derives another law which, for the lack of a better name, we may call the law of *combined development* – by which we mean a drawing together of the different stages of the journey, a combining of separate steps, an amalgam of archaic with more contemporary forms. Without this law, to be taken of course in its whole material content, it is impossible to understand the history of Russia, and indeed of any country of the second, third or tenth cultural class. . . .

The law of combined development reveals itself most indubitably in the history and character of Russian industry. Arising late, Russian industry did not repeat the development of the advanced countries, but inserted itself into this development, adapting their latest achievements to its own backwardness. Just as the economic evolution of Russia as a whole skipped over the epoch of craft-guilds and manufacture, so also the separate branches of industry made a series of special leaps over technical productive stages that had been measured in the West by decades. Thanks to this, Russian industry developed at certain periods with extraordinary speed. Between the first revolution and the war, industrial production in Russia approximately doubled. This has seemed to certain Russian historians a sufficient basis for concluding that 'we must abandon the legend of backwardness and slow growth'. In reality the possibility of this swift growth was determined by that very backwardness which, alas, continued not only up to the moment of liquidation of the old Russia, but as her legacy up to the present day. . . .

At the same time that peasant land-cultivation as a whole remained, right up to the revolution, at the level of the seventeenth century, Russian industry in its technique and capitalist structure stood at the level of the advanced countries, and in certain respects even outstripped them. Small enterprises, involving less than 100 workers, employed in the United States, in 1914, 35 per cent of the total industrial workers, but in Russia anly 17·8 per cent. The two countries had an approximately identical relative quantity of enterprises involving 100 to 1,000 workers. But the giant enterprises, above 1,000 workers each, employed in the United States 17·8 per cent of the workers and in Russia 41·4 per cent! For the most important industrial districts the latter percentage is still higher: for the Petrograd district 44·4 per cent, for the Moscow district even 57·3 per cent. We get a like result if we compare Russian with British or German industry. This fact – first established by the author in 1908 – hardly accords with the banal idea of the economic backwardness of Russia. However, it does not disprove this backwardness, but dialectically completes it. . . .

The social character of the Russian bourgeoisie and its political physiognomy were determined by the condition of origin and the structure of Russian industry. The extreme concentration of this industry alone meant that between the capitalist leaders and the popular masses there was no hierarchy of transitional layers. To this we must add that the proprietors of the principal industrial, banking, and transport enterprises were foreigners, who realised on their investment not only the profits drawn from Russia, but also a political influence on foreign parliaments, and so not only did not forward the struggle for Russian parliamentarism, but often opposed it: it is sufficient to recall the shameful role played by official France. Such are the elementary and irremovable causes of the political isolation and anti-popular character of the Russian bourgeoisie. Whereas in the dawn of its history it was too unripe to accomplish a Reformation, when the time came for leading a revolution it was overripe.

In correspondence with this general course of development of the country, the reservoir from which the Russian working class formed itself was not the craft-guild, but agriculture, not the city, but the country. Moreover, in Russia the proletariat did not arise gradually through the ages, carrying with itself the burden of the past as in England, but in leaps involving sharp changes of environment, ties, relations, and a sharp break with the past. It is just this fact – combined with the concentrated oppressions of czarism – that made the Russian workers hospitable to the boldest conclusions of revolutionary thought – just as the backward industries were hospitable to the last word in capitalist organisation. . . .

The incapacity of the bourgeoisie for political action was immediately caused by its relation to the proletariat and the peasantry. It could not lead after it workers who stood hostile in their everyday life, and had so early learned to generalise their problems. But it was likewise incapable of leading after it the peasantry, because it was entangled in a web of interests with the landlords, and dreaded a shake-up of property relations in any form. The belatedness of the Russian revolution was thus not only a matter of chronology, but also of the social structure of the nation.

England achieved her Puritan revolution when her whole population was not more than $5\frac{1}{2}$ millions, of whom half a million were to be found in London. France, in the epoch of her revolution, had in Paris also only half a million out of a population of 25 million. Russia at the beginning of the twentieth century had a population of about 150 million, of whom more than three million were in Petrograd and Moscow. Behind these comparative figures lurk enormous social differences. Not only England of the seventeenth century, but also France of the eighteenth, had no proletariat in the modern sense. In Russia, however, the working class in all branches of labour, both city and village, numbered in 1905 no less than 10 million, which with their families amounts to more than 25 million – that is to say, more than the whole population of France in the epoch of the great revolution. Advancing from the sturdy artisans and independent peasants of the army of Cromwell – through the Sansculottes of Paris – to the industrial proletarians of St Petersburg, the revolution had deeply changed its social mechanism, its methods, and therewith its aims.

The events of 1905 were a prologue to the two revolutions of 1917, that of February and that of October. In the prologue all the elements of the drama were included, but not carried through. The Russo-Japanese war had made czarism totter. Against the background of a mass movement the liberal bourgeoisie had frightened the monarchy with its opposition. The workers had organised independently of the bourgeoisie, and in opposition to it, in soviets, a form of organisation then first called into being. Peasant uprisings to seize the land occurred throughout vast stretches of the country. Not only the peasants, but also the revolutionary parts of the army tended towards the soviets, which at the moment of highest tension openly disputed the power with the monarchy. However, all the revolutionary forces were then going into action for the first time, lacking experience and confidence. The liberals demonstratively backed away from the revolution exactly at the moment when it became clear that to shake czarism would not be enough, it must be overthrown. This sharp break of the bourgeoisie with the people, in which the bourgeoisie carried with it considerable circles of the democratic intelligentsia, made it easier for the monarchy to differentiate within the army, separating out the loyal units, and to make a bloody settlement with the workers and peasants. Although with a few broken ribs, czarism came out of the experience of 1905 alive and strong enough.

What changes in the correlation of forces were introduced by the eleven years' historical development dividing the prologue from the drama? Czarism during this period came into still sharper conflict with the demands of historical development. The bourgeoisie became economically more powerful, but as we have seen its power rested on a higher concentration of industry and an increased predominance of foreign capital. Impressed by the lessons of 1905, the bourgeoisie had become more conservative and suspicious. The relative weight of the petty and middle bourgeoisie, insignificant before, had fallen still lower. The democratic intelligentsia generally speaking had no firm social support whatever. It could have a transitional political influence, but could play no independent role: its dependence upon bourgeois liberalism had grown enormously. In these circumstances only the youthful proletariat could give the peasantry a programme, a banner and a leadership. The gigantic tasks thus presented to the proletariat gave rise to an urgent necessity for a special revolutionary organisation capable of quickly getting hold of the popular masses and making them ready for revolutionary action under the leadership of the workers. Thus the soviets of 1905 developed gigantically in 1917.

That the soviets, we may remark here, are not a mere child of the historic backwardness of Russia, but a product of her combined development, is indicated by the fact that the proletariat of the most industrial country, Germany, at the time of its revolutionary high point – 1918 to 1919 – could find no other form of organisation.

The revolution of 1917 still had as its immediate task the overthrow of the bureaucratic monarchy, but in distinction from the older bourgeois revolutions, the decisive force was now a new class formed on the basis of a concentrated industry, and armed with new organisations, new methods of struggle. The law of combined development here emerges in its extreme expression: starting with the overthrow of a decayed medieval structure, the revolution in the course of a few months placed the proletariat and the Communist Party in power.

5.13 THE 'PERMANENT REVOLUTION'

From Leon Trotsky, The Permanent Revolution *(1930), translated by John G. Wright, as revised by Brian Pearce (New York, 1969), pp. 130–3.*

The concept of the 'permanent revolution', in the sense of a perpetual process of change, goes back ultimately to Saint-Simon, and to Proudhon. Marx, in his 1850 Address to the Communist League, gave it a special twist to fit the special conditions of Germany with its weak bourgeoisie – and it was in this sense that it was taken up by Lenin and – especially – Trotsky, who added the international dimension.

The permanent revolution, in the sense which Marx attached to this concept, means a revolution which makes no compromise with any single form of class rule, which does not stop at the democratic stage, which goes over to socialist measures and to war against reaction from without; that is, a revolution whose every successive stage is rooted in the preceding one and which can end only in the complete liquidation of class society.

To dispel the chaos that has been created around the theory of the permanent revolution, it is necessary to distinguish three lines of thought that are united in this theory.

First, it embraces the problem of the transition from the democratic revolution to the socialist. This is in essence the historical origin of the theory.

The concept of the permanent revolution was advanced by the great Communists of the middle of the nineteenth century, Marx and his co-thinkers, in opposition to the democratic ideology which, as we know, claims that with the establishment of a 'rational' or democratic state all questions can be solved peacefully by reformist or evolutionary measures. Marx regarded the bourgeois revolution of 1848 as the direct prelude to the proletarian revolution. Marx 'erred'. Yet his error has a factual and not a methodological character. The Revolution of 1848 did not turn into the socialist revolution. But that is just why it also did not achieve democracy. As to the German Revolution of 1918, it was no democratic completion of the bourgeois revolution, it was a proletarian revolution decapitated by the Social Democrats; more correctly, it was a bourgeois *counter-revolution*, which was compelled to preserve pseudo-democratic forms after its victory over the proletariat.

Vulgar 'Marxism' has worked out a pattern of historical development according to which every bourgeois society sooner or later secures a democratic regime, after which the proletariat, under conditions of democracy, is gradually organised and educated for socialism. The actual transition to socialism has been variously conceived: the avowed reformists pictured this transition as the reformist filling of democracy with a socialist content (Jaurès); the formal revolutionists acknowledged the inevitability of applying revolutionary violence in the transition to socialism (Guesde). But both the former and the latter considered democracy and socialism, for all peoples and countries, as two stages in the development of society which are not only entirely distinct but also separated by great distances of time from each other. This view was predominant also among those Russian Marxists who, in the period of 1905, belonged to the Left Wing of the Second International. Plekhanov, the brilliant progenitor of Russian Marxism, considered the idea of the dictatorship of the proletariat a delusion in contemporary Russia. The same standpoint was defended not only by the Mensheviks but also by the overwhelming majority of the leading Bolsheviks, in particular by those present party leaders, without exception, who in their day were resolute revolutionary democrats but for whom the problems of the socialist revolution, not only in 1905 but also on the eve of 1917, still signified the vague music of a distant future.

The theory of the permanent revolution, which originated in 1905, declared war upon these ideas and moods. It pointed out that the democratic tasks of the backward bourgeois nations lead directly, in our epoch, to the dictatorship of the proletariat and that the dictatorship of the proletariat puts socialist tasks on the order of the day. Therein lay the central idea of the theory. While the traditional view was that the road to the dictatorship of the proletariat led through a long period of democracy, the theory of the permanent revolution established the fact that for backward countries the road to democracy passed through the dictatorship of the proletariat. Thus democracy is not a regime that remains self-sufficient for decades, but is only a direct prelude to the socialist revolution. Each is bound to the other by an unbroken chain. Thus there is established between the democratic revolution and the socialist reconstruction of society a permanent state of revolutionary development.

The second aspect of the 'permanent' theory has to do with the socialist revolution as such. For an indefinitely long time and in constant internal struggle, all social relations undergo transformation. Society keeps on changing its skin. Each stage of transformation stems directly from the preceding. This process necessarily retains a political character, that is, it develops through collisions between various groups in the society which is in transformation. Outbreaks of civil war and foreign wars alternate with periods of 'peaceful' reform. Revolutions in economy, technique, science, the family, morals and everyday life develop in complex reciprocal action and do not allow society to achieve equilibrium.

Therein lies the permanent character of the socialist revolution as such.

The international character of the socialist revolution, which constitutes the third aspect of the theory of the permanent revolution, flows from the present state of economy and the social structure of humanity. Internationalism is no abstract principle but a theoretical and political reflection of the character of world economy, of the world development of productive forces and the world scale of the class struggle. The socialist revolution begins on national foundations – but it cannot be completed within these foundations. The maintenance of the proletarian revolution within a national framework can only be a provisional state of affairs, even though, as the experience of the Soviet Union shows, one of long duration. In an isolated proletarian dictatorship, the internal and external contradictions grow inevitably along with the success achieved. If it remains isolated, the proletarian state must finally fall victim to these contradictions. The way out for it lies only in the victory of the proletariat of the advanced countries. Viewed from this standpoint, a national revolution is not a self-contained whole; it is only a link in the international chain. The international revolution constitutes a permanent process, despite temporary declines and ebbs.

5.14 THE NATURE OF DUAL POWER IN REVOLUTIONS

From Leon Trotsky, The History of the Russian Revolution *(1929–30), 3 vols., translated by Max Eastman, vol. 1, pp. 202–07.*

Trotsky here offers a fine comparative analysis of one of the most characteristic features of revolutions. Once more, he is led to conclude that the Russian Revolution half imitates the past, half creates anew.

The political mechanism of revolution consists of the transfer of power from one class to another. The forcible overturn is usually accomplished in a brief time. But no historic class lifts itself from a subject position to a position of rulership suddenly in one night, even though a night of revolution. It must already on the eve of the revolution have assumed a very independent attitude towards the official ruling class; moreover, it must have focused upon itself the hopes of intermediate classes and layers, dissatisfied with the existing state of affairs, but not capable of playing an independent role. The historic preparation of a revolution brings about, in the pre-revolutionary period, a situation in which the class which is called to realise the new social system, although not yet master of the country, has actually concentrated in its hands a significant share of the state power, while the official apparatus of the government is still in the hands of the old lords. That is the initial dual power in every revolution.

But that is not its only form. If the new class, placed in power by a revolution which it did not want, is in essence an already old, historically belated, class; if it was already worn out before it was officially crowned; if on coming to power it encounters an antagonist already sufficiently mature and reaching out its hand towards the helm of state; then instead of one unstable two-power equilibrium, the political revolution produces another, still less stable. To overcome the 'anarchy' of this two-fold sovereignty becomes at every new step the task of the revolution – or the counter-revolution.

This double sovereignty does not presuppose – generally speaking, indeed, it excludes – the possibility of a division of the power into two equal halves, or indeed any formal equilibrium of forces whatever. It is not a constitutional, but a revolutionary fact. It implies that a destruction of the social equilibrium has already split the state superstructure. It arises where the hostile classes are already each relying upon essentially incompatible governmental organisation – the one outlived, the other in process of formation – which jostle against each other at every step in the sphere of government. The amount of power which falls to each of these struggling classes in such a situation is determined by the correlation of forces in the course of the struggle.

By its very nature such a state of affairs cannot be stable. Society needs a concentration of power, and in the person of the ruling class – or, in the situation we are discussing, the two half-ruling classes – irresistibly strives to get it. The splitting of sovereignty foretells nothing less than a civil war. But before the competing classes and parties will go to that extreme – especially in case they dread the interference of a third force – they may feel compelled for quite a long time to endure, and even to sanction, a two-power system. This system will nevertheless inevitably explode. Civil war gives to this double sovereignty its most visible, because territorial, expression. Each of the powers, having created its own fortified drill ground, fights for possession of the rest of the territory, which often has to endure the double sovereignty in the form of successive invasions by the two fighting powers, until one of them decisively installs itself.

The English revolution of the seventeenth century, exactly because it was a great revolution shattering the nation to the bottom, affords a clear example of this alternating dual power, with sharp transitions in the form of civil war.

At first the royal power, resting upon the privileged classes or the upper circles of these classes – the aristocrats and bishops – is opposed by the bourgeoisie and the circles of the squirearchy that are close to it. The government of the bourgeoisie is the Presbyterian Parliament supported by the City of London. The protracted conflict between these two regimes is finally settled in open civil war. The two governmental centres – London and Oxford – create their own armies. Here the dual power takes a territorial form, although, as always in civil war, the boundaries are very shifting. Parliament conquers. The king is captured and awaits his fate.

It would seem that the conditions are now created for the single rule of the Presbyterian bourgeoisie. But before the royal power could be broken, the parliamentary army has converted itself into an independent political force. It has concentrated in its ranks the Independents, the pious and resolute petty bourgeoisie, the craftsmen and farmers. This army powerfully interferes in the social life, not merely as an armed force, but as a Praetorian Guard, and as the political representative of a new class opposing the prosperous and rich bourgeoisie. Correspondingly the army creates a new state organ rising above the military command: a council of soldiers' and officers' deputies ('agitators'). A new period of double sovereignty has thus arrived: that of the Presbyterian Parliament and the Independents' army. This leads to open conflicts. The bourgeoisie proves powerless to oppose with its own army the 'model army' of Cromwell – that is, the armed plebeians. The conflict ends with a purgation of the Presbyterian Parliament by the sword of the Independents. There remains but the rump of a parliament; the dictatorship of Cromwell is established. The lower ranks of the army, under the leadership of the Levellers – the extreme left wing of the revolution – try to oppose to the rule of the upper military levels, the patricians of the army, their own veritably plebeian regime. But this new two-power system does not succeed in developing: the Levellers, the lowest depths of the petty bourgeoisie, have not yet, nor can have, their own historic path. Cromwell soon settles accounts with his enemies. A new political equilibrium, and still by no means a stable one, is established for a period of years.

In the great French revolution, the Constituent Assembly, the backbone of which was the upper levels of the Third Estate, concentrated the power in its hands – without however fully annulling the prerogatives of the king. The period of the Constituent Assembly is a clearly-marked period of dual power, which ends with the flight of the king to Varennes, and is formally liquidated with the founding of the Republic.

The first French constitution (1791), based upon the fiction of a complete independence of the legislative and executive powers, in reality concealed from the people, or tried to conceal a double sovereignty: that of the bourgeoisie, firmly entrenched in the National Assembly after the capture by the people of the Bastille, and that of the old monarchy still relying upon the upper circles of the priesthood, the clergy, the bureaucracy, and the military, to say nothing of their hopes of foreign intervention. In this self-contradictory regime lay the germs of its inevitable destruction. A way out could be found only in the abolition of bourgeois representation by the powers of European reaction, or in the guillotine for the king and the monarchy. Paris and Coblenz must measure their forces.

But before it comes to war and the guillotine, the Paris Commune enters the scene – supported by the lowest city layers of the Third Estate – and with increasing boldness contests the power with the official representatives of the national bourgeoisie. A new double sovereignty is thus inaugurated, the first manifestation of which we observe as early as 1790, when the big and medium bourgeoisie is still firmly seated in the administration and in the municipalities. How striking is the picture – and how vilely it has been slandered! – of the efforts of the plebeian levels to raise themselves up out of the social cellars and catacombs, and stand forth in that forbidden arena where people in wigs and silk breeches are settling the fate of the nation. It seemed as though the very foundation of society, tramped underfoot by the cultured bourgeoisie, was stirring and coming to life. Human heads lifted themselves above the solid mass, horny hands stretched aloft, hoarse but courageous voices shouted! The districts of Paris, bastards of the revolution, began to live a life of their own. They were recognised – it was impossible not to recognise them! – and transformed into sections. But they kept continually breaking the boundaries of legality and receiving a current of fresh blood from below, opening their ranks in spite of the law to those with no rights, the destitute Sansculottes. At the same time the rural municipalities were becoming a screen for a peasant uprising against that bourgeois legality which was defending the feudal property system. Thus from under the second nation arises a third.

The Parisian sections at first stood opposed to the Commune, which was still dominated by the respectable bourgeoisie. In the bold outbreak of 10 August 1792, the sections gained control of the Commune. From then on the revolutionary Commune opposed the Legislative Assembly, and subsequently the Convention, which failed to keep up with the problems and progress of the revolution – registering its events, but not performing them – because it did not possess the energy, audacity and unanimity of that new class which had raised itself up from the depths of the Parisian districts and found support in the most backward villages. As the sections gained control of the Commune, so the Commune, by way of a new insurrection, gained control of the Convention. Each of the stages was characterised by a sharply marked double sovereignty, each wing of which was trying to establish a single and strong government – the right by a defensive struggle, the left by an offensive. Thus, characteristically – for both revolutions and counter-revolutions – the demand for a dictatorship results from the intolerable contradictions of the double sovereignty. The transition from one of its forms to the other is accomplished through civil war. The great stages of a revolution – that is, the passing of power to new classes or layers – do not at all coincide in this process with the succession of representative institutions, which march along after the dynamic of the revolution like a belated shadow. In the long run, to be sure, the revolutionary dictatorship of the Sansculottes unites with the dictatorship of the Convention. But with what Convention? A Convention purged of the Girondists, who yesterday ruled it with the hand of the Terror – a Convention abridged and adapted to the dominion of new social forces. Thus by the steps of the dual power the French revolution rises in the course of four years to its culmination. After the 9th Thermidor it begins – again by the steps of the dual power – to descend. And again civil war precedes every downward step, just as before it had accompanied every rise. In this way the new society seeks a new equilibrium of forces.

The Russian bourgeoisie, fighting with and co-operating with the Rasputin bureaucracy, had enormously strengthened its political position during the war. Exploiting the defeat of czarism, it had concentrated in its hands, by means of the Country and Town unions and the Military-Industrial Committees, a great power. It had at its independent disposition enormous state resources, and was in the essence of the matter a parallel government. During the war the czar's ministers complained that Prince Lvov was furnishing supplies to the army, feeding it, medicating it, even establishing barber shops for the soldiers. 'We must either put an end to this, or give the whole power into his hands,' said Minister Krivoshein in 1915. He never imagined that a year and a half later Lvov would receive 'the whole power' – only not from the czar, but from the hands of Kerensky, Cheidze and Sukhanov. But on the second day after he received it, there began a new double sovereignty: alongside of yesterday's liberal half-government – today formally legalised – there arose an unofficial, but so much the more actual government of the toiling masses in the form of the soviets. From that moment the Russian revolution began to grow up into an event of world-historic significance.

What, then, is the peculiarity of this dual power as it appeared in the February revolution? In the events of the seventeenth and eighteenth centuries, the dual power was in each case a natural stage in a struggle imposed upon its participants by a temporary correlation of forces, and each side strove to replace the dual power with its own single power. In the revolution of 1917, we see the official democracy consciously and intentionally creating a two-power system, dodging with all its might the transfer of power into its own hands. The double sovereignty is created, or so it seems at a glance, not as a result of a struggle of classes for power, but as the result of a voluntary 'yielding' of power by one class to another. In so far as the Russian 'democracy' sought for an escape from the two-power regime, it could find one only in its own removal from power. It is just this that we have called the paradox of the February revolution.

5.15 REVOLUTION WILL PRODUCE A NEW BUREAUCRATIC RULING CLASS

From Robert Michels, Political Parties *(1962 edn.), pp. 347–9, 355.*

Michel's prediction, made in 1911, seemed amply borne out by the course of the Russian Revolution, and his conception is similar in most respects to that later espoused by Milovan Djilas in The New Class.

See 'Introduction', p. 85.

The Marxist theory of the state, when conjoined with a faith in the revolutionary energy of the working class and in the democratic effects of the socialisation of the means of production, leads logically to the idea of a new social order which to the school of Mosca appears utopian. According to the Marxists the capitalist mode of production transforms the great majority of the population into proletarians, and thus digs its own grave. As soon as it has attained maturity, the proletariat will seize political power, and will immediately transform private property into state property.

In this way it will eliminate itself, for it will thus put an end to all social differences, and consequently to all class antagonisms. In other words, the proletariat will annul the state, *qua* state. Capitalist society, divided into classes, has need of the state as an organisation of the ruling class, whose purpose it is to maintain the capitalist system of production in its own interest and in order to effect the continued exploitation of the proletariat. Thus to put an end to the state is synonymous with putting an end to the existence of the dominant class. [Engels].

But the new collectivist society, the society without classes, which is to be established upon the ruins of the ancient state, will also need elective elements. It may be said that by the adoption of the preventive rules formulated by Rousseau in the *Contrat Social*, and subsequently reproduced by the French revolutionists in the *Déclaration des Droits de l'Homme*, above all by the strict application of the principle that all offices are to be held on a revocable tenure, the activity of these representatives may be confined within rigid limits. It is none the less true that social wealth cannot be satisfactorily administered in any other manner than by the creation of an extensive bureaucracy. In this way we are led by an inevitable logic to the flat denial of the possibility of a state without classes. The administration of an immeasurably large capital, above all when this capital is collective property, confers upon the administrator influence at least equal to that possessed by the private owner of capital. Consequently the critics in advance of the Marxist social order ask whether the instinct which today leads the members of the possessing classes to transmit to their children the wealth which they (the parents) have amassed, will not exist also in the administrators of the public wealth of the socialist state, and whether these administrators will not utilise their immense influence in order to secure for their children the succession to the offices which they themselves hold.

The constitution of a new dominant minority would, in addition, be especially facilitated by the manner in which, according to the Marxist conception of the revolution, the social transformation is to be effected. Marx held that the period between the destruction of capitalist society and the establishment of communist society would be bridged by a period of revolutionary transition in the economic field, to which would correspond a period of political transition, 'when the state could not be anything other than the revolutionary dictatorship of the proletariat'. To put the matter less euphemistically, there will then exist a dictatorship in the hands of those leaders who have been sufficiently astute and sufficiently powerful to grasp the sceptre of dominion in the name of

271

socialism, and to wrest it from the hand of the expiring bourgeois society. . . .

The attempt to make dictatorship serve the ends of democracy is tantamount to the endeavour to utilise war as the most efficient means for the defence of peace, or to employ alcohol in the struggle against alcoholism. It is extremely probable that a social group which had secured control of the instruments of collective power would do all that was possible to retain that control. Theophrastus noted long ago that the strongest desire of men who have attained to leadership in a popularly governed state is not so much the acquirement of personal wealth as the gradual establishment of their own sovereignty at the expense of popular sovereignty. The danger is imminent lest the social revolution should replace the visible and tangible dominant classes which now exist and act openly, by a clandestine demagogic oligarchy, pursuing its ends under the cloak of equality. . . .

Thus the social revolution would not effect any real modification of the internal structure of the mass. The socialists might conquer, but not socialism, which would perish in the moment of its adherents' triumph. We are tempted to speak of this process as a tragi-comedy in which the masses are content to devote all their energies to effecting a change of masters. All that is left for the workers is the honour 'of participating in government recruiting'. The result seems a poor one, especially if we take into account the psychological fact that even the purest of idealists who attains to power for a few years is unable to escape the corruption which the exercise of power carries in its train. In France, in working-class circles, the phrase is current, *homme élu, homme foutu*. The social revolution like the political revolution, is equivalent to an operation by which, as the Italian proverb expresses it: 'Si cambia il maestro di cappella, ma la musica è sempre quella.' [There is a new conductor, but the music is just the same.]

5.16 TOTAL TRANSFORMATION ENTAILS TOTALITARIANISM

From Victor Serge (1890–1947), Memoirs of a Revolutionary
1901–1941, *translated and edited by Peter Sedgwick (London, 1967
edn.), pp. 132–5.*

*Serge worked for the Bolshevik Government after the Russian
Revolution. When the sailors of Kronstadt revolted in 1921 against
the dictatorship of the Party, he eventually sided with the Party, but
saw that it lied about the nature of the revolt. The bloody suppression
led him to reflect pessimistically on the current state of the Revolution.*

The truth was that emergent totalitarianism had already gone
half-way to crushing us. 'Totalitarianism' did not yet exist as a
word; as an actuality it began to press hard on us, even without our
being aware of it. I belonged to that pitifully small minority that
realised what was going on. Most of the Party leadership and
activists, in reviewing their ideas about War Communism, came
to the conclusion that it was an economic expedient analogous to
the centralised regimes set up during the war in Germany, France,
and Britain, which they termed 'war capitalism'. They hoped that,
once peace came, the state of siege would fall away spontaneously
and some sort of Soviet democracy, of which nobody had any clear
conception would return. The great ideas of 1917, which had
enabled the Bolshevik Party to win over the peasant masses, the
army, the working class, and the Marxist intelligentsia, were quite
clearly dead. Did not Lenin, in 1917, suggest a Soviet form of free
Press, whereby any group with the support of 10,000 votes could
publish its own organ at the public expense? He had written that
within the Soviets power could be passed from one party to another
without any necessity for bitter conflicts. His theory of the Soviet
state promised a state structure totally different from that of the
old bourgeois states, 'without officials or a police-force distinct
from the people', in which the workers would exercise power
directly through their elected Councils, and keep order themselves
through a militia system.

What with the political monopoly, the Cheka and the Red Army, all that now existed of the 'Commune-State' of our dreams was a theoretical myth. The war, the internal measures against counter-revolution, and the famine (which had created a bureaucratic rationing-apparatus) had killed off Soviet democracy. How could it revive, and when? The Party lived in the certain knowledge that the slightest relaxation of its authority would give the day to reaction.

To these historical features, certain important psychological factors must be added. Capitalist industrial society tends to encompass the whole of the world, fashioning all aspects of life to its design. Consequently, ever since the beginning of the twentieth century, Marxism has aimed to renew and transform everything: the property system, the organisation of work, the map of the world (through the abolition of frontiers), and even the inner life of man (through the extinction of the religious mode of thought). Aspiring to a total transformation, it has consequently been, in the etymological sense of the word, totalitarian. It presents the two faces of the ascendant society, simultaneously democratic and authoritarian. The greatest Marxist party, from 1880 to 1920, the Social-Democratic Party of Germany, is bureaucratically organised on the lines of a State, and functions as a means of achieving power within the State. Bolshevik thinking is grounded in the possession of the truth. The Party is the repository of truth, and any form of thinking which differs from it is a dangerous or reactionary error. Here lies the spiritual source of its intolerance. The absolute conviction of its lofty mission assures it of a moral energy quite astonishing in its intensity – and, at the same time, a clerical mentality which is quick to become Inquisitorial. Lenin's 'pro-letarian Jacobinism' with its detachment and discipline both in thought and action is eventually grafted upon the pre-existing temperament of activists moulded by the old regime, that is by the struggle against despotism; I am quite convinced that a sort of natural selection of authoritarian temperaments is the result.

For all these reasons, even the great popular leaders themselves flounder within inextricable contradictions which dialectics allows them to surmount verbally, sometimes even demagogically. Twenty or maybe a hundred times, Lenin sings the praises of democracy and stresses that the dictatorship of the proletariat is a dictatorship against 'the expropriated possessing classes', and at the same time, 'the broadest possible workers' democracy'. He believes and wants it to be so. He goes to give an account of himself before the factories; he asks for merciless criticism from the workers. He also writes, in 1918, that the dictatorship of the proletariat is not at all incompatible with personal power; thereby justifying, in advance, some variety of Bonapartism. He has Bogdanov, his old friend and comrade, jailed because this outstanding intellectual confronts him with embarrassing objections. He outlaws the Mensheviks because these 'petty-bourgeois' Socialists are guilty of errors which happen to be awkward. He welcomes the anarchist partisan Makhno with real affection, and tries to prove to him that Marxism is right; but he either permits or engineers the outlawing of anarchism. He promises peace to religious believers and orders that the churches are to be respected; but he keeps saying that 'religion is the opium of the people'. We are proceeding towards a classless society of free men; but the Party has posters stuck up nearly everywhere announcing that 'the rule of the workers will never cease'. Over whom then will they rule? And what is the meaning of this word *rule*? Totalitarianism is within us.

5.17 THE SOVIET THERMIDOR

From Leon Trotsky, The Revolution Betrayed *(1936) (London, 1967 edn.), pp. 87–9, 92–3, 105–6, 112–13.*

Forced out of Russia by Stalin, Trotsky now saw the Russian Revolution as completing the pattern of the classic European Revolutions. The rise of a conservative bureaucratic power represented the Thermidorian reaction to the earlier expanding phases of the Revolution.

The February revolution raised Kerensky and Tseretelli to power, not because they were 'cleverer' or 'more astute' than the ruling tsarist clique, but because they represented, at least temporarily, the revolutionary masses of the people in their revolt against the old regime. Kerensky was able to drive Lenin underground and imprison other Bolshevik leaders, not because he excelled them in personal qualifications, but because the majority of the workers and soldiers in those days were still following the patriotic petty bourgeoisie. The personal 'superiority 'of Kerensky, if it is suitable to employ such a word in this connection, consisted in the fact that he did not see farther than the overwhelming majority. The Bolsheviks in their turn conquered the petty bourgeois democrats, not through the personal superiority of their leaders, but through a new correlation of social forces. The proletariat had succeeded at last in leading the discontented peasantry against the bourgeoisie.

The consecutive stages of the great French Revolution during its rise and fall alike, demonstrate no less convincingly that the strength of the 'leaders' and 'heroes' that replaced each other consisted primarily in their correspondence to the character of those classes and strata which supported them. Only this correspondence, and not any irrelevant superiorities whatever, permitted each of them to place the impress of his personality upon a certain historic period. In the successive supremacy of Mirabeau, Brissot, Robespierre, Barras and Bonaparte, there is an obedience to objective law incomparably more effective than the special traits of the historic protagonists themselves.

It is sufficiently well known that every revolution up to this time has been followed by a reaction, or even a counter-revolution. This, to be sure, has never thrown the nation all the way back to its starting point, but it has always taken from the people the lion's share of their conquests. The victims of the first reactionary wave have been, as a general rule, those pioneers, initiators, and instigators who stood at the head of the masses in the period of the revolutionary offensive. In their stead people of the second line, in league with the former enemies of the revolution, have been advanced to the front. Beneath this dramatic duel of 'coryphées' on the open political scene, shifts have taken place in the relations between classes, and, no less important, profound changes in the psychology of the recently revolutionary masses.

Answering the bewildered questions of many comrades as to what has become of the activity of the Bolshevik party and the working class – where is its revolutionary initiative, its spirit of self-sacrifice and plebeian pride – why, in place of all this, has appeared so much vileness, cowardice, pusillanimity and careerism – Rakovsky referred to the life story of the French revolution of the eighteenth century, and offered the example of Babeuf, who on emerging from the Abbaye prison likewise wondered what had become of the heroic people of the Parisian suburbs. A revolution is a mighty devourer of human energy, both individual and collective. The nerves give way. Consciousness is shaken and characters are worn out. Events unfold too swiftly for the flow of fresh forces to replace the loss. Hunger, unemployment, the death of the revolutionary cadres, the removal of the masses from administration, all this led to such a physical and moral impoverishment of the Parisian suburbs that they required three decades before they were ready for a new insurrection.

The axiom-like assertions of the Soviet literature, to the effect that the laws of bourgeois revolutions are 'inapplicable' to a proletarian revolution, have no scientific content whatever. The proletarian character of the October revolution was determined by the world situation and by a special correlation of internal forces. But the classes themselves were formed in the barbarous circumstances of tsarism and backward capitalism, and were anything but made to order for the demands of a socialist revolution. The exact opposite is true. It is for the very reason that a proletariat still backward in many respects achieved in the space of a few months the unprecedented leap from a semi-feudal monarchy to a socialist dictatorship, that the reaction in its ranks was inevitable. This reaction has developed in a series of consecutive waves. External conditions and events have vied with each other in nourishing it. Intervention followed intervention. The revolution got no direct help from the west. Instead of the expected prosperity of the country an ominous destitution reigned for long. Moreover, the outstanding representatives of the working class either died in the civil war, or rose a few steps higher and broke away from the masses. And thus after an unexampled tension of forces, hopes and illusions, there came a long period of weariness, decline and sheer disappointment in the results of the revolution. The ebb of the 'plebeian pride' made room for a flood of pusillanimity and careerism. The new commanding caste rose to its place upon this wave. . . .

It would be naïve to imagine that Stalin, previously unknown to the masses, suddenly issued from the wings fully armed with a complete strategic plan. No indeed. Before he felt out his own

277

course, the bureaucracy felt out Stalin himself. He brought it all the necessary guarantees: the prestige of an old Bolshevik, a strong character, narrow vision, and close bonds with the political machine as sole source of his influence. The success which fell upon him was a surprise at first to Stalin himself. It was the friendly welcome of the new ruling group, trying to free itself from the old principles and from the control of the masses, and having need of a reliable arbiter in its inner affairs. A secondary figure before the masses and in the events of the revolution, Stalin revealed himself as the indubitable leader of the Thermidorian bureaucracy, as first in its midst. . . .

We have defined the Soviet Thermidor as a triumph of the bureaucracy over the masses. We have tried to disclose the historic conditions of this triumph. The revolutionary vanguard of the proletariat was in part devoured by the administrative apparatus and gradually demoralised, in part annihilated in the civil war, and in part thrown out and crushed. The tired and disappointed masses were indifferent to what was happening on the summits. These conditions, however, important as they may have been in themselves, are inadequate to explain why the bureaucracy succeeded in raising itself above society and getting its fate firmly into its own hands. Its own will to this would in any case be inadequate; the arising of a new ruling stratum must have deep social causes.

The victory of the Thermidorians over the Jacobins in the eighteenth century was also aided by the weariness of the masses and the demoralisation of the leading cadres, but beneath these essentially incidental phenomena a deep organic process was taking place. The Jacobins rested upon the lower petty bourgeoisie lifted by the great wave. The revolution of the eighteenth century, however, corresponding to the course of development of the productive forces, could not but bring the great bourgeoisie to political ascendancy in the long run. The Thermidor was only one of the stages in this inevitable process. What similar social necessity found expression in the Soviet Thermidor? . . .

The basis of bureaucratic rule is the poverty of society in objects of consumption, with the resulting struggle of each against all. When there are enough goods in a store, the purchasers can come whenever they want to. When there are few goods, the purchasers are compelled to stand in line. When the lines are very long, it is necessary to appoint a policeman to keep order. Such is the starting point of the power of the Soviet bureaucracy. It 'knows' who is to get something and who has to wait.

A raising of the material and cultural level ought, at first glance, to lessen the necessity of privileges, narrow the sphere of application of 'bourgeois law', and thereby undermine the standing ground of its defenders, the bureaucracy. In reality the opposite thing has happened: the growth of the productive forces has been so far accompanied by an extreme development of all forms of inequality, privilege and advantage, and therewith of bureaucratism. That too is not accidental.

In its first period, the Soviet regime was undoubtedly far more equalitarian and less bureaucratic than now. But that was an equality of general poverty. The resources of the country were so scant that there was no opportunity to separate out from the masses of the population any broad privileged strata. At the same time the 'equalising' character of wages, destroying personal interestedness, became a brake upon the development of the productive forces. Soviet economy had to lift itself from its poverty to a somewhat higher level before fat deposits of privilege became possible. The present state of production is still far from guaranteeing all necessities to everybody. But it is already adequate to give significant privileges to a minority, and convert inequality into a whip for the spurring on of the majority. That is the first reason why the growth of production has so far strengthened not the socialist, but the bourgeois features of the state.

But that is not the sole reason. Alongside the economic factor dictating capitalistic methods of payment at the present stage, there operates a parallel political factor in the person of the bureaucracy itself. In its very essence it is the planter and protector of inequality. It arose in the beginning as the bourgeois organ of a workers' stage. In establishing and defending the advantages of a minority, it of course draws off the cream for its own use. Nobody who has wealth to distribute ever omits himself. Thus out of a social necessity there has developed an organ which has far outgrown its socially necessary function, and become an independent factor and therewith the source of great danger for the whole social organism.

279

The social meaning of the Soviet Thermidor now begins to take form before us. The poverty and cultural backwardness of the masses has again become incarnate in the malignant figure of the ruler with a great club in his hand. The deposed and abused bureaucracy, from being a servant of society, has again become its lord. On this road it has attained such a degree of social and moral alienation from the popular masses, that it cannot now permit any control over either its activities or its income.

6 The Changing Conditions of Revolutionary Action

6.1 SUCCESSIVE REVOLUTIONS STRENGTHEN STATE POWER

For 6.1–6.4, see 'Introduction', pp. 40–2, 84–5.

6.1.1 *From Alexis de Tocqueville,* On the State of Society in France before the Revolution of 1789, *translated by Henry Reeve (1856), pp. 13–16, 110–11.*

(i)

When the Revolution overthrew at once all the institutions and all the customs which up to that time had maintained certain gradations in society and kept men within certain bounds, it seemed as if the result would be the total destruction not only of one particular order of society, but of all order; not only of this or that form of government, but of all social authority; and its nature was judged to be essentially anarchical. Nevertheless, I maintain that this too was true only in appearance.

Within a year from the beginning of the Revolution, Mirabeau wrote secretly to the King:

> Compare the new state of things with the old rule; there is the ground for comfort and hope. One part of the acts of the National Assembly, and that the more considerable part, is evidently favourable to monarchical government. Is it nothing to be without parliament? without the *pays d'état*? without a body of clergy? without a privileged class?

without a nobility? The idea of forming a single class of all the citizens would have pleased Richelieu; this equality of the surface facilitates the exercise of power. Several successive reigns of an absolute monarchy would not have done as much for the royal authority as this one year of revolution.

Such was the view of the Revolution taken by a man capable of guiding it.

As the object of the French Revolution was not only to change an ancient form of government, but also to abolish an ancient state of society, it had to attack at once, every established authority, to destroy every recognised influence, to efface all traditions, to create new manners and customs, and, as it were, to purge the human mind of all the ideas upon which respect and obedience had hitherto been based. Thence arose its singularly anarchical character.

But, clear away the ruins, and you behold an immense central power, which has attracted and absorbed into unity all the fractions of authority and influence which had formerly been dispersed amongst a host of secondary powers, orders, classes, professions, families and individuals, and which were disseminated throughout the whole fabric of society. The world had not seen such a power since the fall of the Roman empire. This power was created by the revolution, or rather it arose spontaneously out of the ruins which the revolution had left. The governments which it founded are more perishable, it is true, but a hundred times more powerful than any of those which it overthrew; we shall see hereafter that their fragility and their power were owing to the same causes.

It was this simple, regular, and imposing form of power which Mirabeau perceived through the dust and rubbish of ancient, half-demolished institutions. This object, in spite of its greatness, was still invisible to the eyes of the many, but time has gradually unveiled it to all eyes. At the present moment it especially attracts the attention of rulers: it is looked upon with admiration and envy, not only by those whom the Revolution has created, but by those who are the most alien and the most hostile to it; each endeavours, within his own dominions, to destroy immunities and to abolish privileges. They confound ranks, they equalise classes, they supersede the aristocracy by public functionaries, local franchises by uniform enactments, and the diversities of authority by the unity of a central government. They labour at this revolutionary task with unwearied industry, and, when they meet with occasional obstacles, they do not scruple to copy the measures as well as the maxims of the revolution. They have even stirred up the poor against the rich, the middle classes against the nobility, the peasants against their feudal lords. The French Revolution has been at once their curse and their instructor.

(ii)

The Revolution which was approaching, and which had already begun to agitate the mind of the whole French people, suggested to them a multitude of new ideas, which the central power of the Government could alone realise. The Revolution developed that power before it overthrew it, and the agents of the Government underwent the same process of improvement as everything else. This fact becomes singularly apparent from the study of the old administrative archives. The Comptroller-General and the Intendant of 1780 no longer resemble the Comptroller-General and the Intendant of 1740; the administration was already transformed, the agents were the same, but they are impelled by a different spirit. In proportion as it became more minute and more comprehensive, it also became more regular and more scientific. It became more temperate as its ascendancy became universal; it oppressed less, it directed more.

The first outbreak of the Revolution destroyed this grand institution of the monarchy; but it was restored in 1800. It was not, as has so often been said, the principles of 1789 which triumphed at that time and ever since in the public administration of France, but, on the contrary, the principles of the administration anterior to the Revolution, which then resumed their authority and have since retained it.

If I am asked how this fragment of the state of society anterior to the Revolution could thus be transplanted in its entirety, and incorporated into the new state of society which had sprung up, I answer that if the principle of centralisation did not perish in the Revolution, it was because that principle was itself the precursor and the commencement of the Revolution; and I add that when a people has destroyed Aristocracy in its social constitution, that people is sliding by its own weight into centralisation. Much less exertion is then required to drive it down that declivity than to hold it back. Amongst such a people all powers tend naturally to unity, and it is only by great ingenuity that they can still be kept separate. The democratic Revolution which destroyed so many of the institutions of the French monarchy, served therefore to consolidate the centralised administration, and centralisation seemed so naturally to find its place in the society which the Revolution had formed that it might easily be taken for its offspring.

6.1.2 *From Karl Marx, 'The Eighteenth Brumaire of Louis Napoleon', Marx and Engels,* Selected Works in Two Volumes, *vol.* 1, *pp. 332–3.*

This executive power with its enormous bureaucratic and military organisation, with its ingenious state machinery, embracing wide strata, with a host of officials numbering half a million, besides an army of another half million, this appalling parasitic body, which enmeshes the body of French society like a net and chokes all its pores, sprang up in the days of the absolute monarchy, with the decay of the feudal system, which it helped to hasten. The seigniorial privileges of the landowners and towns became transformed into so many attributes of the state power, the feudal dignitaries into paid officials and the motley pattern of conflicting medieval plenary powers into the regulated plan of a state authority whose work is divided and centralised as in a factory. The first French Revolution, with its task of breaking all separate local, territorial, urban and provincial powers in order to create the civil unity of the nation, was bound to develop what the absolute monarchy had begun: centralisation, but at the same time the extent, the attributes and the agents of governmental power. Napoleon perfected this state machinery. The Legitimist monarchy and the July monarchy added nothing but a greater division of labour, growing in the same measure as the division of labour within bourgeois society created new groups of interests, and, therefore, new material for state administration. Every *common* interest was straightaway severed from society, counterposed to it as a higher, *general* interest, snatched from the activity of society's members themselves and made an object of government activity, from a bridge, a schoolhouse and the communal property of a village community to the railways, the national wealth and the national university of France. Finally, in its struggle against the revolution, the parliamentary republic found itself compelled to strengthen, along with the repressive measures, the resources and centralisation of governmental power. All revolutions perfected this machine instead of smashing it. The parties that contended in turn for domination regarded the possession of this huge state edifice as the principal spoils of the victor.

6.2 REVOLUTION AND BUREAUCRATIS-ATION

From Gaetano Mosca (1858–1931), The Ruling Class (1896), translated by Hannah D. Kahn, edited by Arthur Livingstone (New York, 1939), pp. 214–19.

Considered as social phenomena, the revolutions that broke out in France during the nineteenth century are especially interesting as due to very special political conditions, notably to the phenomenon of over-bureaucratisation.

Not of this type was the great Revolution of 1789. That was a real collapse of the classes and political forces which had ruled in France down to that time. During the Revolution government administration and the army completely broke down, owing to inexperience in the National Assembly, to emigration and to the propaganda of the clubs. For some time they were unable to enforce respect for the decisions of any government. By July 1789, whole regiments had gone over to the cause of the Revolution. From then on, noncommissioned officers and soldiers were carefully lured into the clubs, where they received the watchword of obedience to the resolutions of the revolutionary committees rather than to the commands of their officers. The Marquis de Bouille, commanding the Army of the East, had been unable to suppress a dangerous military insurrection at Metz. He wrote late in 1790 that, with the exception of a regiment or two, the army was 'rotten', that the soldiers were disposed to follow the party of disorder or, rather, whoever paid them best, and that they were talking in such terms openly. The powers, therefore, that had fallen from the hands of the king were not gathered up by any ministry that had the confidence of the Constituent Assembly. It belonged in turn to the clique, or to the man, who on the given day could get himself followed to Paris by a show of armed force, whether he were a Lafayette at the head of the National Guard, or a Danton with a suburban mob armed with clubs and iron bars.

Nevertheless, apparent even in those early days were the beginnings of a tendency that was to become stronger and stronger during the first half of the nineteenth century. Leaders of insurrections always tried to become masters of the individual or individuals who impersonated the symbol, or the institution, to which in France, whether because of ancient tradition or because of faith in new principles, was inclined to defer; and, once successful in that intent, they were actually masters of the country.

That is what the rioters of 6 October 1789, did when, obviously in obedience to a watchword, they went to Versailles and seized the person of the king. With the monarchy abolished, the National Convention became the goal of all surprises, such as the coup of 31 May 1793, which made the Assembly that represented all France slave to a handful of Paris guttersnipes. The provinces tried to react, but in vain, because the army remained obedient to the orders that emanated from the capital in the name of the Convention, though everybody knew that the Convention was acting under compulsion.

The same general acquiescence in everything that happened at the seat of government contributed greatly to the favourable outcome of the various coups d'état that took place under the Directory, and down to the establishment of the Napoleonic empire.

But even more characteristic, perhaps, is what occurred in 1830, then again in 1848, and finally in 1870. First of all comes a battle, more or less protracted and sometimes relatively insignificant, with the detachment of soldiers that is guarding the buildings in the capital in which are assembled the representatives of the supreme power that has previously been recognised as legitimate. The famous February Revolution of 1848, which overthrew the monarchy of Louis Philippe, cost the lives of 72 soldiers and 287 civilians, either rioters or bystanders! Next, the mob, armed or unarmed, puts sovereigns and ministers to flight, dissolves the assemblies and riotously forms a government. This government is made up of names more or less widely known to the country. The men mentioned take desks in the offices from which the former heads of the government have been wont to govern, and then, almost always with the connivance or acquiescence of the ordinary clerks, they telegraph to all France that, by the will of the victorious people, they have become masters of the country. The country, the administrative departments, the army, promptly obey. It all sounds like a story of Aladdin's wonderful lamp. When by chance or by guile that lamp fell into the hands of someone, even a mere child or an ignorant boy, at once the genii were his blind slaves and made him richer and more powerful than any sultan of the East. And no one, furthermore, ever asked how or why the precious talisman came into the boy's possession.

It may be objected that in 1830 the government had become an obedient tool of the Legitimist party, that it had given up all pretense to legality, that a large part of France was definitely opposed to the political policy which the government was following, and even that a party of the army responded feebly, or not at all, at the decisive moment. Also, the catastrophe of 1870 might account in part for the change of government that took place in France at that time.

But no element of that sort figured in the sudden revolution of 1848. Neither the Chambers nor the bureaucracy nor the army were sympathetic to the republican government at that time. The majority of the departments were frankly opposed to it. Louis Blanc himself confesses as much. After rejecting as insulting the hypothesis that the republic had a minority in its favour, he admits that a nationwide vote might have declared against a republican form of government. And again he says, no more, no less: 'Why not face the facts? Most of the departments in February 1848, were still monarchical.' Lamartine, too, in speaking of the impression that the revolution of 1848 made in France, admits that it was surrounded by an 'atmosphere of uneasiness, doubt, horror and fright that had never been equalled, perhaps, in the history of mankind'. In Paris itself the National Guard had been wavering in February because it wanted to see an end put to the Guizot ministry. However, it was manifesting a reactionary frame of mind in the following March and April. A few hours of vacillation were none the less enough to drive Louis Philippe, his family and his ministers not only from Paris but from France, to abolish two chambers and to enable a provisional government – a mere list of names shouted at a tumultuous crowd that was milling about the Palais Bourbon – to assume from one moment to the next full political control over a great country – France!

Citizen Caussidière, 'wanted' by the police the day before, went to police headquarters on the afternoon of 20 February 1848, at the head of a group of insurgents, his hands still smudged with gunpowder. That evening he became chief of police, and the next day all the heads of branches in the service promised him loyal co-operation and, willing or unwilling, kept their promises. Police headquarters were, moreover, the only office where the rank and file of the personnel was changed, the old municipal guards being dismissed and replaced by Montagnards, former comrades in conspiracy and at the barricades of the new chief, who afterwards uttered the famous epigram that he stood for 'order through disorder'.

In the preface to his history of 1848, Louis Blanc decides that Louis Philippe fell mainly because his sponsors were supporting him for selfish reasons and not because of personal devotion. According to Blanc, the 'bourgeois king' had very few enemies and many confederates but at the moment of danger failed to find one friend. That reasoning, it seems to us, has only a very moderate value. Not all the people who support a given form of government have to feel a personal affection, or have a disinterested friendship, for the individual who stands at the head of that form of government. Actually, such sentiments can be sincerely felt only by the few persons, or the few families, who are actually intimate with him. Political devotion to a sovereign, or even to the president of a republic, is quite another matter. The main cause of the frequent sudden upheavals in France was the excessive bureaucratic centralisation of that country, a situation that was made worse by the parliamentary system itself. Public employees had grown accustomed to frequent changes in chiefs and policies, and they had learned from experience that much was to be gained by pleasing anyone who was seated at the top and that much was to be lost by displeasing such a person.

Under such a system what the great majority in the army and the bureaucracy want – and also the great majority in that part of the public that loves order, whether by interest or by instinct – is just a government, not any particular government. Those, there-fore, who stand de facto at the head of the state machine always find conservative forces ready to sustain them, and the whole political organism moves along in about the same way whatever the hand that sets it in motion.

Certainly, under such a system, it is easier to change the person-nel that holds supreme power, as happened in France after 1830, 1848 and 1870, than it is to change the actual political trend of a society. For if the more radical change is the object, governors who have emerged from the revolution itself are forced to prevent it by the conservative elements which are their instruments and at the same time their masters. That was the case in June 1848 and in 1871.

Unquestionably, also, a strong sense of the legality and legit-imacy of an earlier government would prevent submissive obedience to a new regime issuing from street rioting. But for a feeling of that sort to rise and assert itself requires time and tradition, and for France the changes that had occurred down to 1870 were too rapid to enable any tradition to take root. In France and in a large part of Europe, during the nineteenth century, revolutionary minorities were able to rely not only on the sympathy of the poor and unlettered masses but also, and perhaps in the main, upon the sympathies of the fairly well-educated classes. Rightly or wrongly, young people in Europe were taught for the better part of a century that many of the most important conquests of modern life had been obtained as a consequence of the great Revolution, or by other revolutions. Given such an education, it is not to be wondered at that revolution-ary attempts and successful revolutions were not viewed with any great repugnance by the majority of the people, at least as long as they offered no serious menace or actual injury to material interests. Naturally, such feelings will be stronger and more widespread in countries where the de facto or legal governments themselves have issued from revolutions, so that, while condemning rebellions in general, they are obliged to glorify the one good, the one holy insurrection from which they sprang themselves.

6.3 ADMINISTRATION AND REVOLUTION

From Alexis de Tocqueville, On the State of Society in France before the Revolution of 1789, *translated by Henry Reeve, pp. 367–71.*

The first English Revolution, which overthrew the whole political constitution of this country and abolished the monarchy itself, touched but superficially the secondary laws of the land and changed scarcely any of the customs and usages of the nation. The administration of justice and the conduct of public business retained their old forms and followed even their past aberrations. In the heat of the Civil Wars the twelve judges of England are said to have continued to go the circuit twice a year. Everything was not, therefore, abandoned to agitation at the same time. The Revolution was circumscribed in its effects, and English society, although shaken at its apex, remained firm upon its base.

France herself has since 1789 witnessed several revolutions which have fundamentally changed the whole structure of her government. Most of them have been very sudden and brought about by force, in open violation of the existing laws. Yet the disorder they have caused has never been either long or general; scarcely have they been felt by the bulk of the nation, sometimes they have been unperceived.

The reason is that since 1789 the administrative constitution of France has ever remained standing amidst the ruins of her political constitutions. The person of the sovereign or the form of the government was changed, but the daily course of affairs was neither interrupted nor disturbed: every man still remained submissive, in the small concerns which interested himself, to the rules and usages with which he was already familiar; he was dependent on the secondary powers to which it had always been his custom to defer; and in most cases he had still to do with the very same agents; for, if at each Revolution the administration was decapitated, its trunk still remained unmutilated and alive; the same public duties were discharged by the same public officers, who carried with them through all the vicissitudes of political legislation the same temper and the same practice. They judged and they administered in the name of the King, afterwards in the name of the Republic, at last in the name of the Emperor. And when Fortune had again given the same turn to her wheel, they began once more to judge and to administer for the King, for the Republic, and for the Emperor, the same persons doing the same thing, for what is there in the name of a master? Their business was not so much to be good citizens as to be good administrators and good judicial officers. As soon as the first shock was over, it seemed, therefore, as if nothing had stirred in the country.

6.4 BUREAUCRACY EQUALS THE END OF REVOLUTION

From Max Weber (1864–1920), 'Bureaucracy', in From Max Weber: Essays in Sociology, translated and edited by H. H. Gerth and C. Wright Mills (London, 1948), pp. 228–30.

Once it is fully established, bureaucracy is among those social structures which are the hardest to destroy. Bureaucracy is *the* means of carrying 'community action' over into rationally ordered 'societal action'. Therefore, as an instrument for 'societalising' relations of power, bureaucracy has been and is a power instrument of the first order – for the one who controls the bureaucratic apparatus.

Under otherwise equal conditions, a 'societal action', which is methodically ordered and led, is superior to every resistance of 'mass' or even of 'communal action.' And where the bureaucratisation of administration has been completely carried through, a form of power relation is established that is practically unshatterable.

The individual bureaucrat cannot squirm out of the apparatus in which he is harnessed. In contrast to the honorific or avocational 'notable', the professional bureaucrat is chained to his activity by his entire material and ideal existence. In the great majority of cases, he is only a single cog in an ever-moving mechanism which prescribes to him an essentially fixed route of march. The official is entrusted with specialised tasks and normally the mechanism cannot be put into motion or arrested by him, but only from the very top. The individual bureaucrat is thus forged to the community of all the functionaries who are integrated into the mechanism. They have a common interest in seeing that the mechanism continues its functions and that the societally exercised authority carries on.

The ruled, for their part, cannot dispense with or replace the bureaucratic apparatus of authority once it exists. For this bureaucracy rests upon expert training, a functional specialisation of work, and an attitude set for habitual and virtuoso-like mastery of single yet methodically integrated functions. If the official stops working, or if his work is forcefully interrupted, chaos results, and it is difficult to improvise replacements from among the governed who are fit to master such chaos. This holds for public administration as well as for private economic management. More and more the material fate of the masses depends upon the steady and correct functioning of the increasingly bureaucratic organisations of private capitalism. The idea of eliminating these organisations becomes more and more utopian.

The discipline of officialdom refers to the attitude-set of the official for precise obedience within his *habitual* activity, in public as well as in private organisations. This discipline increasingly becomes the basis of all order, however great the practical importance of administration on the basis of the filed documents may be. The naïve idea of Bakuninism of destroying the basis of 'acquired rights' and 'domination' by destroying public documents overlooks the settled orientation of *man* for keeping to the habitual rules and regulations that continue to exist independently of the documents. Every reorganisation of beaten or dissolved troops, as well as the restoration of administrative orders destroyed by revolt, panic, or other catastrophes, is realised by appealing to the trained orientation of obedient compliance to such orders. Such compliance has been conditioned into the officials, on the one hand, and, on the other hand, into the governed. If such an appeal is successful it brings, as it were, the disturbed mechanism into gear again.

The objective indispensability of the once-existing apparatus, with its peculiar, 'impersonal' character, means that the mechanism – in contrast to feudal orders based upon personal piety – is easily made to work for anybody who knows how to gain control over it.

A rationally ordered system of officials continues to function smoothly after the enemy has occupied the area; he merely needs to change the top officials. This body of officials continues to operate because it is to the vital interest of everyone concerned, including above all the enemy.

During the course of his long years in power, Bismarck brought his ministerial colleagues into unconditional bureaucratic dependence by eliminating all independent statesmen. Upon his retirement, he saw to his surprise that they continued to manage their offices unconcerned and undismayed, as if he had not been the master mind and creator of these creatures, but rather as if some single figure had been exchanged for some other figure in the bureaucratic machine. With all the changes of masters in France since the time of the First Empire, the power machine has remained essentially the same. Such a machine makes 'revolution', in the sense of the forceful creation of entirely new formations of authority, technically more and more impossible, especially when the apparatus controls the modern means of communication (telegraph, etc.) and also by virtue of its internal rationalised structure. In classic fashion, France has demonstrated how this process has substituted *coups d'état* for 'revolutions': all successful transformations in France have amounted to *coups d'état*.

6.5 THE OBSOLESCENCE OF STREET-FIGHTING AND BARRICADES

From Friedrich Engels, 'Introduction' (1895) to Marx's The Class Struggles in France *1848–50, in Marx and Engels, Selected Works in Two Volumes, vol. 1, pp. 122–5, 128–34.*

See 'Introduction', p. 89.

(i)

When the February Revolution broke out, all of us, as far as our conceptions of the conditions and the course of revolutionary movements were concerned, were under the spell of previous historical experience, particularly that of France. It was, indeed, the latter which had dominated the whole of European history since 1789, and from which now once again the signal had gone forth for general revolutionary change. It was, therefore, natural and unavoidable that our conceptions of the nature and the course of the 'social' revolution proclaimed in Paris in February 1848, of the revolution of the proletariat, should be strongly coloured by memories of the prototypes of 1789 and 1830. Moreover, when the Paris uprising found its echo in the victorious insurrections in Vienna, Milan and Berlin; when the whole of Europe right up to the Russian frontier was swept into the movement; when thereupon in Paris, in June, the first great battle for power between the proletariat and the bourgeoisie was fought; when the very victory of its class so shook the bourgeoisie of all countries that it fled back into the arms of the monarchist-feudal reaction which had just been overthrown – there could be no doubt for us, under the circumstances then obtaining, that the great decisive combat had commenced, that it would have to be fought out in a single, long and vicissitudinous period of revolution, but that it could only end in the final victory of the proletariat. . . .

But history has shown us to have been wrong, has revealed our point of view of that time to have been an illusion. It has done even more: it has not merely dispelled the erroneous notions we then held; it has also completely transformed the conditions under which the proletariat has to fight. The mode of struggle of 1848 is today obsolete in every respect, and this is a point which deserves closer examination on the present occasion.

All revolutions up to the present day have resulted in the displacement of one definite class rule by another; but all ruling classes up to now have been only small minorities in relation to the ruled mass of the people. One ruling minority was thus overthrown; another minority seized the helm of state in its stead and refashioned the state institutions to suit its own interests. This was on every occasion the minority group qualified and called to rule by the given degree of economic development; and just for that reason, and only for that reason, it happened that the ruled majority either participated in the revolution for the benefit of the former or else calmly acquiesced in it. But if we disregard the concrete content in each case, the common form of all these revolutions was that they were minority revolutions. Even when the majority took part, it did so – whether wittingly or not – only in the service of a minority; but because of this, or even simply because of the passive, unresisting attitude of the majority, this minority acquired the appearance of being the representative of the whole people.

As a rule, after the first great success, the victorious minority divided; one half was satisfied with what had been gained, the other wanted to go still further, and put forward new demands, which, partly at least, were also in the real or apparent interest of the great mass of the people. In individual cases these more radical demands were actually forced through, but often only for the moment; the more moderate party would regain the upper hand, and what had last been won would wholly or partly be lost again; the vanquished would then shriek of treachery or ascribe their defeat to accident. In reality, however, the truth of the matter was largely this: the achievements of the first victory were only safeguarded by the second victory of the more radical party; this having been attained, and, with it, what was necessary for the moment, the radicals and their achievements vanished once more from the stage.

All revolutions of modern times, beginning with the great English Revolution of the seventeenth century, showed these features, which appeared inseparable from every revolutionary struggle. They appeared applicable, also, to the struggle of the proletariat for its emancipation; all the more applicable, since precisely in 1848 there were but a very few people who had any idea at all of the direction in which this emancipation was to be sought. The proletarian masses themselves, even in Paris, after the victory, were still absolutely in the dark as to the path to be taken. And yet the movement was there, instinctive, spontaneous, irrepressible. Was not this just the situation in which a revolution had to succeed, led, true, by a minority, but this time not in the interest of the minority, but in the veriest interest of the majority? If, in all the longer revolutionary periods, it was so easy to win the great masses of the people by the merely plausible false representations of the forward-thrusting minorities, why should they be less susceptible to ideas which were the truest reflection of their economic condition, which were nothing but the clear, rational expression of their needs, of needs not yet understood but merely vaguely felt by them? To be sure, this revolutionary mood of the masses had almost always, and usually very speedily, given way to lassitude or even to a revulsion of feeling as soon as illusion evaporated and disappointment set in. But here it was not a question of false representations, but of giving effect to the highest special interests of the great majority itself, interests which, true, were at that time by no means clear to this great majority, but which soon enough had to become clear to it in the course of giving practical effect to them, by their convincing obviousness. And when, as Marx showed in his third article, in the spring of 1850, the development of the bourgeois republic that arose out of the 'social' Revolution of 1848 had even concentrated real power in the hands of the big bourgeoisie – monarchistically inclined as it was into the bargain – and, on the other hand, had grouped all the other social classes, peasantry as well as petty bourgeoisie, round the proletariat, so that, during and after the common victory, not they but the proletariat grown wise by experience had to become the decisive factor – was there not every prospect then of turning the revolution of the minority into a revolution of the majority?

History has proved us, and all who thought like us, wrong. It has made it clear that the state of economic development on the Continent at that time was not, by a long way, ripe for the elimination of capitalist production; it has proved this by the economic revolution which, since 1848, has seized the whole of the Continent, and has caused big industry to take real root in France, Austria, Hungary, Poland and, recently, in Russia, while it has made Germany positively an industrial country of the first rank – all on a capitalist basis, which in the year 1848, therefore, still had great capacity for expansion. But it is just this industrial revolution which has everywhere produced clarity in class relations, has removed a number of intermediate forms handed down from the period of manufacture and in Eastern Europe even from guild handicraft, has created a genuine bourgeoisie and a genuine large-scale industrial proletariat and has pushed them into the foreground of social development.

(ii)

But the German workers rendered a second great service to their cause in addition to the first, a service performed by their mere existence as the strongest, best disciplined and most rapidly growing Socialist Party. They supplied their comrades in all countries with a new weapon, and one of the sharpest, when they showed them how to make use of universal suffrage.

There had long been universal suffrage in France, but it had fallen into disrepute through the misuse to which the Bonapartist government had put it. After the Commune there was no workers' party to make use of it. It also existed in Spain since the republic, but in Spain boycott of elections was ever the rule of all serious opposition parties. The experience of the Swiss with universal suffrage was also anything but encouraging for a workers' party. The revolutionary workers of the Latin countries had been wont to regard the suffrage as a snare, as an instrument of government trickery. It was otherwise in Germany. The *Communist Manifesto* had already proclaimed the winning of universal suffrage, of democracy, as one of the first and most important tasks of the militant proletariat, and Lassalle had again taken up this point. Now, when Bismarck found himself compelled to introduce this franchise as the only means of interesting the mass of the people in his plans, our workers immediately took it in earnest and sent August Bebel to the first, constituent Reichstag. And from that day on, they have used the franchise in a way which has paid them a thousandfold and has served as a model to the workers of all countries. The franchise has been, in the words of the French Marxist programme, *transformé, de moyen de duperie qu'il a été jusqu'ici, en intsrument d'émancipation* – transformed by them from a means of deception, which it was before, into an instrument of emancipation. And if universal suffrage had offered no other advantage than that it allowed us to count our numbers every three years; that by the regularly established, unexpectedly rapid rise in the number of our votes it increased in equal measure the workers' certainty of victory and the dismay of their opponents, and so became our best means of propaganda; that it accurately informed us concerning our own strength and that of all hostile parties, and thereby provided us with a measure of proportion for our actions second to none, safeguarding us from untimely timidity as much as from untimely foolhardiness – if this had been the only advantage we gained from the suffrage, it would still have been much more than enough. But it did more than this by far. In election agitation it provided us with a means, second to none, of getting in touch with the mass of the people where they still stand aloof from us; of forcing all parties to defend their views and actions against our attacks before all the people; and, further, it provided our representatives in the Reichstag with a platform from which they could speak to their opponents in parliament, and to the masses without, with quite other authority and freedom than in the press or at meetings. Of what avail was their Anti-Socialist Law to the government and the bourgeoisie when election compaigning and socialist speeches in the Reichstag continually broke through it?

With this successful utilisation of universal suffrage, however, an entirely new method of proletarian struggle came into operation, and this method quickly developed further. It was found that the state institutions, in which the rule of the bourgeoisie is organised, offer the working class still further opportunities to fight these very state institutions. The workers took part in elections to particular Diets, to municipal councils and to trades courts; they contested with the bourgeoisie every post in the occupation of which a sufficient part of the proletariat had a say. And so it happened that the bourgeoisie and the government came to be much more afraid of the legal than of the illegal action of the workers' party, of the results of elections than of those of rebellion.

For here, too, the conditions of the struggle had essentially changed. Rebellion in the old style, street-fighting with barricades, which decided the issue everywhere up to 1848, was to a considerable extent obsolete.

Let us have no illusions about it: a real victory of an insurrection over the military in street-fighting, a victory as between two armies, is one of the rarest exceptions. And the insurgents counted on it just as rarely. For them it was solely a question of making the troops yield to moral influences which, in a fight between the armies of two warring countries, do not come into play at all or do so to a much smaller extent. If they succeed in this, the troops fail to respond, or the commanding officers lose their heads, and the insurrection wins. If they do not succeed in this, then, even where the military are in the minority, the superiority of better equipment and training, of single leadership, of the planned employment of the military forces and of discipline makes itself felt. The most that an insurrection can achieve in the way of actual tactical operations is the proper construction and defence of a single barricade. Mutual support, the disposition and employment of reserves – in short, concerted and co-ordinated action of the individual detachments, indispensable even for the defence of one section of a town, not to speak of the whole of a large town, will be attainable only to a very limited extent, and most of the time not at all. Concentration of the military forces at a decisive point is, of course, out of the question here. Hence passive defence is the prevailing form of fighting; the attack will rise here and there, but only by way of exception, to occasional thrusts and flank assaults; as a rule, however, it will be limited to occupation of positions abandoned by retreating troops. In addition, the military have at their disposal artillery and fully equipped corps of trained engineers, resources of war which, in nearly every case, the insurgents entirely lack. No wonder then, that even the barricade fighting conducted with the greatest heroism – Paris, June 1848; Vienna, October 1848; Dresden, May 1849 – ended in the defeat of the insurrection as soon as the leaders of the attack, unhampered by political considerations, acted from the purely military standpoint, and their soldiers remained reliable.

The numerous successes of the insurgents up to 1848 were due to a great variety of causes. In Paris, in July 1830 and February 1848, as in most of the Spanish street-fighting, a citizen's guard stood between the insurgents and the military. This guard either sided directly with the insurrection, or else by its lukewarm, indecisive attitude caused the troops likewise to vacillate, and supplied the insurrection with arms into the bargain. Where this citizens' guard opposed the insurrection from the outset, as in June 1848 in Paris, the insurrection was vanquished. In Berlin in 1848, the people were victorious partly through a considerable accession of new fighting forces during the night and the morning of [March] the 19th, partly as a result of the exhaustion and bad victualling of the troops, and, finally, partly as a result of the paralysis that was seizing the command. But in all cases the fight was won because the troops failed to respond, because the commanding officers lost the faculty to decide or because their hands were tied.

Even in the classic time of street-fighting, therefore, the barricade produced more of a moral than a material effect. It was a means of shaking the steadfastness of the military. If it held out until this was attained, victory was won; if not, there was defeat. This is the main point, which must be kept in view, likewise, when the chances of possible future street-fighting are examined.

Already in 1849, these chances were pretty poor. Everywhere the bourgeoisie had thrown in its lot with the governments, 'culture and property' had hailed and feasted the military moving against insurrection. The spell of the barricade was broken; the soldier no longer saw behind it 'the people', but rebels, agitators, plunderers, levellers, the scum of society; the officer had in the course of time become versed in the tactical forms of street-fighting, he no longer marched straight ahead and without cover against the improvised breastwork, but went round it through gardens, yards and houses. And this was now successful, with a little skill, in nine cases out of ten.

But since then there have been very many more changes, and all in favour of the military. If the big towns have become considerably bigger, the armies have become bigger still. Paris and Berlin have, since 1848, grown less than fourfold, but their garrisons have grown more than that. By means of the railways, these garrisons can, in twenty-four hours, be more than doubled, and in forty-eight hours they can be increased to huge armies. The arming of this enormously increased number of troops has become incomparably more effective. In 1848 the smooth-bore, muzzle-loading percussion gun, today the small calibre, breech-loading magazine rifle, which shoots four times as far, ten times as accurately and ten times as fast as the former. At that time the relatively ineffective round shot and grape-shot of the artillery; today the percussion shells, of which one is sufficient to demolish the best barricade. At that time the pick-axe of the sapper for breaking through fire-walls; today the dynamite cartridge.

On the other hand, all the conditions of the insurgents' side have grown worse. An insurrection with which all sections of the people sympathise will hardly recur; in the class struggle all the middle strata will probably never group themselves round the proletariat so exclusively that in comparison the party of reaction gathered round the bourgeoisie will well-nigh disappear. The 'people', therefore, will always appear divided, and thus a most powerful lever, so extraordinarily effective in 1848, is gone. If more soldiers who have seen service came over to the insurrectionists, the arming of them would become so much the more difficult. The hunting and fancy guns of the munitions shops – even if not previously made unusable by removal of part of the lock by order of the police – are far from being a match for the magazine rifle of the soldier, even in close fighting. Up to 1848 it was possible to make the necessary ammunition oneself out of powder and lead; today the cartridges differ for each gun, and are everywhere alike only in one point, namely, that they are a complicated product of big industry, and therefore not to be manufactured *ex tempore*, with the result that most guns are useless as long as one does not possess the ammunition specially suited to them. And, finally, since 1848 the newly built quarters of the big cities have been laid out in long, straight, broad streets, as though made to give full effect to the new cannon and rifles. The revolutionist would have to be mad who himself chose the new working-class districts in the North or East of Berlin for a barricade fight.

Does that mean that in the future street-fighting will no longer play any role? Certainly not. It only means that the conditions since 1848 have become far more unfavourable for civilian fighters and far more favourable for the military. In future, street-fighting can, therefore, be victorious only if this disadvantageous situation is compensated by other factors. Accordingly, it will occur more seldom in the beginning of a great revolution than in its further progress, and will have to be undertaken with greater forces. These, however, may then well prefer, as in the whole great French Revolution or on 4 September and 31 October 1870, in Paris, the open attack to the passive barricade tactics.

Does the reader now understand why the powers that be positively want to get us to go where the guns shoot and the sabres slash? Why they accuse us today of cowardice, because we do not betake ourselves without more ado into the street, where we are certain of defeat in advance? Why they so earnestly implore us to play for once the part of cannon fodder?

The gentlemen pour out their prayers and their challenges for nothing, for absolutely nothing. We are not so stupid. They might just as well demand from their enemy in the next war that he should accept battle in the line formation of old Fritz, or in the columns of whole divisions à la Wagram and Waterloo, and with the flint-lock in his hands at that. If conditions have changed in the case of war between nations, this is no less true in the case of the class struggle.

The time of surprise attacks, of revolutions carried through by small conscious minorities at the head of unconscious masses, is past. Where it is a question of a complete transformation of the social organisation, the masses themselves must also be in it, must themselves already have grasped what is at stake, what they are going in for, body and soul. The history of the last fifty years has taught us that. But in order that the masses may understand what is to be done, long, persistent work is required, and it is just this work that we are now pursuing, and with a success which drives the enemy to despair.

6.6 REVOLUTIONARY ILLUSIONS

From Albert Camus (1923–60), 'Neither Victims Nor Executioners' (1946), translated by Dwight MacDonald, and reprinted in Liberation, *February 1960.*

In a series of newspaper articles just after the Second World War, Camus argued that the classical European concept of revolution had become a dangerous illusion in the context of contemporary world politics.

[E]verybody talks about revolution, and quite sincerely too. But sincerity is not in itself a virtue: some kinds are so confused that they are worse than lies. Not the language of the heart but merely that of clear thinking is what we need today. Ideally, a revolution is a change in political and economic institutions in order to introduce more freedom and justice; practically, it is a complex of historical events, often undesirable ones, which brings about the happy transformation.

Can one say that we use this word today in its classical sense? When people nowadays hear the word, 'revolution', they think of a change in property relations (generally collectivisation) which may be brought about either by majority legislation or by a minority coup.

This concept obviously lacks meaning in present historical circumstances. For one thing, the violent seizure of power is a romantic idea which the perfection of armaments has made illusory.

Since the repressive apparatus of a modern State commands tanks and airplanes, tanks and airplanes are needed to counter it. 1789 and 1917 are still historic dates, but they are no longer historic examples.

And even assuming this conquest of power were possible, by violence or by law, it would be effective only if France (or Italy or Czechoslovakia) could be put into parentheses and isolated from the rest of the world. For, in the actual historical situation of 1946, a change in our own property system would involve, to give only one example, such consequences to our American credits that our economy would be threatened with ruin. A right-wing coup would be no more successful, because of Russia with her millions of French Communist voters and her position as the dominant continental power. The truth is – excuse me for stating openly what everyone knows and no one says – the truth is that we French are not free to make a revolution. Or at least that we can be no longer revolutionary all by ourselves, since there no longer exists any policy, conservative or socialist, which can operate exclusively with a national framework.

Thus we can only speak of world revolution. The revolution will be made on a world scale or it will not be made at all. But what meaning does this expression still retain? There was a time when it was thought that international reform would be brought about by the conjunction or the synchronisation of a number of national revolutions – a kind of totting-up of miracles. But today one can conceive only the extension of a revolution that has already succeeded. This is something Stalin has very well understood, and it is the kindest explanation of his policies (the other being to refuse Russia the right to speak in the name of revolution).

This viewpoint boils down to conceiving of Europe and the West as a single nation in which a powerful and well-armed minority is struggling to take power. But if the conservative forces – in this case, the USA – are equally well armed, clearly the idea of revolution is replaced by that of ideological warfare. More precisely, world revolution today involves a very great danger of war. Every future revolution will be a foreign revolution. It will begin with a military occupation – or, what comes to the same thing, the blackmail threat of one. And it will become significant only when the occupying power has conquered the rest of the world.

6.7 'THIRD WORLD' REVOLUTION: THE PEASANTRY AND GUERRILLA WARFARE

From Mao Tse-tung, Selected Works in Five Volumes (New York, 1954), vol. 1, pp. 116–17, 122–4. From a letter to a party comrade, 1930.

See 'Introduction', pp. 89–90.

The theory that we should, on a nation-wide scale and in all regions, win over the masses first and establish political power afterwards, does not fit in with the actual situation of the Chinese revolution. It stems in the main from the failure to understand clearly that China is a semi-colony contended for by many imperialist powers. If one clearly understands this, then first, one can understand why in China alone in the world there is such an unusual thing as a prolonged strife within the ruling classes, why the fight intensifies and expands day by day, and why no unified political power has ever come into being. Secondly, one can understand how important the peasant problem is, and consequently why rural uprisings have developed on such a nation-wide scale as at present. Thirdly, one can understand the correctness of the slogan about a workers' and peasants' democratic political power. Fourthly, one can understand another unusual thing which corresponds to and arises out of the unusual thing that in China alone in the world there is a prolonged strife within the ruling classes, and that is the existence and development of the Red Army and guerrilla troops, and, together with them, the existence and development of small Red areas that have grown amid the encirclement of the White political power (no such unusual thing is found anywhere except in China). Fifthly, one can also understand that the formation and development of the Red Army, the guerrilla units and the Red areas are the highest form of the peasant struggle under the leadership of the proletariat in semi-colonial China, the inevitable outcome of the growth of the peasant struggle in a semi-colony, and are undoubtedly the most important factors in accelerating the revolutionary upsurge throughout the country. And sixthly, one can also understand that the policy of purely mobile guerrilla-like activities cannot accomplish the task of accelerating the nation-wide revolutionary upsurge, while the kind of policies adopted by Chu Teh and Mao Tse-tung and by Fang Chih-min are undoubtedly correct – policies such as establishing base areas; building up political power according to plan; deepening the agrarian revolution; and expanding the people's armed forces by developing in due order first the township Red guards, then the district Red guards, then the county Red guards, then the local Red Army, and then a regular Red Army; and expanding political power by advancing in a series of waves, etc., etc. Only thus can we win the confidence of the revolutionary masses throughout the country, just as the Soviet Union has done throughout the world. Only thus can we create tremendous difficulties for the reactionary ruling classes, shake their very foundations, and precipitate their internal disintegration. And only thus can we really create a Red Army that will be our chief weapon in the coming great revolution. In short, only thus can we accelerate the revolutionary upsurge. . . .

Proletarian leadership is the sole key to the victory of the revolution. The laying of the Party's proletarian basis and the establishment of the Party branches in industrial enterprises in key districts are the important organisational tasks of the Party at present; but at the same time the development of struggles in the countryside, the establishment of the Red political power in small areas, and the creation and expansion of the Red Army, are in particular the main conditions for helping the struggle in the cities and accelerating the revolutionary upsurge. It is therefore a mistake to abandon the struggle in the cities, and in our opinion it is also a mistake for any of our Party members to fear the development of the power of the peasants lest it become stronger than that of the workers and hence detrimental to the revolution. For the revolution in semi-colonial China will fail only if the peasant struggle is deprived of the leadership of the workers, and it will never suffer just because the peasants, through their struggle, become more powerful than the workers. . . .

The tactics we have worked out during the last three years in the course of the struggle are indeed different from any employed in ancient or modern times, in China or elsewhere. With our tactics, the struggles of the masses are daily expanding and no enemy, however powerful, can cope with us. Ours are guerrilla tactics. They consist mainly of the five following points:

Disperse the forces among the masses to arouse them, and concentrate the forces to deal with the enemy.

The enemy advances, we retreat: the enemy halts, we harass; the enemy tires, we attack; the enemy retreats, we pursue.

In an independent regime with stabilised territory, we adopt the policy of advancing in a series of waves. When pursued by a powerful enemy, we adopt the policy of circling around in a whirling motion.

Arouse the largest numbers of the masses in the shortest possible time and by the best possible methods.

These tactics are just like casting a net; we should be able to cast the net wide or draw it in at any moment. We cast it wide to win over the masses and draw it in to deal with the enemy. Such are the tactics we have applied in the past three years.

6.8 THE INTELLIGENTSIA AND TWENTIETH-CENTURY REVOLUTIONS

From Hugh Seton-Watson, 'Twentieth Century Revolutions', The Political Quarterly, vol. XXII, no. 3 (July–Sept. 1951), pp. 251–9.

For this and the following extract, see 'Introduction', p. 88.

The first half of the twentieth century is richer than any previous period of human history in the activities of revolutionary movements. Some have failed, others are still engaged in the struggle. A few have achieved revolutions of historic importance. But there is one important feature of the twentieth century revolutionary movements which distinguishes them from those of the nineteenth century. The earlier movements arose in culturally and economically advanced countries, while those of the present century have for the most part affected backward regions and peoples.

These movements are much discussed at present by journalists and politicians, but have received little attention from historians. In current discussions the main emphasis is usually placed on the mass aspect of the movements and on economic factors. It is assumed that their strength comes mainly from the unrest of subject nations, industrial proletariats and impoverished peasants. The victories which they have won are usually attributed to mass support. The conclusion is that revolutions can best be averted if the wealthier nations invest large sums in the development of backward economies. Better food crops, new jobs in industry and more extensive trade will reduce the mass poverty and deprive the revolutionaries of their opportunity.

It would be absurd to deny that revolutionary movements thrive on mass poverty and mass discontent, or that improvement in the standard of living of the masses makes for political stability. But two further factors deserve consideration. The first is the origin and the nature of revolutionary leadership. The second is the political framework within which revolutionary movements develop. Both these factors have of course been minutely studied by historians of the revolutions of the eighteenth and nineteenth centuries in Western Europe and North America. They have, however, been somewhat neglected in connection with the twentieth-century movements in Eastern Europe, Asia and Africa. Such attempts as have been made are too often the work of uncritical admirers or passionate adversaries. Yet even a brief examination of these two factors may make possible some significant conclusions about the twentieth-century revolutionary movements of backward peoples.

West European and American political commentators and economists are too inclined to consider world problems from the point of view of the economics and political traditions of Western Europe and North America. But the 'western society' on which their ideas are based is not the typical society of the world. It exists only in Scandinavia, north-west Europe, North America, and the British Dominions of the Pacific. If northern Italy and Germany are added, the whole area has a population of less than 400 million out of a world population of more than 2,000 million.

The society of this 'north-western corner' of the world, which has grown up since the end of the Middle Ages, has certain specific features. The class structure is balanced. The level of skill and the standard of living of workers and farmers are on the whole high. There is a numerous and influential middle class, in which the three subdivision of business, free professions and administration play

307

their parts. Education is widespread and long established. The tradition of representative institutions, both national and local, is deeply rooted. Though there are great differences in wealth, all citizens belong to the same century. Class structure, education and constitutional forms vary considerably within different regions and countries of the north-west corner, but all share these general characteristics, in contrast to the lands outside the corner.

If the typical classes of the north-west corner are skilled workers, educated farmers and business men, the typical classes of the outside world are unskilled labourers, uneducated peasants and bureaucrats. In southern and eastern Europe, Asia, Africa and Latin America the great majority of the population are primitive and poverty-stricken peasants. In the last decades the rapid industrialisation of certain regions has reduced the number of peasants and increased the number of unskilled workers in mines or factories, little if at all less primitive or poor. One reason for the poverty of the peasants has been the survival of great landed estates and of various semi-feudal legal forms. This was the case in Russia before 1917 and in Hungary until 1945. It is still the case in southern Italy, Spain, Egypt and large parts of Asia, Africa and Latin America. But experience has shown that the distribution of landlords' estates among the peasants – which was done in parts of Eastern Europe after 1918, in other parts after 1945, and in Japan, Korea and China after the Second World War – is not the end of the peasants' poverty. A more basic cause of poverty is rural over-population. The numbers of people in the villages have grown more rapidly than the output of the soil has been increased or than new jobs in industry have been created. Overpopulation means under-employment for the peasants, and a reserve of half-employed peasants keeps down the level of wages for all but the skilled minority among the urban workers.

For those sons of peasants who are able by ability or good fortune to rise in the social scale the best opportunities have usually lain in the state service. But the growing influx of recruits from below inflates the bureaucracy intolerably. As the numbers of bureaucrats grow faster than the national wealth, their material conditions deteriorate. An enormous underpaid civil service breeds corruption: only by bribery can the poor official feed his family. To corruption must be added a tradition of arrogance and brutality. The official is accustomed to despise and bully the human cattle whom it is his duty to push, pull or drive whither his masters bid. This has certainly long been the practice in Spain, Hungary, Poland, the Balkans and Russia. It is still more so in Turkey, Persia, China or Japan. In colonial countries the situation has been somewhat different. The West European administrators have tried, with varying success, to bring to their colonies the more civilised methods of administration prevalent in their own countries, and have also resisted the pressure to inflate the numbers of officials. But the lower ranks of their administration have been filled with local people who have imperfectly acquired the higher standards, while the limitation of numbers has contributed above all to the frustration of the subject nations. As soon as they attain independence the colonial peoples rapidly expand their civil services. The world must be shown that they are not 'unfit to govern', and jobs must be found for the boys. Corruption increases faster than ever, and the new bureaucrats feel even more strongly than the old how distinct and superior a caste they are.

In this type of society, which until recently was typical of most of the world outside the north-west corner, the masses were too inert and the bureaucrats too powerful. If there was to be radical change, leadership must be found. The source of such leadership has been the small educated class – the 'intelligentsia'.

The intelligentsia is a product of western influence. Already in the eighteenth-century western ideas and ways of life were known to the aristocracies of Poland, Hungary and Russia. During the nineteenth century schools and universities developed in these countries, slowly it is true, but with important effects. The professional class was formed from two directions, from the children of the landed gentry for whom there was no place on the family estate, and from the children of small officials, merchants and village shop-keepers who had just enough money, ability or 'connections' to mount the educational ladder. Even the reactionary but incompetent Ministers of Education of mid-nineteenth-century Russia were unable either to reserve higher education to members of the nobility or to purge it of progressive ideas. In the Balkan countries liberated from Turkish rule no social hierarchy barred the way to education. The Balkan governments were keen to extend education: the obstacle was the meagre wealth of the states. Though the intention was education for all, the more prosperous families were in fact privileged. The children of the army officers, officials, innkeepers, pig-merchants and village usurers from whom the ruling class of the new states was formed, had better chances than the children of peasant smallholders, miners, railwaymen or factory workers. In Asia the process started later. In the Middle East the Islamic system of education was open to comparatively poor children, but it was more or less unrelated to the needs of the nineteenth and twentieth centuries. The same was true of the Confucian system in China. The introduction of western ideas and influences was largely the work of such institutions as the French schools in the Levant, the American Robert College at Constantinople, the American University of Beirut, and European and American missions in China. Japan alone among Asiatic countries systematically copied European education and diffused it among her subjects. In Latin America considerable efforts had been made in education ever since the Spanish and Portuguese conquests.

The best education available at the most modern schools and universities in Eastern Europe, Asia and Latin America has been little inferior to that available at the same time anywhere in the western world. Some institutions in Africa have recently approached or attained the same standard. The best scientists, writers, doctors or engineers produced by this education have been as good at their jobs as their western counterparts. They have entered the twentieth century, while their peoples, suffering from social injustice and political oppression, have remained in the eighteenth, or fifteenth, or tenth century.

Many, probably most, members of the East European and Asian intelligentsias accepted this fact. Some believed that by becoming twentieth-century people, and doing twentieth-century jobs, they were working for their own nations' good, and would help to raise their nations to their level. Others were so engrossed in their special skill that the wider issues did not occur to them. Others simply enjoyed the life of a French lawyer or an American engineer, rather than that of a Hungarian worker, a Lebanese peasant or a Chinese coolie. Their lives were more agreeable than those of their compatriots: let the latter fend for themselves.

But a minority, and in some countries a very numerous minority, rebelled. They were horrified by the contrast between themselves and their peoples, between the fifteenth and twentieth centuries. The social injustices were intolerable, and the political factors which perpetuated them – the dominance of a privileged class or a privileged nation – must be swept away. There were young Slovaks who were not content, by learning the Magyar language and so reaching a Magyar university, to merge themselves in the Hungarian ruling class, but insisted on fighting for the national and social liberation of the submerged Slovak nation. There were Russian or Chinese intellectuals, of both distinguished and humble birth, who could not ignore the land-hunger in the villages, the maltreatment of peasants by landlords or police, the dead weight of a bureaucracy suspicious of every generous initiative.

To these idealist motives must be added personal motives for revolt. Semi-feudal legal survivals of foreign rule were not only socially or nationally unjust: they were also obstacles to the ambitions of the local intellectuals. Poles, Ukrainians, Balts and Caucasians in the Russian Empire; South Slavs, Slovaks and Roumanians in Hungary; the Asiatic and African subjects of European colonial empires found their way to power and wealth barred by members of the dominant nations. In Hungary, Roumania and Poland between the world wars many of the best posts in business and the free professions were held by Jews. University graduates who found no jobs attributed their difficulties to a sinister Jewish conspiracy. Idealism and interest alike led them to anti-semitic fascism. Chinese in Siam and Malaya, Indians in East Africa, Greeks in the Middle East, and Europeans throughout Asia, form a host of 'Jewish problems', seem to the young intellectuals of each country to have robbed them of their birthright, and drive them to revolutionary nationalism. Balkan university students denounced their professors as 'reactionary' because they failed in their examinations. Egyptian or Indian students have beaten or murdered invigilators who objected to their bringing cribs into the examination hall. To join an extremist party – fascist, nationalist or communist – was emotionally satisfying and required less sustained mental effort than plain hard work. For most of the revolutionary intellectuals of the backward countries the broader and the personal motives existed side by side. The personal motive is perhaps more powerful in colonial countries, where the presence of the foreign Power is a constant irritant, and where the level of education is lower than in Eastern Europe, Japan or even the Middle East. The half-educated are perhaps more frustrated, and more inclined to revolutionary short-cuts, than the fully educated.

It was through the intelligentsia, created by the development of western types of education, that the modern political ideas of Western Europe reached the countries of Eastern Europe, Asia and Africa. It should be noted that the ideas reached the backward countries ready-made, before the economic social and political conditions to which they were related had arisen. Examples are Russia in the 1870s, Bulgaria in the 1890s and China in the 1920s. Even nationalism was preached by the intelligentsia when national consciousness hardly existed among the masses. Examples from Europe are the Slovaks and the Ukrainians. In Asia and Africa this has been still more the case. . . .

The impact of ready-made West European political ideas on these various types of backward societies had effects at least as far-reaching as the impact of West European trade and technique. The political ideas were reflected in political movements, in which inevitably the leadership came from the intelligentsia. In Russia, China, the Ottoman Empire and the Balkan states the radical intellectuals were forced by the repressive policy of dictatorial governments to resort to more or less revolutionary and conspiratorial methods. In Austria-Hungary, Japan and the British and French empires they enjoyed greater freedom of action, though this fell short of 'western democracy' as understood in Britain and France. In general, the radicalism of the intellectuals and their importance in the revolutionary movements varied in inverse proportion to the economic and cultural development of their peoples. As the masses became more prosperous, more skilled and more educated, broadly based mass movements became more possible, the leadership of intellectuals became less essential, and it became more reasonable to hope for improvement by comparatively peaceful means. It is the combination of backward masses, extremist intellectuals and despotic bureaucrats which creates the most conspiratorial movements. . . .

Communism is today the most important of the revolutionary movements among the backward peoples, but it is not and will not necessarily be the only one. Communism, as developed by Stalin and Mao Tse-tung, is only the most important example of a wider phenomenon, the revolt of the backward peoples, led by a section of their intelligentsia, against the West.

6.9 THE FATE OF THE MARXIAN REVOLUTIONARY IDEA: THE REVOLUTION OF UNDERDEVELOPMENT

From Robert C. Tucker, The Marxian Revolutionary Idea *(London, 1970), pp. 135–8.*

It has often been noted – and remains notable – that communist revolutions have not occurred on the model projected by classical Marxism. For Marx and Engels the revolutionary overthrow of bourgeois society was something inherent in the very dynamics of capitalism as a mode of production based on wage labour and the drive to maximise profit. . . . Capitalist economic development, in Marx's view, necessarily brings a proletarianisation of the masses of factory workers and a progressive worsening of their living and working conditions. Marx formulated it as the 'absolute general law of capitalist accumulation' that

the accumulation of wealth at one pole of society involves a simultaneous accumulation of poverty, labour torment, slavery, ignorance, brutalisation, and moral degradation, at the opposite pole – where dwells the class that produces its own product in the form of capital.

At the postulated point in this process at which conditions become wholly intolerable, the masses of workers revolt and the communist revolution occurs with the seizure and socialisation of private property. Thus, classical Marxism envisaged the communist revolution as a *revolution of capitalist breakdown* occurring in the most advanced stage of development of the capitalist system. This was the assumption underlying the expectation of Marx and Engels that communist revolutions would come first in the countries of Western Europe where capitalism was most highly developed.

History has diverged in two fundamental ways from their theory. First, capitalist societies, instead of suffering self-destruction in a proletarian upheaval, have gone through a process of self-modification that Marx would not have thought possible and for which his theory in any event made no provision. In violation of the 'absolute general law of capitalist accumulation', the industrial worker has won improved conditions and has tended to grow more integrated into the society rather than more alienated from it. Capitalist economies have evolved into postcapitalist mixed economies with self-stabilising tools of fiscal regulation and planning. Although significant communist movements still exist in some of these societies, Italy and France in particular, what prospects they may have of coming to power do not derive from the dynamics of capitalist development. No communist revolution has taken place on the classical Marxist model, and no such revolution seems likely. Indeed, societies that have experienced thoroughgoing capitalist development appear to be among the least likely prospects for communist revolution.

If classical Marxism erred in projecting the communist revolution in a form in which it would not occur, it likewise erred in failing to foresee it in the form in which it *would* occur. The communist revolution has not come about as a revolution of capitalist breakdown; large-scale industrialisation has been among its consequences rather than its causes. It does, however, show a certain general pattern. With but two exceptions (Czechoslovakia and East Germany), the typical habitat of communist revolution has been a country of precapitalist or at most semicapitalist economic formation, and one that has shown a tendency to stagnate in its further economic development and modernisation. It has been a country heavily populated by peasants and dependent upon agriculture, although usually with at least a small industrial working class and some development of modern industrial economy; a socially and politically as well as economically backward country, with very sharp class divisions and political institutions of traditional authoritarian complexion. Finally, it has been a country with chronic social unrest and a radical intelligentsia ready to furnish the leadership of a mass-based revolutionary movement to overthrow the old order in the name of national renovation and development. Russia and China are both classic cases in all these respects.

The communist revolution – in so far as we can draw a generalisation concerning its nature on the basis of these facts – is a *revolution of underdevelopment*, and this in two senses: (1) the revolution typically comes about in the setting of underdevelopment as just described; and (2) it becomes, after the achievement of power by the communist movement, a long-term effort to overcome the country's underdevelopment, a revolution of modernisation. The communist revolution is not the sole or necessary form of the revolution of underdevelopment. In some countries, particularly since the end of the Second World War, there have been attempts to carry through such a revolution under non-communist national leadership, which, however, usually borrows some aspects of communist experience and organisational technique. The most that communism might reasonably claim is to have been so far the most influential and in certain respects the most efficacious form of the revolution of underdevelopment. The notable disadvantage of communism lies in the peculiarly great difficulty that it experiences in coming to power. In the Arab Middle East, for example, the revolution of underdevelopment has proceeded – where it has proceeded at all – under nationalist rather than communist auspices, not because the nationalist political forces can carry it through most successfully but because no indigenous communist movement has been capable of competing with nationalist revolutionary groups in the contest for power.

6.10 PROSPECTS FOR REVOLUTION IN INDUSTRIAL SOCIETIES: TWO VIEWS

For the following two extracts, see 'Introduction', pp. 85–6.

6.10.1 *From Raymond Aron,* The Opium of the Intellectuals, *translated by Terence Kilmartin (London, 1957), pp. 310–14.*

The theory of the class struggle, which is still current today, is falsified by a spurious analogy: the rivalry between bourgeoisie and proletariat differs in essence from the rivalry between aristocracy and bourgeoisie.

Certain nineteenth-century thinkers transfigured into a promethean exploit the overthrow of the French monarchy and the blood-stained, terror-haunted, faction-ridden adventure of the Republic. Hegel claimed to have seen the spirit of the world passing on horseback, in the form of an officer risen from the ranks whom the god of battles had crowned. Marx and then Lenin painted dream-pictures of the Jacobins, the active minority which stirs up the stagnant pool of popular feeling, the missionary order in the service of the socialist revolution. There could be no doubt about it – the proletariat would finish the work begun by the bourgeoisie.

The ideologists of the proletariat are bourgeois intellectuals. The bourgeoisie, whether it derived its ideas from Montesquieu, Voltaire or Jean-Jaques Rousseau, set up its own conception of human existence and the political order in opposition to the *Ancien Régime* and the Catholic vision of the world. *The proletariat has never had a conception of the world opposed to that of the bourgeoisie; there has been an ideology of what the proletariat should be or should do, an ideology whose historical ascendancy was most powerful when the number of industrial workers was smallest.* The so-called proletarian party, in the countries where it has seized power, has had peasants rather than factory workers as its troops, and intellectuals, exasperated by the traditional hierarchy or by national humiliation, as its leaders.

The values to which the working class spontaneously subscribes differ from those of the bourgeoisie. It is not impermissible to construct antitheses between the two: the sense of solidarity against the desire for possessions, participation in the community against individualism or egoism, the generosity of the penniless against the avarice of the rich, etc. In any case there is no denying the obvious fact that the system and style of living in working-class districts are very different from those of the wealthy middle classes. So-called proletarian regimes, that is regimes governed by Communist parties, owe practically nothing to authentic working-class culture, to the parties or unions whose leaders themselves belong to the working class.

Popular culture in our century has succumbed to the blows of *Pravda, France-Soir* or the *Readers' Digest*. Revolutionary syndicalist or anarchist movements cannot resist the unconscious coalition of employers' organisations which fear them, and socialist, especially communist, parties which detest them. The latter have been affected by the thought and action of the intellectuals.

It was in the hope of accomplishing fully the ambitions of the bourgeoisie – the conquest of Nature, social equality or equality of opportunity – that the ideologists handed on the torch to the proletariat. The contrast between technological progress and the misery of the workers was a crying scandal. How could one help but impute to private ownership and the anarchy of the market the survival of ancestral poverty which was in fact due to the exigencies of accumulation (capitalist or socialist), insufficient productivity and increases in population. Soft-hearted intellectuals, revolted by injustice, seized on the idea that capitalism, being in itself evil, would be destroyed by its contradictions and that its victims would eventually overthrow the privileged. Marx achieved an improbable synthesis between the Hegelian metaphysic of history, the Jacobin interpretation of the Revolution, and the pessimistic theory of the market economy developed by British authors. To maintain the continuity between the French Revolution and the Russian Revolution, it was only necessary to call Marxist ideology proletarian. But one has merely to open one's eyes to be rid of the illusion.

The market economy and total planning are rival models – which no existing economy actually reproduces – not successive stages in evolution. There is no necessary link between the phases of industrial development and the predominance of one model or the other. Backward economies approximate more to the mode of the planners than do advanced economies. Mixed systems are not monsters incapable of surviving, or transitional forms on the way to the pure type; they are the normal thing. In a planned system one will find most of the categories of the market economy, more or less modified. As the standard of living rises and the Soviet consumer has more freedom of choice, the benefits and the problems of Western prosperity will appear on the other side of the Iron Curtain.

The revolutions of the twentieth century have not been proletarian revolutions; they have been thought up and carried out by intellectuals. They have overthrown the traditional power, ill-adapted to the exigencies of the technological age. The prophets imagined that capitalism would precipitate a revolution comparable to the one which convulsed France at the end of the eighteenth century. Nothing of the sort happened. On the contrary, wherever the ruling classes have been unable or unwilling to reform themselves quickly enough, the dissatisfaction of the bourgeoisie, the impatience of the intellectuals and the immemorial aspirations of the peasants have provoked an explosion.

Neither Russia nor the United States ever fully experienced the struggle between the aristocracy and the bourgeoisie. Tsarism sought to borrow the technical civilisation of the West while discarding its democratic ideas. It has been replaced by a power which has re-established the identification between society and the State, the administrators constituting the only privileged class.

The United States became conscious of its identity through the progressive ideas of the European eighteenth century. It sought to put them into practice on virgin soil which had to be conquered not so much in the face of the Indians, who were doomed to extinction by the gap between their tribal culture and that of the European immigrants, as in the face of recalcitrant Nature and the elements. There was no aristocracy, clinging to its privileges, to restrain the impetus of reason and industry. American religion taught moral strictness, not a creed or othodoxy. It urged the citizens both to intransigence and conformism, but it did not unite with the State to put a brake on the movement of modern thought. No event comparable to the French Revolution and the secession of the proletariat came to belie the eighteenth-century optimism of the New World. The Civil War was interpreted by the historians – the spokesmen of the victors – as a triumph, proving that the world cannot live half free and half enslaved. The American workers accepted the promises of the American idea and did not believe in the necessity of an Apocalypse.

Armed with a doctrine which condemned their enterprise in advance, the Bolsheviks were the builders of an industrial society of a kind hitherto unknown. The State took over the responsibility for distributing the collective resources, for managing the factories, for savings and investments. The Western working class in the nineteenth century rose against the employers, not directly against the State. Where the employers and the State are identical, revolt against the one would involve dissidence towards the other. The Marxist ideology offered an admirable justification for the necessities of a State economy: the proletarians owed unconditional obedience to their own collective will embodied in the Party.

Certainly, if criticism had been tolerated, the intellectuals would have denounced the misery of the slums of Leningrad and Moscow in the Russia of 1930, just as their colleagues had denounced those of Manchester or Paris a century earlier. The contrast between the growth of the means of production and the aggravation, apparent or real, of the sufferings of the people would have inspired familiar Utopian visions of progress without tears or of fecund catastrophes.

In any case, what possible programme could the oppositionists offer as an alternative to the Soviet reality? They might demand political liberties, the participation of the workers in the management of industry, but not the individual appropriation of the instruments of production, except perhaps in agriculture. Under a capitalist regime the masses can at least imagine that public ownership would cure or attenuate the evils of industry, but under a collectivist regime they cannot expect the same miracle from a restoration of private ownership. The malcontents dream of a return to Leninism, of a truly proletarian State; in other words they aspire to institutions and a way of life which would be a more faithful expression of the reigning ideology.

In the United States, the proletariat does not think of itself as such. The workers' organisations demand and obtain many of the reforms which in Europe are associated with the Welfare State or socialism; the leaders of the masses are satisfied with the position accorded to them under the present regime, and the masses themselves do not aspire to a different society or different values. Unanimity on 'free enterprise', on competition and the 'circulation of the élites' does not mean that the American reality accords with these ideas any more than the obligatory teaching of Marxist-Leninism ensures that Russian society conforms to the official ideology.

Thus, by different routes, either spontaneously or with the help of the police, the two great societies of our time have come to suppress the workers, and imposed a unanimous adherence to the principles of the regime.

6.10.2 *Herbert Marcuse,* An Essay on Liberation, *(London, 1969), pp. 49–60, 79–82.*

Marcuse in a number of places has argued that the 'repressive tolerance' of advanced industrial societies makes necessary a re-definition of the traditional Marxist concept of revolution under

319

capitalism. In particular, the way in which the working class has been integrated into late capitalist society makes it unlikely that it will play any initiating role in transforming society. Exploitation of the ruled by the rulers now takes the form of a willing captivity on the part of the ruled, where their very 'biological' need-structures have been determined by the institutions controlled by the ruling class. A revolution therefore must mean a transformation of these basic need-structures, and the creation of a society where work and leisure both have the character of artistic creativity and enjoyment: 'society as a work of art'.

The notion of 'aesthetic form' as the Form of a free society would indeed mean reversing the development of socialism from scientific to utopian unless we can point to certain tendencies in the infrastructure of advanced industrial society which may give this notion a realistic content. We have repeatedly referred to such tendencies: first of all the growing technological character of the process of production, with the reduction of the required physical energy and its replacement by mental energy – dematerialisation of labor. At the same time, an increasingly automated machine system, no longer used as the system of exploitation, would allow that 'distantiation' of the labourer from the instruments of production which Marx foresaw at the end of capitalism: the workers would cease to be the 'principal agents' of material production and become its 'supervisors and regulators' – the emergence of a free subject within the realm of necessity. Already today, the achievements of science and technology permit the play of the productive imagination: experimentation with the possibilities of form and matter hitherto enclosed in the density of unmastered nature: the technical transformation of nature tends to make things lighter, easier, prettier – the loosening up of reification. The material becomes increasingly susceptible and subject to aesthetic forms, which enhance its exchange value (the artistic, modernistic banks, office buildings, kitchens, salesrooms, and salespeople, etc.). And within the framework of capitalism, the tremendous growth in the productivity of labor enforces the ever-enlarged production of 'luxuries': wasteful in the armament industry, and in the marketing of gadgets, devices, trimmings, status symbols.

This same trend of production and consumption, which makes

for the affluence and attraction of advanced capitalism, makes for the perpetuation of the struggle for existence, for the increasing necessity to produce and consume the non-necessary: the growth of the so-called 'discretionary income' in the United States indicates the extent to which income earned is spent on other than 'basic needs'. Former luxuries become basic needs, a normal development which, under corporate capitalism, extends the competitive business of living to newly created needs and satisfactions. The fantastic output of all sorts of things and services defies the imagination, while restricting and distorting it in the commodity form, through which capitalist production enlarges its hold over human existence. And yet, precisely through the spread of this commodity form, the repressive social morality which sustains the system is being weakened. The obvious contradiction between the liberating possibilities of the technological transformation of the world, the light and free life on the one hand and the intensification of the struggle for existence on the other, generates among the underlying population that diffused aggressiveness which, unless steered to hate and fight the alleged national enemy, hits upon any suitable target: white or black, native or foreigner, Jew or Christian, rich or poor. This is the aggressiveness of those with the mutilated experience, with the false consciousness and the false needs, the victims of repression who, for their living, depend on the repressive society and repress the alternative. Their violence is that of the Establishment and takes as targets figures which, rightly or wrongly seem to be different, and to represent an alternative.

But while the image of the libertarian potential of advanced industrial society is repressed (and hated) by the managers of repression and their consumers, it motivates the radical opposition and gives it its strange unorthodox character. Very different from the revolution at previous stages of history, this opposition is directed against the totality of a well-functioning, prosperous society – a protest against its Form – the commodity form of men and things, against the imposition of false values and a false morality. This new consciousness and the instinctual rebellion isolate such opposition from the masses and from the majority of organised labor, the integrated majority, and make for the concentration of radical politics in active minorities, mainly among the young middle-class intelligentsia, and among the ghetto populations.

Here, prior to all political strategy and organisation, liberation becomes a vital, 'biological' need.

It is of course nonsense to say that middle-class opposition is replacing the proletariat as the revolutionary class, and that the *Lumpenproletariat* is becoming a radical political force. What is happening is the formation of still relatively small and weakly organised (often disorganised) groups which, by virtue of their consciousness and their needs, function as potential catalysts of rebellion within the majorities to which, by their class origin, they belong. In this sense, the militant intelligentsia has indeed cut itself loose from the middle classes, and the ghetto population from the organised working class. But by that token they do not think and act in a vacuum: their consciousness and their goals make them representatives of the very real common interest of the oppressed. As against the rule of class and national interests which suppress this common interest, the revolt against the old societies is truly international: emergence of a new, spontaneous solidarity. This struggle is a far cry from the ideal of humanism and humanitas; it is the struggle for life – life not as masters and not as slaves, but as men and women.

For Marxian theory, the location (or rather contraction) of the opposition appears as an intolerable deviation – as does the emphasis on biological and aesthetic needs: regression to bourgeois or, even worse, aristocratic, ideologies. But, in the advanced monopoly-capitalist countries, the displacement of the opposition (from the organised industrial working classes to militant minorities) is caused by the internal development of the society; and the theoretical 'deviation' only reflects this development. What appears as a surface phenomenon is indicative of basic tendencies which suggest not only different prospects of change, but also a depth and extent of change far beyond the expectations of traditional socialist theory. Under this aspect, the displacement of the negating forces from their traditional base among the underlying population, rather than being a sign of the weakness of the opposition against the integrating power of advanced capitalism, may well be the slow formation of a new base, bringing to the fore the new historical Subject of change, responding to the new objective conditions, with qualitatively different needs and aspirations. And on this base (probably intermittent and preliminary) goals and strategies take shape which re-examine the concepts of democratic-parliamentary as well as of revolutionary transformation.

The modifications in the structure of capitalism alter the basis for the development and organisation of potentially revolutionary forces. Where the traditional laboring classes cease to be the 'gravediggers' of capitalism, this function remains, as it were, suspended, and the political efforts toward change remain 'tentative', preparatory not only in a temporal but also in a structural sense. This means that the 'addressees' as well as the immediate goals and occasions of action will be determined by the shifting situation rather than by a theoretically well-founded and elaborated strategy. This determinism, direct consequence of the strength of the system and the diffusion of the opposition also implies a shift of emphasis toward 'subjective factors': the development of awareness and needs assumes primary importance. Under total capitalist administration and introjection, the social determination of consciousness is all but complete and immediate: direct implantation of the latter into the former. Under these circumstances, radical change in consciousness is the beginning, the first step in changing social existence: emergence of the new Subject. Historically, it is again the period of enlightenment prior to material change – a period of education, but education which turns into praxis: demonstration, confrontation, rebellion.

The radical transformation of a social system still depends on the class which constitutes the human base of the process of production. In the advanced capitalist countries, this is the industrial working class. The changes in the composition of this class, and the extent of its integration into the system alter, not the potential but the actual political role of labor. Revolutionary class 'in-itself' but not 'for-itself', objectively but not subjectively, its radicalisation will depend on catalysts outside its ranks. The development of a radical political consciousness among the masses is conceivable only if and when the economic stability and the social cohesion of the system begin to weaken. It was the traditional role of the Marxist-Leninist party to prepare the ground for this development. The stabilising and integrating power of advanced capitalism, and the requirements of 'peaceful coexistence', forced this party to 'parliamentarise' itself, to integrate itself into the bourgeois-democratic process, and to concentrate on economic demands, thereby inhibiting rather than promoting the growth of a radical political consciousness. Where the latter broke through the party and trade union apparatus, it happened under the impact of 'outside' forces – mainly from among the intelligentsia; the apparatus only followed suit when the movement gained momentum, and in order to regain control of it.

No matter how rational this strategy may be, no matter how sensible the desperate effort to preserve strength in the face of the sustained power of corporate capitalism, the strategy testifies to the 'passivity' of the industrial working classes, to the degree of their integration – it testifies to the facts which the official theory so vehemently denies. Under the conditions of integration, the new political consciousness of the vital need for radical change emerges among social groups which, on objective grounds, are (relatively) free from the integrating, conservative interests and aspirations, free for the radical transvaluation of values. Without losing its historical role as the basic force of transformation, the working class, in the period of stabilisation, assumes a stabilising, conservative function; and the catalysts of transformation operate 'from without'.

This tendency is strengthened by the changing composition of the working class. The declining proportion of blue-collar labor, the increasing number and importance of white-collar employees, technicians, engineers, and specialists, divides the class. This means that precisely those strata of the working class which bore, and still bear, the brunt of brute exploitation will perform a gradually diminishing function in the process of production. The intelligentsia obtains an increasingly decisive role in this process – an instrumentalist intelligentsia, but intelligentsia nevertheless. This 'new working class', by virtue of its position, could disrupt, reorganise, and redirect the mode and relationships of production. However, they have neither the interest nor the vital need to do so: they are well integrated and well rewarded. To be sure, monopolistic competition and the race for intensifying the productivity of labor may enforce technological changes which may come into conflict with still prevailing policies and forms of private capitalist enterprise, and these changes may then lead to a technocratic reorganisation of large sectors of the society (even of its culture and ideology). But it is not clear why they would lead to an abolition of the capitalist system, of the subjugation of the under-lying population to the apparatus of profitable production for particular interests. Such a qualitative change would presuppose the control and redirection of the productive apparatus by groups with needs and goals very different from those of the technocrats. Technocracy, no matter now 'pure', sustains and streamlines the continuation of domination. This fatal link can be cut only by a revolution which makes technology and technique subservient to the needs and goals of free men: in this sense, and in this sense only, it would be a revolution against technocracy.

Such a revolution is not on the agenda. In the domain of cor-porate capitalism, the two historical factors of transformation, the subjective and objective, do not coincide: they are prevalent in different and even antagonistic groups. The objective factor, i.e., the human base of the process of production which reproduces the established society, exists in the industrial working class, the human source and reservoir of exploitation; the subjective factor, i.e., the political consciousness exists among the nonconformist young intelligentsia; and the vital need for change is the very life of the ghetto population; and of the underprivileged sections of the laboring classes in backward capitalist countries. The two historical factors do coincide in large areas of the Third World, where the National Liberation Fronts and the guerrillas fight with the support and participation of the class which is the base of the process of production, namely, the predominantly agrarian and the emerging industrial proletariat.

The constellation which prevails in the metropoles of capitalism, namely, the objective necessity of radical change, and the paralysis of the masses, seems typical of a non-revolutionary but pre-revolutionary situation. The transition from the former to the latter presupposes a critical weakening of the global economy of capital-ism, and the intensification and extension of the political work: radical enlightenment. It is precisely the preparatory character of this work which gives it its historical significance: to develop, in the exploited, the consciousness (and the unconscious) which would loosen the hold of enslaving needs over their existence – the needs which perpetuate their dependence on the system of exploitation. Without this rupture, which can only be the result of political education in action, even the most elemental, the most immediate force of rebellion may be defeated, or become the mass basis of counter-revolution.

The ghetto population of the United States constitutes such a force. Confined to small areas of living and dying, it can be more easily organised and directed. Moreover, located in the core cities of the country, the ghettos form natural geographical centres from which the struggle can be mounted against targets of vital economic and political importance; in this respect, the ghettos can be compared with the *faubourgs* of Paris in the eighteenth century, and their location makes for spreading and 'contagious' upheavals. Cruel and indifferent privation is now met with increasing resistance, but its still largely unpolitical character facilitates suppression and diversion. The racial conflict still separates the ghettos from the allies outside. While it is true that the white man is guilty, it is equally true that white men are rebels and radicals. However, the fact is that monopolistic imperialism validates the racist thesis: it subjects ever more non-white populations to the brutal power of its bombs, poisons, and moneys; thus making even the exploited white population in the metropoles partners and beneficiaries of the global crime. Class conflicts are being superseded or blotted out by race conflicts: color lines become economic and political realities – a development rooted in the dynamic of late imperialism and its struggle for new methods of internal and external colonisation.

The long-range power of the black rebellion is further threatened by the deep division within this class (the rise of a Negro bourgeoisie), and by its marginal (in terms of the capitalist system) social function. The majority of the black population does not occupy a decisive position in the process of production, and the white organisations of labor have not exactly gone out of their way to change this situation. In the cynical terms of the system, a large part of this population is 'expendable', that is to say, it makes no essential contribution to the productivity of the system. Consequently, the powers that be may not hesitate to apply extreme measures of suppression if the movement becomes dangerous. The fact is that, at present in the United States, the black population appears as the 'most natural' force of rebellion.

Its distance from the young middle-class opposition is formidable in every respect. The common ground: the total rejection of the existing society, of its entire value system, is obscured by the obvious class difference – just as, within the white population, the community of 'real interest' between the students and the workers is vitiated by the class conflict. However, this community did realize itself in political action on a rather large scale during the May rebellion in France – against the implicit injunction on the part of the Communist Party and the CGT (*Confédération Générale du Travail*), and the common action was initiated by the students, not by the workers. This fact may be indicative of the depth and unity of the opposition underneath and across the class conflicts. With respect to the student movement, a basic trend in the very structure of advanced industrial society favors the gradual development of such a community of interests. The long-range process which, in large areas of material production, tends to replace heavy physical labor by technical, mental energy, increases the social need for scientifically trained, intelligent workers; a considerable part of the student population is prospective working class – 'new working class', not only not expendable, but vital for the growth of the existing society. The student rebellion hits this society at a vulnerable point; accordingly, the reaction is venomous and violent.

The 'student movement' – the very term is already ideological and derogatory: it conceals the fact that quite important sections of the older intelligentsia and of the non-student population take active part in the movement. It proclaims very different goals and aspirations; the general demands for educational reforms are only the immediate expression of wider and more fundamental aims. The most decisive difference is between the opposition in the socialist and that in the capitalist countries. The former accepts the socialist structure of society but protests against the repressive-authoritarian regime of the state and party bureaucracy; while, in the capitalist countries, the militant (and apparently increasing) part of the movement is anti-capitalist: socialist or anarchist. Again, within the capitalist orbit, the rebellion against fascist and military dictatorships (in Spain, in Latin American countries) has a strategy and goals different from the rebellion in the democratic countries. And one should never forget the one student rebellion which was instrumental in perpetrating the most despicable mass murder in the contemporary world: the massacre of hundreds of thousands of 'communists' in Indonesia. The crime has not yet

REVOLUTION

been punished; it is the only horrible exception from the libertarian, liberating function of student activism.

In the fascist and semi-fascist countries, the militant students (a minority of the students everywhere) find support among the industrial and agrarian proletariat; in France and Italy, they have been able to obtain precarious (and passing!) aid from powerful leftist parties and unions; in West Germany and in the United States, they meet with the vociferous and often violent hostility of 'the people' and of organised labor. Revolutionary in its theory, in its instincts, and in its ultimate goals, the student movement is not a revolutionary force, perhaps not even an avant-garde so long as there are no masses capable and willing to follow, but it is the ferment of hope in the overpowering and stifling capitalist metropoles: it testifies to the truth of the alternative – the real need, and the real possibility of a free society. . . .

The preceding attempt to analyze the present opposition to the society organised by corporate capitalism was focused on the striking contrast between the radical and total character of the rebellion on the one hand, and the absence of a class basis for this radicalism on the other. This situation gives all efforts to evaluate and even discuss the prospects for radical change in the domain of corporate capitalism their abstract, academic, unreal character. The search for specific historical agents of revolutionary change in the advanced capitalist countries is indeed meaningless. Revolutionary forces emerge in the process of change itself; the translation of the potential into the actual is the work of political practice. And just as little as critical theory can political practice orient itself on a concept of revolution which belongs to the nineteenth and early twentieth century, and which is still valid in large areas of the Third World. This concept envisages the 'seizure of power' in the course of a mass upheaval, led by a revolutionary party acting as the avant-garde of a revolutionary class and setting up a new central power which would initiate the basic social changes. Even in industrial countries where a strong Marxist party has organised the exploited masses, strategy is no longer guided by this notion – witness the long-range Communist policy of 'popular fronts'. And the concept is altogether inapplicable to those countries in which the integration of the working class is the result of structural economic-political processes (sustained high productivity; large markets; neo-colonialism; administered democracy) and where the masses themselves are forces of conservatism and stabilisation. It is the very power of this society which contains new modes and dimensions of radical change.

The dynamic of this society has long since passed the stage where it could grow on its own resources, its own market, and on normal trade with other areas. It has grown into an imperialist power which, through economic and technical penetration and outright military intervention, has transformed large parts of the Third World into dependencies. Its policy is distinguished from classical imperialism of the preceding period by effective use of economic and technical conquests on the one hand, and by the political-strategic character of intervention on the other: the requirements of the global fight against communism supersede those of profitable investments. In any case, by virtue of the evolution of imperialism, the developments in the Third World pertain to the dynamic of the First World, and the forces of change in the former are not extraneous to the latter; the 'external proletariat' is a basic factor of potential change within the dominion of corporate capitalism. Here is the coincidence of the historical factors of revolution: this predominantly agrarian proletariat endures the dual oppression exercised by the indigenous ruling classes and those of the foreign metropoles. A liberal bourgeoisie which would ally itself with the poor and lead their struggle does not exist. Kept in abject material and mental privation, they depend on a militant leadership. Since the vast majority outside the cities is unable to mount any concerted economic and political action which would threaten the existing society, the struggle for liberation will be a predominantly military one, carried out with the support of the local population, and exploiting the advantages of a terrain which impedes traditional methods of suppression. These circumstances, of necessity, make for guerrilla warfare. It is the great chance, and at the same time the terrible danger, for the forces of liberation. The powers that be will not tolerate a repetition of the Cuban example; they will employ ever more effective means and weapons of suppression, and the indigenous dictatorships will be strengthened with the ever more active aid from the imperialist metropoles. It would be romanticism to underrate the strength of this deadly alliance and its resolution to contain subversion. It seems that not the features of the terrain, nor the unimaginable resistance of the men and women of Vietnam, nor considerations of 'world opinion', but fear of the other nuclear powers has so far prevented the use of nuclear or semi-nuclear weapons against a whole people and a whole country.

Under these circumstances, the preconditions for the liberation and development of the Third World must emerge in the advanced capitalist countries. Only the internal weakening of the super-power can finally stop the financing and equipping of suppression in the backward countries. The National Liberation Fronts threaten the life line of imperialism; they are not only a material but also an ideological catalyst of change. The Cuban revolution and the Viet Cong have demonstrated: it can be done; there is a morality, a humanity, a will, and a faith which can resist and deter the gigantic technical and economic force of capitalist expansion. More than the 'socialist humanism' of the early Marx, this violent solidarity in defense, this elemental socialism in action, has given form and substance to the radicalism of the New Left; in this ideological respect too, the external revolution has become an essential part of the opposition within the capitalist metropoles. However, the exemplary force, the ideological power of the external revolution, can come to fruition only if the internal structure and cohesion of the capitalist system begin to disintegrate. The chain of exploitation must break at its strongest link.